Trafford Park

The First Hundred Years

'Trafford Park Reduces Transit Costs'—a typical interwar Estates Company advertisement for the 'Industrial Arcady' in Trafford Park.

Trafford Park

The First Hundred Years

Robert Nicholls

Phillimore

1996

Published by
PHILLIMORE & CO. LTD.
Shopwyke Manor Barn, Chichester, West Sussex

ISBN 1 86077 013 4

Printed and bound in Great Britain by
BUTLER AND TANNER LTD.
London and Frome

To my father —
with thanks for everything

Contents

List of Illustrations

Frontispiece: 'Trafford Park Reduces Transit Costs'

Illustration Acknowledgements

The author wishes to thank the following for permission to reproduce photographs and illustrations in this book:
Trafford Park Estates plc; Trafford Park Development Corporation; The Documentary Photograph Archive; Manchester Evening News; Local Studies Unit, Manchester Central Reference Library; Salford Local Studies Library; St Antony's Centre; Derby Local Studies Library; Manchester United Football Club museum collection; Sir Dermot de Trafford, Bart.; Manchester Ship Canal Company plc; Phil Evans Photography (Andover); Hunting Aerofilms Ltd; Donald Thorpe; Procter & Gamble plc (Manchester); Cerestar plc; FMC Process Additives plc; Carborundum (U.K.) plc; GEC Alsthom plc; H. & J. Quick plc; Rank Hovis McDougall plc; Trafford Edible Oils plc; Ford of Europe plc.

And thanks to Ian Howarth of Touchdown Photography at Manchester Airport for undertaking a superb job of copying many of the photographs.

Acknowledgements

The author wishes to acknowledge the generous help and wealth of information that he has been given by official bodies, Park industries and individuals.

From Trafford Park Estates plc–Sir Neil Westbrook, Roy Winsby, Graham Hope and Geoff Roe; Trafford Metropolitan Borough–Roger Dodsworth, John Wingad and Ken Wainman; Trafford Park Development Corporation–Dave Perkins, Alison Reid, Derek Farmer and Lynn Sheppard; Department of Trade and Industry–Brian Eaton.

The local history librarians and staff of Manchester Central Reference Library, Salford Local Studies Library, libraries at Sale, Stretford and Urmston. Staff at the Greater Manchester County Record Office, Lancashire County Record Office, the Public Record Office, Kew, and the House of Lords Record Office. Marianne Goodman at the Royal Institution of Chartered Surveyors' Library and Audrey Linkman at the Documentary Photograph Archive.

Suzanne Miles, Helen Lee and Mike Unger at the *Manchester Evening News*. The Chief Executive's Department (Committee Services) of Manchester City Council.

From Park firms: Acrison–Doug Henry, Carborundum–Des Towers; Cerestar–Jackie Hanson;, FMC–Robin Galloway; GEC Alsthom–Stan Nelson, Mark Alman and Neil Gregory; Manchester United Football Club–Marc Wylie; Procter & Gamble–Rodger Green and John Newhill; Rank Hovis MacDougall–Alan Ayling; H. & J. Quick Ltd–Jim Quick; Trafford Edible Oils–Steve Crick; Turner & Newall–Ian Speakman; and Zeneca–Ken Magee.

Kevin Flanagan from St Antony's Centre, Father James OFMConV from All Saints, Barton, Don Thorpe for information on railways, Brian Robinson for information on the aerodrome, Jason Bull of Salford & Trafford Groundwork for information on the Ecology Park, Sir Dermot de Trafford for information about his predecessors, Bill Ashton, J.G. Atherton, Charles Brien, Enid Halliday, Elizabeth Hatton, Mr. and Mrs. J. Littlewood, Richard Perrin, Mr. A. Stevens and Frank Walsh.

The Trafford Park Centenary Steering Committee and Trafford Park Development Corporation for financial help.

Trafford Park Development Corporation

The emergence of Trafford Park in 1896 gave the world its first and largest industrial park. In the mid-1980s the UK's largest industrial estate Trafford Park was in decline with just some 600 companies and a workforce of about 19,000 remaining. In its heyday it had been heralded as the most important centre for manufacturing and, at its peak in 1945, 75,000 people were employed in the Park.

Radical steps were needed to reverse the downward trend and on 10 February 1987 Trafford Park Development Corporation was established to bring about an exciting programme of regeneration to the area. Thanks to a broad based strategy implemented by the Corporation, Trafford Park's reputation as a leading and successful commercial and industrial location has come full circle.

In almost nine years, the Development Corporation has encouraged development and inward investment; modernised the infrastructure; provided training and employment initiatives for local people with local companies; created a better working environment and marketed the available opportunities. Therefore, in the Centenary Year of Trafford Park, it is fitting that the Development Corporation plays a major rôle together with Trafford Park Estates plc and the Trafford and Salford Councils to celebrate not only the successes and achievements of the last 100 years but also to consolidate the future of Trafford Park as a world-wide centre of industrial and commercial excellence.

TRAFFORD PARK
DEVELOPMENT CORPORATION
MANCHESTER

Introduction

Trafford Park is a name that is known throughout North West England, and probably beyond. The name remains in the collective memory because the 'Trafford' part has found its way into the venues of both a First Class County Cricket team and one of the world's greatest football clubs. It has also since 1974 been adopted in the name of the local authority, Trafford Metropolitan Borough.

The name 'Trafford' is allegedly a Norman adaptation of the old Saxon name 'Stretford', although some say that the derivation is in fact the other way round. Nevertheless, the area is particularly endowed with place-names ending with 'ford', stemming from the fact that it was bounded in ancient times by both the river Mersey to the south and the frequently meandering Irwell to the north, necessitating a large number of forded river crossings.

Most Mancunians know where Trafford Park is, and all will agree that it is a very distinctive place. On local maps, it is easily identifiable as being a sort of island of roughly triangular shape, bounded to its north by the Manchester Ship Canal, and to the south east and south west by the Bridgewater Canal.

The Trafford Park of today is in a period of great change, with areas of industrial dereliction and decay, accompanied by areas of wholesale redevelopment, and the pro-

1 *Trafford Hall viewed in 1896, showing the main south frontage, and the older ivy-clad part of the building to the rear.*

1

2 *The large conservatory and formal gardens of Trafford Hall in 1896. The conservatory was moved to the Village in 1910 to be used as the Recreation Hall and cinema.*

3 *The stables behind Trafford Hall, 1896.*

vision of new roads and landscaping. The large empty Edwardian factory stands across the road from yet another business park, containing the usual mixture of small firms providing high technology, service industry, warehousing or transport functions.

In fact, the area has for the last 100 years been more or less in a state of continuous change and development, with relatively few periods of stability. The various redevelopment initiatives of the last 20 years are no more than another phase of this process, the new growing Phoenix-like from the ruins of the old.

Trafford Park is a lot older than the events of the last 100 years, and the name itself takes us back in time when the Estate was the seat of the de Trafford family, and was truly a rural estate of the minor nobility with meadows, farms and woodlands.

The Park was somewhat of an island even before the arrival of the Manchester Ship Canal and the Industrial Estate. Since 1761, it had been bounded on two of its three sides by the Bridgewater Canal, and its northern boundary had always been the circuitous River Irwell, latterly the Mersey and Irwell Navigation. Possessing no great features of terrain or landscape, it was either flat or gently undulating, except at its northerly margins, where steep wooded slopes led down to the river.

Geologically, the area is underlain by Triassic Bunter Sandstone, which acts as an aquifer, and has been tapped at Trafford Park for use by artesian wells. The overlying 'drift' is mainly late glacial flood gravels, with some areas of alluvium, and peat at the western end of the Estate in the area once known as Trafford Moss.

The mid to late 19th century saw Trafford Park as a rural estate at the height of its development. The central area was described in 1896 as a 'beautifully timbered deer park',[1] and the remainder comprised two extensive outer parks. Despite the flattish terrain the expanses were pleasantly broken up by extensive wooded areas, both natural and planted, with evocative names like Warren Wood, Deer Shed Wood, Long Wood and Hatton's Wood. The wooded slopes, mainly made up of common poplars, that adjoined the River Irwell near Barton, were called Whittleswick Wood, recalling the earlier Saxon village of the same name. Oaks, elms, beech and Spanish Chestnuts were to be found at the western end of the Estate. The beeches were said to be particularly fine examples of their type.

The trees also lined the two main avenues to the Hall from Old Trafford and Barton, itself located close to the river on a slightly higher area of ground. Ash, together with limes and sycamores, formed these avenues, some reputedly planted in the late 18th century, others as late as the 1860s. The stretch from the Hall to the Barton entrance was thought to be the most beautiful part of the Park, with trees of 'splendid growth'.[2]

As for the surroundings of the Hall itself: 'The long reaches of greensward which stretch between the shady plantations and clusters of forest trees are very delightful to the eye, while fallow deer and grazing cattle find here fuel and shelter in peace and plenty.'[3] The forty to fifty deer were elsewhere described as being 'exceptionally tame'.[4]

The Hall was surrounded by an ornamental garden and there was a large glass conservatory and a kitchen garden. Behind the Hall was extensive stabling and a model farm, complete with piggeries, pulping and chaff house, mill and grinding house, slaughter house, fire engine house, smithy, carpenter's shop and kennels etc.

The front of the Hall, which faced south-east, comprised the newer part. It dated from c.1762, and had a classical frontage with a pediment supported by four Corinthian columns, built in a pleasantly coloured buff sandstone or 'freestone'. The rear part of the Hall was ivy-clad and dated from Elizabethan times.

Inside the Hall were eight main reception rooms, described as being in the 'Adam' style, including a drawing room, library, billiards room, study and an oval-shaped morning room. There was also a glass fernery. The main entrance hall was nearly 1,200 square feet in area. It led to a staircase hall connecting to the rear part of the Hall, which contained the servants' quarters, including a servants' hall, kitchen, bakery, brewery, larder and dairy.

On the first floor were the bedrooms, over forty in number. Near the north-western corner of the older part of the building on the first floor was the de Trafford's private Catholic Chapel, called (in 1896) the 'Chapelle Ardente', complete with a gothic arched roof, five stained glass windows, confessional chamber and sacristy.

By 1896, the Hall had been furnished with hot water, central heating and the telephone, but not with electricity. It did however contain paintings by Van Artois, Ansdell, Calvert, and Keeling, together with 'The Four Elements' by Brueghel, and a painting of the fourth Sir Humphrey de Trafford. Examples of Dresden china, Capo di Monte, Chinese rugs and ornaments could also be found.

Elsewhere in the Park, there were three full-sized farms, called respectively Park Farm, adjoining the main carriage drive from the east, Moss Farm, on the westerly boundary and Waters Meeting Farm at the southern end of the Estate near the junction of the same name on the Bridgewater Canal. Also in the west was the large Trafford Moss House. Smaller keepers' cottages complete with aviaries and kennels, ice houses and a snipe ground could be found dotted around the Estate. Game was bred, a pair of hawks were kept and hawking was practised. Three entrance lodges, at Throstle Nest, Old Trafford (opposite the Botanical Gardens entrance on Chester Road), and at Barton guarded the main entrances to the Estate. The lodges at Throstle Nest and Chester Road were reputedly built in the late 1860s, and replaced a set of lodges further along the carriage drive towards the Hall. Public access was not normally permitted, and the Park was completely free of any public rights of way.

On the banks of the river was a large ornamental lake—'a favourite resort for wildfowl, with a pretty wooded island in the centre, and sloping grounds clothed with rhododendrons'.[5] Having an area of about eight acres, it is thought to have been dug *c*.1860. A rustic boat house on the western side completed the scene.

The established park during the 19th century did well to resist the encroachments of the ever expanding industrial city on its doorsteps, although a paper mill had been established, partly on de Trafford land, on the banks of the Mersey and Irwell Navigation at Throstle Mill in 1765 at the extreme north-eastern edge of the Estate. During the 1880s, debates in learned circles took place on the damage to the park caused by the pollution of the day. Some stated that hawthorns, which adjoined the carriage drive, and some of the oaks were showing 'painful signs of air poison'.[6] The birds on the lake were said to be 'uncomfortable near so great an industrial centre'. Others however, poured scorn on these suggestions, maintaining that only the old oaks were affected by the 'bad vapours' and that otherwise the trees were all very healthy. These were small matters, however, when compared with what was to happen to the Estate after 1896.

Before we examine that, it will be necessary to have a brief look at the family which created Trafford Park, the de Traffords.

Notes

1. Sale particulars prepared by Chinnock Galsworthy & Chinnock, May 1896.
2. 'Manchester Faces & Places', Vol. 8, p.166.
3. Transactions of the Lancashire & Cheshire Antiquarian Society, 1888.
4. Manchester Local Studies Library, ref:F942.7389 Sc10.
5. Chinnock Galsworthy & Chinnock, sale particulars.
6. Transactions of the Lancashire & Cheshire Antiquarian Society, 1888.

Chapter I

The de Traffords and Trafford Park
up to 1896

Early origins of the family

The de Traffords, an old land-owning family, are claimed to have been associated with Trafford Park 'to time whereof the memory of man runneth not to the contrary',[1] i.e. in legal terms 'since time immemorial'. An article written in 1887[2] states that they were probably one of the oldest families in the country.

Their association with the area has been traced with some certainty to the late 12th century.[3] The traditional myths and legends of the family's origins, now considered to be of doubtful provenance, were set out in a pedigree established in 1664, and were still being promulgated by some 19th-century antiquarians, for whom studies of the family were a favourite topic. These first identify the family in late Saxon times when Randolph de Trafford[4] is mentioned in the service of King Canute (1016 to 1035). He is said to have defeated the local Saxon rebel, Wolfermote, and received his lands at Stretford as reward.

Randolph died about 1050 during the reign of Edward the Confessor, and his son, Ralph, is reputed to have defended a ford on the River Bollin with vigour against the invading Normans after the Conquest. Shortly after, according to one version of popular legend, Ralph fled to a barn, where his pursuers found him aimlessly threshing corn with the wrong end of a flail. When questioned, he pretended to be a local simpleton, and answered only with the words 'Now Thus'. His pursuers left him alone. This legend is reputed to be the source of both the motto 'Now Thus', and the representations of a man threshing wheat that appear at the top of the family's Coat of Arms.[5]

Unlike many other Saxon landowners after the Conquest, the de Traffords (the use of the prefix to the name would shortly fall out of use) did not suffer. At first, William the Conqueror awarded all the land between the Ribble and the Mersey to Roger de Poitiers.[6] He, in turn, granted part of this large area to Hamon de Massy, Baron of Dunham Massey.[7] About 1080, Hamon de Massy obtained William the Conqueror's pardon, peace and protection for the de Trafford family, and confirmed, for the grant of four marks, Ralph in his holding of the lands formerly possessed by Wolfermote. He also granted to his son, Robert, an oxgang of land in Stretford.

Although some have stated otherwise, Trafford Park is not mentioned in Domesday Book (1086). Over the next few centuries, the family expanded their estates and status through grants, acquisitions and marriage, although the inheritance was inevitably divided at times. Richard Trafford, in the time of King John, acquired the township of Stretford from the Earls of Derby and Chester, and land at Stretford from Richard Fitz Ade de Urmston.[8] Richard divided his lands between his two sons. His elder son, the third Henry, received Trafford and Stretford between 1190 and 1212. The fifth Henry was one of the witnesses to the granting of the charter of Manchester in 1301. A chantry in the Trafford Chapel of the Manchester Church[9] was founded by the sixth Henry in 1349. The eighth Henry died in 1396, to be succeeded by his son, the ninth Henry, aged six. He died in 1403,[10] the estates falling to his uncle, Edmund.

Edmund Trafford

Edmund Trafford was knighted at the Coronation of Henry VI at Whit 1426 in recognition of his conduct at the battle of Verneuil. In May 1409, he had married the 11-year-old Alice Venables, the elder daughter of Sir William Venables of Bolyn, who on the death of her brother inherited valuable land near Wilmslow and the estate of Whittleswick, or Wiggleswick, the western part of Trafford Park as a dowry. Alice's younger sister, Dulcie, married a Booth of Barton, a local land-owning family. This acquisition probably included the earliest Whittleswick Hall, reputedly built on the site of a village that dated from Saxon times. In 1422, Edmund was one of the parishioners who gave their consent to the proposal of Thomas de la Warre that a Collegiate Church be established in Manchester.

Edmund was also noted as an alchemist, and on 7 April 1446 he and his friend, Sir Thomas Assheton, of Ashton under Lyne, were able to persuade a weak and debt-ridden Henry VI to grant them a licence to discover the means of transforming baser metals into gold and silver as a way of paying off royal debts. He also claimed to have discovered an elixir for restoring youth, although it failed to prevent his own death in January 1458.

His son, the first Sir John, fought on the Lancastrian side during the Wars of the Roses, serving the Earl of Warwick, sometimes known as the 'Kingmaker'. He married Elizabeth, daughter of his father's friend, Sir Thomas Assheton. A succession of Sir Edmunds now followed. The third Edmund was a feoffee of Manchester Grammar School on its foundation in 1524. Several Sir Edmunds served as High Sheriffs of Lancashire. The fourth Edmund served under Henry VIII and joined the Earl of Hertford's expedition to Scotland, when on 8 May 1544 he captured and then burned Edinburgh. Later the same year he took part in the siege of Boulogne, for which he received a knighthood. He later became brother-in-law to the King and joined a force of 20,000 raised by the Earl of Derby to support Mary Tudor against the claim of the throne by the Earl of Northumberland and Lady Jane Grey. About this time, a Henry Trafford was rector of Wilmslow, building the chancel of Wilmslow Church. He was Chancellor of York during the Dissolution of the Monasteries.

The fifth Edmund, born in 1526, married firstly Mary Howard, grand-daughter of the Second Duke of Norfolk and sister to Catherine Howard, the fifth wife of Henry VIII. He became a staunch protestant serving Queen Elizabeth, and signed a petition against the desecration of the Sabbath, against the general desecration of the hours of divine service and in favour of cutting down the number of ale houses in Manchester. In 1580, he sent information to Elizabeth on the 'contemptuous and disobedient attitude of the county's Catholics'. This led to an Ecclesiastical Commission being set up against certain recusants or practising catholics. He served as High Sheriff of Lancashire no less than three times. His second wife was Elizabeth, daughter of Sir Ralph Leicester and widow of Sir Randal Mainwaring of Peover. In 1584, Edmund was called upon to levy a force of 200 men commanded by his son for military service in Ireland.

The sixth Edmund, who inherited in 1590, married Margaret Booth of Barton. The marriage was the result of a rather curious agreement dated 6 January 1564 between his father and John Booth of Barton, whereby both agreed that Edmund would marry

Margaret and, in the event of either child dying before the marriage took place, then the survivor would marry the next male Trafford or female Booth and vice versa. The Booth property at Barton would pass in the event of the marriage. The arrangement was later disputed by Booth under pressure from his father-in-law, Sir Piers Legh of Lyme Park, and proceedings took place in Chancery to have the agreement set aside. In due course, the Lord Keeper, Sir Nicholas Bacon, directed Thomas Stanley to arrange for both Edmund and Margaret to meet to ascertain whether the two had a genuine liking for each other. This duly occurred and the marriage took place shortly after, Margaret being only 12 at the time. Their son, John, died aged ten. In 1592, a complaint was made to the Bishop of Chester that Edmund and Margaret did not live together as man and wife. Edmund later decided to disinherit the daughters of his marriage to Margaret, and settled his estates on Cecil, the son of his second wife, Lady Mildred Cecil, daughter of the first Earl of Exeter.[11] In 1603, Edmund Trafford and his father-in-law, Cecil Lord Burleigh, met the first Stuart King, James I, at York, on his way from Scotland to assume the English throne. For this he was knighted.

Religious Persecution and the Civil War

In the early 1630s, it is said[12] that Cecil Trafford bought Whittleswick Hall from Dorothy Liversidge of Dunham Massey. It is suggested that the family moved from Trafford Old Hall (at Old Trafford) to Whittleswick Hall about this time. The older part of Trafford Hall was certainly built around this time, on the site of the earlier Whittleswick Hall, and supports this view.

Cecil Trafford was at first as fervent a protestant as his predecessors, but in 1636 he took the family back to the old catholic faith. This is said to have taken place when he met Francis Downs of Wardley, whose brother was to marry Cecil's sister. Downs himself had reverted to catholicism in 1632, and Cecil was determined to persuade him of the error of his ways. After prolonged arguments, it was Downs who prevailed and the Trafford family again became catholics.[13] He was received back into the catholic church by Father Richard Huddlestone, a Benedictine monk. Cecil was later included on a proscribed list of recusants, and in 1638 a third of his estates was seized by the Crown and granted on lease to farmers.

Sir Cecil sided with the Crown during the Civil War, when both he and Edward Ashton supplied arms to the inhabitants of Manchester and urged them to use them. The inhabitants were less inclined to follow this line and after the war the remaining two-thirds of his estates were sequestered by Parliament. On 2 December 1642, he was arrested on the order of Sir John Seaton and is said to have been imprisoned on a ship at Hull for several months without being able to see daylight. Another suggestion is that this imprisonment took place in Manchester.

From now on, the Traffords' rôle in local affairs would be more low key, most public offices being denied to them. They were obliged, for instance, to relinquish their right of presenting benefices at Manchester Cathedral, and the cathedral fellows took over their responsibilities for appointing curates for the Traffords' own local church in Stretford.

The family's tenacity and ability to survive soon enabled them to regain most of their estates as Sir Cecil successfully begged leave in 1653 under the Recusants Act for the return of the two-thirds of the estates sequestered in 1642. He died in 1672. The 1673 Hearth Tax returns showed Trafford Hall as having 33 hearths, clearly by then a substantial building. His marriage to Penelope, the daughter of Sir Humphrey Davenport, Lord Chief Baron of the Exchequer, introduced the name Humphrey into usage by the family.

The early 18th century saw further consolidation of the Estate by the Traffords. In 1762, during the tenure of the third Sir Humphrey, the Hall was extended to a design allegedly by the celebrated architect, Robert Adam. By the 1790s, the family were so secure that they permitted local catholics from Eccles, on the opposite side of the river, to ferry themselves over to attend services in the Trafford's private chapel. In 1789, a catholic mission was established for Barton; this meant in practice that the Trafford chaplain who had served the family since the days of Charles I now also served as priest in charge of a wide area. In 1807, due to the number of people attending services in the private chapel in Trafford Hall, John Trafford built a separate chapel, the St John's Chapel, at a cost of £5,000, close to the Hall on the site of the later glass conservatory.

Trafford Old Hall

Tradition maintains that, until the early years of the 18th century at least, the Traffords lived not at Whittleswick Hall, but at Trafford Old Hall, which stood on the eastern side of Chester Road, close to the later Henshaw's Blind Asylum. Originally a 'quaint black and white structure', its precise age was uncertain, being variously described as dating back to either Norman or Tudor times. A wooden beam evident in the early 1920s bore a 15th-century date. Some of its walls were of heavy timber-framed construction. Built on rising ground, it had been surrounded by a moat, still visible in 1857. At one time, it was locally called 'The Moat House' or ' The Moat'. Subterranean passages are said to have linked the building to Ordsall Hall in Salford (owned by the catholic Radcliffe family) and to Whittleswick Hall.

4   *Trafford Old Hall, Chester Road, in the 1920s.*

At a later date, the black-and-white timber work was plastered over. The building is mentioned twice in Harrison Ainsworth's 'Guy Fawkes'. It is not known precisely when the family moved to Whittleswick Hall, but it is thought to have taken place between 1672 and 1720[14] and certainly by the time of publication of the first *Manchester Directory* in 1772.

After its vacation, it appears to have been used as a Dower House by the family. In 1898, it was used by Mr. Bailey when Barnum and Bailey's Circus appeared in Trafford Park. Early in the 20th century, it was divided into three residences, and in the early 1920s its front garden is reported to have contained several Gothic pinnacles, apparently taken from a church or chapel. The building was finally demolished by Stretford Corporation in 1939.

The Bridgewater Canal

The Estate was affected by the building of the Bridgewater Canal in the middle decades of the 18th century. The canal was originally intended to run from the Duke of Bridgewater's Worsley mines to Hollins Ferry on the Mersey and Irwell Navigation, and also to Salford, where it would terminate on the western side of the river. Work on the first two miles, from Worsley to Patricroft, had been started in spring 1759 and was completed by the end of 1759. By October of that year, however, the Duke had clearly changed his mind, and now wished to gain access directly to Manchester by a completely different route, which involved crossing the Irwell by aqueduct and reaching Manchester via Trafford Park and Stretford. The Duke's stated reasons for the change were to avoid the rocky terrain of a difficult route to Salford on the

5　The Barton entrance lodges were originally located on the banks of the Bridgewater Canal, but had been moved to Redcliffe Road by the end of the 19th century. The lodge and gateway were finally demolished in the early 1920s when Barton Power Station was built.

southside of a hill, with the consequent difficulties of holding water in the canal, and 'to provide a route more beneficial to his grace and to the public, the execution of which would be less difficult and precarious'. Other reasons were to avoid concentrations of 'enclosed' land on the Salford route and instead traverse two miles of mossland in Trafford Park, which the canal would help to drain and reclaim through the transport of marl.

More pertinent reasons, which outweighed the cost of the aqueduct, would be the wishes of the Duke both to gain easier access to the market for coal in Manchester, without produce having to cross the Irwell by the narrow and unsatisfactory bridges of the time, and to link his canal to potential canal routes through Cheshire to the south.

In order to obtain the necessary powers, a second Bill was submitted to Parliament in January 1760. It was supported by 'inspired' Petitions from traders and 'gentlemen' in Altrincham, Stretford and Manchester, and opposed by the Commissioners for the road from Crossford Bridge (a branch canal was intended to reach Longford Bridge in Stretford) through Stretford and Hulme to Manchester. The Bill had its first reading on

7 February and its second on 13 February. It is during the Parliamentary proceedings that James Brindley is reputed to have faced his doubting questioners on the ability of the proposed stone aqueduct at Barton to hold water. He confounded his opponents by demonstrating his ideas with a model made from cheese, with which he described the principle of clay puddling by which the canal and aqueduct would hold water. Notwithstanding this, it is alleged that Brindley largely absented himself from problems encountered in building the aqueduct, and that the responsibility for seeing to its successful construction is largely that of John Gilbert, the Duke's agent.

It is not known whether the Traffords opposed the canal, and other writers have asserted that the family would have done so on account of its threat to their enjoyment of the estate. There is no evidence for this, however, and it is possible that they were supporters of the new route, even to the extent of encouraging both Bridgewater and Brindley to think of it as a favourable alternative to the original line. Despite the physical difficulties of cutting the canal through Trafford Moss and the cost of the aqueduct, the presence of a willing owner along much of the new route would have aided the progress of the scheme considerably. The theory is supported by the fact that the canal passed through land in Trafford ownership on both the south-eastern and south-western side of the Estate, helping to give the Park its island-like quality. For the Traffords, the availability of the canal would have helped them—as indicated to Parliament—to drain the Moss and to reclaim large parts of it through the transport of marl and agricultural produce.

The new Act was passed fairly speedily on 23 March 1760, with work starting on the aqueduct in September, which was completed on 17 July 1761. The canal opened to Cornbrook by September 1761 and to Castlefield in Manchester by 1765.

John Trafford and Land Reclamation

The death of the third Humphrey Trafford in 1779 without issue caused the transfer of the estates to John Trafford of Croston, a relative. He began the first real attempt to reclaim Trafford Moss, and in 1792 entered into arrangements with William Wakefield and William Roscoe, the Liverpool attorney, banker, man of letters and sometime M.P. As the estate was 'entailed', he was unable to let land for leases of more than 21 years and it was necessary for him to obtain an Act in 1793[15] allowing him to let 'waste lands' or mosses on long 'improvement' leases to encourage tenants to reclaim them for agriculture. Trafford Moss was first dealt with from 1794 as a trial area, followed in 1798 by the much larger area of Chat Moss, on the northern side of the river, the latter by a 99-year lease. Both areas saw a genuine start on reclamation; enough work on Trafford Moss had been started for a lengthy description to be included by John Holt in his *General View of the Agriculture of the County of Lancashire* published in 1795. As well as giving details of a portable railway in use, he stated that some 10 acres had been manured with nightsoil and had produced a successful crop of barley. Writing shortly after, Dr. Aiken[16] states that approximately one hundred acres were then under cultivation.

The de Traffords

John Trafford was succeeded by his son, Thomas, in 1815. In 1823, at the Fancy Dress Ball held at the Preston Guild, it is reported that Thomas Trafford was 'remarkably dressed in his own crest—a clown in parti-coloured clothes, a flail in his hand, and the motto "Now Thus" '.[17]

In 1818, the St John's Chapel was demolished and the materials were used to build a mission church, called All Saints, on a site on Redcliffe Road.

During the 1820s and 1830s, Thomas Trafford became involved in litigation with the Bridgewater Canal Trustees. It was alleged that the archway in the Barton aqueduct was too narrow to allow the river to flow freely in times of flood, causing floods in parts of the Park. In order to protect his land, Thomas built up the river banks in the Park. In turn, the resulting pressure of water caused damage to the canal arch. Judgement was given in 1829 to the Trustees, but three years later the Court of Exchequer set aside the decision and a new trial was ordered. The litigation dragged on without success for either side until 1838, when a compromise was reached. A new weir was built with a low lip to allow overflow water via a by-pass channel to rejoin the river at Urmston. The cost of the works, some £4,000, was divided between the Bridgewater Trustees, Thomas Trafford (who paid £100), Wilbraham Egerton of Tatton (another affected landowner) and the Turnpike Commissioners.

Thomas Trafford, like many of his predecessors, served as High Sheriff of Lancashire and was created a baronet in 1841, receiving at the same time a royal licence to use the prefix 'de' before the surname, reviving a usage that had lain dormant for several centuries.

In 1842, he donated the land at Barton for the erection of St Catherine's anglican church. His wife, Laura Ann, laid the foundation stone on 22 July 1842 and was one of the church's first trustees. Built at a cost of £3,835, St Catherine's was consecrated on 25 October of the following year.

Thomas de Trafford died in November 1852, only three weeks after his wife, after falling off his horse. He is the last de Trafford to be buried in Manchester Cathedral.[18]

Sir Humphrey de Trafford and the Manchester Ship Canal

Thomas de Trafford was succeeded by the fourth Sir Humphrey de Trafford. He served as High Sheriff in 1861, and on 17 January 1855 he married Lady Mary Annette Talbot, eldest sister and co-heiress of the 17th Earl of Shrewsbury. Their marriage, celebrated at Rugby, and following closely the restoration of the catholic hierarchy in 1850, is said to have been the first since the Reformation to have been solemnised with the full catholic ceremonial. In 1856-8, All Saints catholic school was built on Redcliffe Road at Sir Humphrey's expense.[19] Like his father, Sir Humphrey also became involved in local church building. He paid for the erection of the new catholic church for Stretford and gave £20,000 to a new catholic parish in Eccles. Swinton and Irlam also benefited from the family's generosity. In 1863, he built at a cost of £3,000 a family chantry on Redcliffe Road. Alongside, in 1865-8, the catholic church of All Saints,[20] Barton, designed by Edward Welby Pugin (the son of the more famous Augustus Pugin), was built at his expense at a cost of £25,000. It is considered by many to be Pugin's masterwork and replaced the earlier mission church which was then rebuilt in Eccles. The All Saints bell was inscribed:

> When I ring God's praises sing,
> When I toll, pray for the soul
> of Sir H. de Trafford the Founder.

In the 'New Domesday Book' of 1873, Sir Humphrey is entered as owning some 6,454 acres of land, with a gross estimated rental of £22,158 7s. per annum.

6 *The fourth Sir Humphrey de Trafford, his wife Lady Annette, other family members, retainers and hounds in Trafford Park, with the Hall in the background, from a painting by Henry Barraud, c.1860.*

Sir Humphrey owned the Estate at the time of the greatest threat it had ever faced. In 1882, an historic meeting took place at the Didsbury home of the industrialist Daniel Adamson, out of which the Manchester Ship Canal proposal was born. It was attended by a young Plymouth man, Marshall Stevens, then working as a steamship agent at Garston, near Liverpool. Stevens became Adamson's right-hand man for the scheme, and became the main commercial witness in the Parliamentary proceedings that were to follow before the scheme could proceed. We will return to Marshall Stevens later.

The next three years saw the establishment of the Ship Canal Company, and the battles in Parliament over the Private Acts that would enable the Company to buy land compulsorily for the scheme, and to operate the Canal. Sir Humphrey was an implacable opponent of the scheme, and engaged one of the foremost lawyers of the day, Sir Ralph Littler KC, to appear on his behalf. In the House of Commons in 1883, it was said: '... his ancestors had resided on the Trafford Estate for centuries. That the Canal would alter the natural boundary of his park and bring polluted water close to his residence. Also damage his Barton entrance and interfere with his drainage.'

The first Ship Canal Bill passed successfully through the Commons in July 1883. In the Lords, Sir Humphrey's agent, Francis Ellis, stated that: 'the Canal would render Trafford Hall, the seat of Sir Humphrey de Trafford, uninhabitable, ... and would have to give up his home and leave the place'.

Under cross examination, however, Ellis was forced to admit that the river was not now in a satisfactory condition, and that the canal would be further from the house than the river was at present. Notwithstanding this, the weight of opposition from landowners, the Port of Liverpool, and the railway companies ensured that the Bill was rejected by the Lords on 9 August 1883.

A second Bill was submitted in December 1883, and debated in the Lords the following year. This time, Sir John Bowman, a civil engineer, appeared on Sir Humphrey's behalf. He made a new point that the promoters, in order to appease the City of Salford, had agreed to let them have a sewage wharf on the northerly bank of the Canal opposite Trafford Hall, and that it would constitute a nuisance to his client. This time, the Bill was passed by the Lords, but failed on 1 August to get through the Commons. The Canal Company's third and final Bill was deposited on 16 December 1884. It passed through the Lords on 7 May 1885, and the Commons on 3 August, finally receiving the Royal Assent on 6 August.

Sir Humphrey's representations managed to secure special conditions for the protection of his lands in Section 126 of the Act. Although some of the Estate would be lost, other land on the northern side of the river but to be on the southern side of the completed canal would be conveyed to him to partly compensate for land lost. The Canal Company could only buy land off him for construction purposes, areas required for spoil deposit were to be rented and returned on completion. Sir Humphrey was allowed to build lay byes on his land for the use of his agents and tenants, provided that these did not interfere with the operation of the canal or diminish its available width. The Company was to construct two wharves on his land for his own use, his tenants and agents, for the transport of farmyard manure, nightsoil, ashpit refuse, cinders etc., such materials being toll free when carried via the canal. The Company was also, if required by the de Traffords, to restore and make fit for agricultural use old parts of the river bed left within the new boundaries of the Estate, on terms to be agreed. Rights of drainage and the free use of canal water were also reserved to the de Traffords.

The most important protection for Sir Humphrey was the requirement on the Company to build a slope to the side of the canal, at an angle of 22.5 degrees, the top of which would mark the new boundary between the Canal Company and de Trafford ownerships. Fifteen feet behind the boundary, on the Estate's land, the Company were to build a wall, not less than nine feet high, to protect the estate. Elsewhere, land owned by the de Traffords would be protected by a fence four feet six inches in height.

Sir Humphrey Francis de Trafford

Sir Humphrey did not live to see the construction of the canal, on which work started in late 1888. After suffering for two years with paralysis he died on 4 May 1886, being succeeded by his eldest son, Sir Humphrey Francis de Trafford, who had been born in 1862 and whose coming of age celebration in 1883 had been celebrated at the Pomona Gardens, themselves soon to be swept away by the Ship Canal. Humphrey Francis's attitude to the family landholdings was to be less possessive than his father's, and in 1889 he allowed the sale of land at Davyhulme for Manchester Corporation's new large sewage works. In January 1888, he entered into a second agreement with the Canal

7   *Sir Humphrey Francis de Trafford, from a photograph taken in 1913 at the time of his own son's coming-of-age celebrations, held at Belle Vue, Manchester.*

Company, enabling the Company to buy more land for dock purposes at the Manchester end of the Park, and also to take ownership of the 15-foot strip between the top of the slope and the wall, which originally would have remained with the Estate. These terms were covered by Section 28 of the Canal Company's 1888 Act. Sir Humphrey Francis also gave up the special right to have wharves as secured by his father in Clause 126 of the 1885 Act. Instead, he agreed to have only the more general right to have free private wharves, given to all adjoining landowners in Clause 62 of the 1885 Act. These alterations were to be debated at some length in 1904, as will be seen later.

In all, the Canal Company took 323 acres off Sir Humphrey Francis de Trafford, of which 202 acres were from Trafford Park itself. In return, he received some land in exchange, and the sum of £182,000 in compensation.

Sir Humphrey made other agreements between 1888 and 1894 that affected Trafford Park. A number of these were with Manchester Corporation, who were able to route their main Outfall Sewer from the City to the new Davyhulme Sewage Works through the Park. The size of this facility was colossal, the main pipe being described as being the size of a London Undergound tunnel. Future development would benefit substantially from the easy availability of such drainage, thereby avoiding the need for a separate sewage works for the estate. A further agreement was entered into with the Cheshire Lines Committee, who were proposing to build a dock branch line to what would become Trafford Wharf Road. This entailed selling a small part of the park, although the actual railway was never built.

The Sale of the Estate

Sir Humphrey Francis de Trafford's easier relations with the Ship Canal Company were also accompanied by his apparent willingness to dispose eventually of the Estate itself. Writing in 1909, Bosdin Leech indicates that at the time the family were under pressure to sell by the mortgagees of the Estate, although one source indicates that the mortgage only amounted to £10,000, hardly a reason for selling the entire estate. One of the most obvious purchasers at the time was Manchester Corporation, then engaged in a rapid expansion of its area, facilities and services, a phase which others have described as constituting an example of Victorian 'Municipal Enterprise' at its best.

The idea that Trafford Park be taken over by a local authority for use as a public park was first given airing in a local newspaper article in November 1889.[21] Entitled 'Trafford Park for Greater Manchester', it canvassed support for Trafford Park as a 'Bois de Boulogne' for Manchester. The article stated that there were reasons to believe that Sir Humphrey would soon leave the Park, and that recently the estate had been opened to the public on occasions. The notion of the Park being taken over by Manchester Corporation would naturally be bound up with the City's plans to extend its powers to incorporate the Stretford area, whose local authority were opposed to the idea.

Nothing more was heard of the idea until 1893, when in February the proposal started to receive formal consideration by Manchester Corporation. Its Open Spaces Committee expressed a resolution that:

> so unique an opportunity for securing a great and lasting source of health and innocent enjoyment for the inhabitants of this large and growing city may not be allowed to slip away unused and that future generations may have reason to commend the wisdom and foresight of those to whom the welfare of the community is at present entrusted.

Reference was also made to a letter received from the War Office seeking a suitable drill ground for military exercises. Previously, Manchester Racecourse, adjoining the River Irwell, had been hired but the Secretary of State had recently been served with a notice from the owners requiring the military to give up possession in April.

The Corporation set up a Special Committee under the Chairmanship of the Mayor, Alderman Marshall, to investigate the proposal. Mr. Dunlop of Manchester surveyors Dunlop, Lightfoot and Wallis (who were also charged with buying land for the Ship Canal scheme) was appointed to open dialogue with Sir Humphrey's representatives. The Mayor was also asked to ascertain the terms and extent to which the Stretford Local Board would be willing to participate in the purchase and subsequent maintenance of the property, either on the basis of their amalgamation with Manchester or otherwise.

Preliminary discussions were held with Mr. Chinnock, of Messrs Chinnock Galsworthy and Chinnock, Sir Humphrey's agents. The initial asking price was £450,000, later reduced to £350,000. A figure of £300,000 suggested by Dunlop to Sir Humphrey's agents was declined, and Dunlop commented to the Corporation that he felt that the Estate was worth at least £320,000. The Special Committee recommended against purchase on account of the asking price, which they felt was excessive, especially as the Estate was some distance from the City boundary. The Committee's recommendations were not well received elsewhere within the Corporation; its report was described as an 'arid and scanty document'. Parallels were drawn with the successful purchase, for refuse disposal purposes, from Sir Humphrey, of the large Chat Moss Estate at a price of £52 per acre. The Special Committee was asked to think again, but its view was unchanged and the Council did not take the matter any further.

The proposal was not allowed to rest for long. In March 1894, another Special Committee was appointed. The *Manchester Guardian* argued that the success of the recently opened Ship Canal would eventually surround Trafford Park with 'housing of the poorer kind'[22] which would slowly overrun such a valuable 'breathing space'. The idea was floated that only half the Estate need be kept as a park, with the remainder being used for building, allowing some of the initial purchase costs to be recouped. There was: 'no place about Manchester from where a more striking view of the City can be obtained than from the slightly raised ground near the Old Trafford gate'.

The Corporation this time decided to make an approach to the Lewis Trustees, a local charity, seeking financial support for the proposed purchase. The Trustees declined to get involved, citing heavy commitments elsewhere. The War Office made further representations seeking a drill ground. Again, the Special Committee recommended that they were unable to entertain the Corporation's purchase of the Estate, and eventually their view was accepted by the Council in October.

8   *Park House Farm, off the main entrance driveway, in 1896.*
The farmhouse and its outbuildings were one of the Estates
Company's first disposals in 1897, being taken by Nuttalls, the
contractors, who occupied it until the mid-1930s. The buildings
still existed in the early 1980s.

The matter was again briefly considered by the Council in 1895, with the same outcome. However, in December an agreement was entered into between Sir Humphrey and the Corporation for holding the 1897 meeting of the Royal Agricultural Society. This agreement allowed the Corporation, for a rent of £5 per acre, to have a large site in the eastern part of the Estate between the Bridgewater Canal and Park House Farm, from the end of June 1896 to 1 September 1897. It was said to have been the largest site that the Show had ever enjoyed, and the provisions of the agreement were to delay the start on the subsequent industrial estate by at least a year.

The idea of the Corporation buying Trafford Park received its final and most dramatic consideration in 1896. This time, Sir Humphrey took the initiative by putting the Estate up for auction. This was held on Thursday 7 May at 3 p.m. in the *Grand Hotel,* Manchester, with Messrs Chinnock Galsworthy and Chinnock as auctioneers. An impressive illustrated set of sale particulars was prepared. The Estate was described in great detail, and vacant possession would be given for most of the property. The exceptions were the area covered by the Corporation's agreement, and Trafford Moss House, to be retained rent free by the resident land agent. Completion of the sale was set for 6 August. Press reports at the time indicated that, if the auction was not successful, Sir Humphrey had a scheme of his own for the development of the Park or would consider offering the estate in separate lots.

The auction was duly held. Only two bids were made, neither being from the Corporation. The auctioneer named a price of £300,000, which he said was not a reserve price. The best bid was only £295,000 and the property was withdrawn. The *Manchester Guardian* regretted that the public had not been allowed more access, otherwise popular feeling in favour of purchase by the local authority would have been overwhelming.

Expounding on this theme a few days later, the paper continued its campaign. For the asking price of £350,000, the Corporation would gain 1,180 acres. This compared favourably with the total cost of £148,000 paid for the 311 acres that then made up the City's public parks. The Inner Park, nearest to the Hall, was the most attractive part of the Park, and included the lake. The outer parks could be developed, as could the land closest to the Ship Canal. The cost on the Manchester rates after a few years would be no more than 1d. in the £1. Comparisons were drawn with the City's Thirlmere water scheme, costing some £3 million, which had not added a single penny to the rates. Why could not the City's Parks Committee achieve a similar result?

In the middle of May, a special meeting of the Council was held. Divisions now began to appear amongst the members of the Council, who were less of one mind than in earlier years. Alderman Gibson, previously a fierce opponent of purchase, demanded a Town's Meeting to consider the idea. He thought that the cost on the rates would be no more than $1\frac{1}{4}$d. Councillor Southern was not in favour of the Corporation acting alone: he wanted Salford, Eccles and Stretford to join in. Another Councillor thought that the cost on the rates would be only $\frac{3}{4}$d. in the £1.

Allegations were made that both the recent auction and the bids made were bogus, and were a device to force the Corporation's hand, but Alderman Gibson had a letter from the auctioneers stating that both bids were genuine, and that the vendor was now negotiating with both parties and that a syndicate had now become involved. The latter was willing to stand aside if the Corporation was willing to buy the central part of the Estate at £300 to £350 per acre. The old justifications of the military training ground and development of the Ship Canal frontages were repeated.

Fast and furious debate also ensued within the Council about the alleged cost to the ratepayers if the purchase went ahead. Some thought that the richest and poorest ratepayers would be the ones that would benefit most, with the hardest burden falling on the middle classes. One Councillor disputed this, saying that the burden would fall mostly on the poor, and that a Town's Meeting could be 'packed' either way to swing such a decision. He wanted other local authorities to join in, with voting powers on a joint body to be in proportion to moneys invested.

The most outspoken opponent of purchase was Alderman Clay—himself an advocate of the purchase of Heaton Park on the city's northern outskirts where the Earl of Wilton was also understood to be seeking a sale. He considered Heaton Park much more suitable for a public park, and at only half the price. Trafford Park was neither cheap nor magnificent. Smoke from the Ship Canal was having a disastrous effect on the trees. It was a place for manufacturing premises and cottage property. Alderman Clay also thought that Government sanction for the loan necessary to effect the purchase would not be forthcoming and dismissed as 'fairy tales' Alderman Gibson's view that the park could be secured on 'easy terms'. Manchester could ill afford such a plan and already had the highest municipal indebtedness per head of population of any English city.

At the end of May, further pressure was put on the Corporation when Sir Humphrey opened the Park to the public for Whit Week.

The Corporation's response was to appoint another Special Committee, this time chaired by Sir John Harwood, who headed the influential and successful Waterworks Committee. Alderman Gibson was his deputy. Their task was to ascertain the lowest price Sir Humphrey wanted for the entire Estate. On 11 June, a letter was sent to the local authorities of Salford, Eccles and Stretford seeking their cooperation in a joint purchase. Eccles replied first, saying they could not consider the matter until their full Council met on 6 July. Salford replied in the negative on 25 June. In the meantime, Stretford had replied positively on 16 June 'provided it can be accomplished without imposing a heavy burden on the ratepayers'.

Discussions now with Sir John Bowden on behalf of Sir Humphrey revealed that neither side wished to negotiate for the Inner Park only. Bowden did however offer to seek Sir Humphrey's views on whether the strip of land fronting Trafford Wharf Road could be excluded: the Corporation's people could not commit themselves on that idea.

Matters now came to a head for the Corporation. Two Memorials or Petitions were presented. The first was from 300 or so prominent property owners and ratepayers, headed by Lord Egerton of Tatton, and including such signatories as Sir William Houldsworth, the Dean of Manchester, Rylands and Sons Ltd. and Kendal Milne & Co.:

It is in our opinion that such a valuable opportunity for acquiring ... a property of the highest value not only for the recreation of large numbers of people but also in part for judicious development for commercial and residential purposes ought not to be thrown away ... provided that the property in question can be secured on reasonable terms.

The second Memorial came from the Manchester and Salford Sanitary Association:

... unless the park can be purchased and the mode in which it is laid out and used is controlled by the City Council, the area will soon be covered by buildings many of which will emit dense smoke and chemical fumes and greatly increase the existing impurity of the air reaching the centre and eastern portion of the City.
Your memorialists recognise the financial magnitude of the undertaking which they advocate, but having regard to the conditions which cause the high death rate in Manchester, they are firmly convinced that the great value of the park from a health point of view makes the acquisition of it necessary from the health point of view.

On Tuesday 23 June, whilst the Thirlmere Sub Committee was meeting, Sir John Bowden called at the Town Hall, and stated that Sir Humphrey's London solicitors, Messrs Burch, Whitehead and Davidsons wanted an immediate meeting. As there was no time to call a Special Committee meeting, an impromptu gathering was arranged consisting of Sir John Harwood, Aldermen Southern, Worthington and MacDougall, Councillor Needham (Chairman of the Parks Committee) and the Town Clerk. Representing Sir Humphrey were Sir John Bowden, Francis Ellis, Mr. Whitehead and Henry Taylor, his surveyors and solicitors respectively.

9   *View along the main entrance driveway, soon to form Trafford Park Road, from Trafford Road in 1896, with the Throstle Nest entrance lodge on the right. From 1897-1900, the lodge was used as an office by the Estates Company, before it was let to the District Bank for a few years.*

The Corporation's representatives were told that Sir Humphrey had received an offer for the whole Estate, to which a reply had to be given by noon the following day. The Corporation's delegation were not in a position to make an offer there and then, but undertook to call a Special Committee meeting on Thursday 25 June, two days later. Faced with this response, Sir Humphrey's representatives withdrew and decided to proceed immediately with the sale to the other interested party, and a contract was exchanged later that day, 23 June.

On Wednesday, 24 June, Sir John Harwood and the Town Clerk each received the following telegrams:

'Have sold Trafford Park–Whitehead.'

Notes

1. From *Trafford Park Past and Present* (1902).
2. Manchester Local Studies Library ref: F942.7389 Sc10.
3. In particular see W.S.G. Richards', *The History of the De Traffords of Trafford.*
4. Alternative names are given as Radulphus, Ranulph, or Randulph. Confusingly, he is also referred to as Ralph.
5. The family's motto is 'Gripe, Griffin, Hold Fast'. A later version puts this story in puritan times, when the family staunchly defended their catholicism. This theory is supported by the fact that the family crest was not granted until the end of the 16th century.
6. Also referred to as Roger de Poictiers.
7. Also referred to as Hamo de Macy or Massie.
8. *Victoria County History* (1911) states that he acquired it from Margery de Macy.
9. None of the current chapels in Manchester Cathedral bears the name Trafford.
10. Other sources say he died in 1412. *Trafford Park Past and Present* says he died without issue.
11. *Trafford Park Past and Present* says he disinherited his surviving sons of the first marriage.
12. *Manchester City News*, 27 November 1909. Article by Sir Bosdin Leech.
13. Edward Baines gives a slightly different version of this story, saying that Cecil was converted by the arguments he met with while studying the case in order to bring Downs back to the protestant faith. He also indicates that Cecil was increasingly apprehensive about the growing rift between Charles I and his puritanical Parliament and wished to demonstrate his loyalty to the King through his re-adoption of the catholic faith.
14. An article in *Manchester Courier*, 4 July 1883 suggests that Trafford Old Hall was vacated between 1672 and 1703.
15. 33 GEO 3 58.
16. In *A description of the country 30 to 40 miles around Manchester* (1795)
17. Manchester Local Studies Library ref: Q942.7389 m83.
18. His grave is not now marked in the Cathedral.
19. The school was demolished in 1890 as part of the Ship Canal scheme. It was replaced by another All Saints School, on Trafford Road in Salford, on land donated by the de Traffords.
20. The church's official name is The Church of the City of Mary Immaculate.
21. *Manchester City News*, 2 November 1889.
22. The *Manchester Guardian*, 8 March 1894.

Chapter II

The Start of the Industrial Estate
1896-1914

E.T. Hooley and the formation of Trafford Park Estates

The local Press was quick to report the sale. The purchasers were described vaguely as a 'London Syndicate', but the real purchaser was Ernest Terah Hooley, a speculator and financier from Risley Hall, near Derby. The contract signed by Hooley on 23 June provided for the sale of the estate to him for £360,000, with completion on 29 September.

Hooley, with typical tendency to exaggerate, publicly stated:

> I have bought Trafford Park for nearly half a million sterling. It was only last Saturday, that I heard that this magnificent property had been allowed to go begging for so long. I have never seen the place. We intend to develop the Estate and make a centre of the cycle and rubber trade. We propose to set up works along the water ... Our syndicate is the same that bought Dunlop Tyre for £3 million. We also launched Singer Cycle and other undertakings. We have not yet chosen the Directors (for Trafford Park), but they will be men of position and influence even locally. The development will be left in the hands of Col. Edis, the Prince of Wales's architect. Some suggest that parts be given to the City, for the future, or they could come to terms with us for something larger.

Other press reports put the syndicate as including a baronet and a leading 'northern agriculturalist'. Hooley poured scorn on the Corporation's failure to secure the Estate: 'The Corporation have been very much asleep in the matter'.[1]

Privately, the Corporation was probably relieved that the Estate had been sold to another party. Despite clear support within the Council, it was felt that the Corporation's hand was being forced by pressure groups and those willing to influence public opinion. Although the Corporation was in an expansive phase, its commitment to Trafford Park was never strong because of the likely capital cost of purchase coupled with the Estate's distance from the city's boundaries, and the apparent lack of support from neighbouring local authorities. Certainly there was no inquest into the failure to secure the purchase. The Council was not, however, to be allowed to ignore the pleas made for the provision of a large open space for the benefit of the city. In early July, they received a letter from London surveyors, Messrs Weatherall and Green, enquiring whether the Corporation was interested in buying Heaton Park. This approach was eventually to prove successful, as the City Council purchased Heaton Park in June 1902, its 617 acres costing £230,000, a lesser sum than the sale price of Trafford Park.

The rôle and background of E.T. Hooley deserves further enquiry. He was born in 1859 at Long Eaton, Derbyshire, the son of a small lace manufacturer. Beginning his working life as a mill hand, at the age of 22, Hooley inherited £35,000 on the death of his mother. With this, he set himself up in Nottingham as a stockbroker where he made a success of himself, claiming later that for several years he earned £20,000 per annum. Hooley's ambitions then turned to company promotion and he moved to London. He realised the potential of the rapidly expanding cycle and rubber trades in particular, and in the years 1894-7 was involved in the promotion of Raleigh Cycles, Dunlop Tyres, Bovril, Schweppes and many other pioneering companies whose names survive today. With Dunlops, he and 'one or two friends' bought the tyre patents for £3 million, and then floated a company to take them over for £5 million. In these ventures, he formed alliances with the rich and famous: '... [he] bought guinea pig directors with titles as other men buy boxes of matches. Peers, politicians and pretty women buzzed around him like flies.'[2]

In four and a half years, Hooley created 26 companies with a total capital value of over £18 million.

Hooley lived a fairly extravagant lifestyle: at one time he was estimated to be making £1 million profit a year, all of which he spent on his mode of living, which involved the best hotels, and ownership of several country houses with fully filled wine cellars. At the time of the Trafford Park purchase, he was claimed to be the largest sheep farmer in the country, owning over 20,000 acres spread over six counties. His possessions extended to a yacht and he claimed also to know over 300 horses by sight. At one time, his political ambitions nearly won him the Parliamentary constituency of Ilkeston.

On the other hand, Hooley was never the archetypal City financier, and he himself said that he had none of the City's 'looks and graces'. Later in his career, after one of his several bankruptcies, he was described as 'the most likeable of all the fallen financiers'.[3] Of good height and moderate build, he had a neatly trimmed beard, bright piercing eyes, and a quick, hearty and unpretentious manner. Rather surprisingly, in view of what he said about Trafford Park, it was said that he had no 'boastfulness' or 'side' and once declared: 'I am a countryman. I hate town sharks with their tricks and lies'.[4]

Occasionally, Hooley had a generous streak, giving at various times £400,000 to the widows and orphans of his own county, and a £10,000 service of solid gold to St Paul's Cathedral, although this was later returned to his creditors after one of his bankruptcies.

10 *Title page of the 1896 Sales Particulars, prepared by Chinnock Galsworthy & Chinnock.*

Hooley's initial interest in Trafford Park has an element of mystery. Although the local press had reported several times in the preceding weeks the possible interest of syndicates, Hooley later claimed that his interest arose at the very last minute and quite by accident. In his autobiographical *Hooley's Confessions*, published in 1925, he states that he was in London staying at the *Midland Grand Hotel* with his young clerk from Nottingham, Harold Ellis. Also staying at the same hotel was Francis Ellis, Sir Humphrey de Trafford's land agent. A letter was despatched from Sir Humphrey's solicitors to Ellis advising that the Corporation was not willing to pay more than £350,000, and seeking Ellis's advice on the next step that Sir Humphrey should take.[5] Needless to say, this letter was mis-delivered, i.e. to Hooley's young assistant. Hooley's interest in a 'deal' was at once aroused, and he immediately sought the advice of one of his contacts, Sir Jacob Wilson. Asked by Hooley whether Trafford Park was worth £360,000, he received the advice, 'It's worth half a million'. Within the hour, Hooley was talking to Mr. Chinnock of Sir Humphrey's auctioneers, and on 23 June the contract was signed, with a deposit of 10 per cent of the sale price paid by Hooley. All this took place within days, and Hooley had not then personally visited the property. Asked in the press why he had bought Trafford Park, he replied with complete honesty, 'Land is at the bottom, it can only go up. In five years' time, the landed property I have bought will be worth £1M more than I gave for it.'[6]

The signing of the contract did not complete the sale to Hooley. This was scheduled for 29 September, and Sir Humphrey would continue as owner until the sale was completed. The conveyance would also be subject to Sir Humphrey's agreement with the Corporation for the Royal Agricultural Show. The total area to be sold was 1,183 acres, mostly bounded by the Ship Canal and Bridgewater Canal, but with two outlying areas around the two main entrances at Throstle Nest and Barton. Sir Humphrey retained ownership of large areas to the west of the Bridgewater Canal south of the Barton entrance.

The Park was to remain in Sir Humphrey's hands rather longer than anticipated, in fact until 14 April 1897. This was because, in line with his way of working, Hooley himself was quite incapable of buying the property. He needed financial partners to put up some of the capital for the initial purchase. He would then form a company and sell the Estate to the Company, the sale price being in the form of shares in the new company. In a simultaneous transaction, Hooley would acquire the Estate from Sir Humphrey, and sell it to the new company. If the terms of the sale were right, Hooley would earn himself a profit. This he achieved, but the process would take time, and Sir Humphrey would have to wait for his £360,000.

By 9 July, Hooley had rectified his omission of not visiting the Estate when he, his architect, Robert Edis, and his colleague, Martin Ricker, carried out an inspection. Somewhat contradictory statements were issued by Edis and Hooley, the former stating that there was no truth in the rumour of a cycle works being built on the Estate, which would be developed for superior houses. A slightly later report did include zones for the cycle and rubber trades, use of the Ship Canal frontages for 'all types of trade including timber' and residential development. The central core of the Estate would largely remain as at present. A plan was produced for publication by Edis along similar lines, which included a racecourse. This plan, no doubt, was provided for Hooley's purpose of raising the finance to form the proposed development company. Edis, one of the most prominent architects of the day, was to play no further rôle in Trafford Park, and little regard was had to his layout in the subsequent development of the Estate.

The company Hooley was to form, Trafford Park Estates Ltd., was first registered on 17 August 1896. A document dated 10 August 1896 shows how Hooley raised his finance for the purchase and how the Company was initially owned. It appears that Hooley put up £155,000 of the purchase price, with the remainder being supplied in different proportions by the other initial shareholders of the new company. The largest shareholder was to be Lord Ashburton, of the Baring banking family. His contribution was £60,000, and Baring's would remain involved with the company for decades in raising its finance. Other contributors were Frederick McCabe of Dublin (described as a 'gentleman'), Frederick Cuthbert of Hampton in Arden (a stockbroker), William Wright of Nottingham (described as 'a gentleman', but known to be a director of Moore & Robinson's Nottinghamshire Banking Company), Weston Webb of Nottingham (a merchant), Robert Hemingway of Nottingham (a contractor) and Arthur du Cros of Regent Street, London. The Company itself was to have a capital shareholding of 650,000 shares, each with a nominal value of £1, and the estate was to be sold to the new company for £900,000. This was to be

11 *Ernest Terah Hooley, the initial purchaser of Trafford Park, photographed in 1897, the year of both the sale and his first bankruptcy.*

mainly a paper transaction, the sale moneys payable by the company to the consortium being paid by the issue of shares to the various parties who put up money to fund the initial purchase from Sir Humphrey. These would be in direct proportion to the notional profit made from the sale of the estate to the company. Thus Lord Ashburton received 127,500 shares for his £60,000 invested. Hooley himself would receive only 40,000 shares, but he would also receive from the company on completion of the sale a debenture of a further £350,000, redeemable at six months' notice with interest at five per cent. Out of this, he would supply £100,000 of working capital for the company, in return for a further 100,000 shares.

Matters seem then to have gone quiet for a while, during which time the problems of how to raise the money needed to pay Hooley his debenture and to raise working capital would have been foremost in the promoters' minds. Allied to this would have been the nature and timing of the development plans for the estate. The proposed sale date of 29 September came and went without the sale being completed.

Hooley's stroke of luck came when he met Marshall Stevens, the General Manager of the Ship Canal, which had opened in full in 1894. The Ship Canal, despite its initial promise, had enjoyed a lean couple of years since opening and traffic, so optimistically predicted by Stevens and others before Parliament 10 years earlier, had largely failed to materialise. The words 'White Elephant' would occasionally appear in the press. At once, both Hooley and Stevens saw the opportunity that Trafford Park and the Ship Canal could provide for each other. In discussions, Stevens was offered a substantial increase on his £1,500 salary by Hooley (reputedly £2,500, the same as the Town Clerk of Manchester) to become Managing Director of the new company. He accepted the offer during the first week of December, and told J.K. Bythell, the Ship Canal Chairman, who asked him to keep the matter to himself whilst the Ship Canal Board considered a successor. By 7 December, news was beginning to leak out and Bythell urged Stevens to make a formal announcement, which was made the following day. Stevens finally took up his duties on 1 January 1897.

Marshall Stevens

Marshall Stevens was born on 18 April 1852, the eldest son of Sandars and Emma Stevens. The Stevens were a West Country family with a strong shipping tradition. His father was a shipbroker, and his grandfather, Thomas Stevens, had operated two shipping lines and had been Mayor of Plymouth in 1854. His great-grandfather, John Stevens, was also a ship owner. One of his great uncles, John Lee Stevens, was the editor and founding proprietor of the *Shipping Gazette*, as well as being a poet and responsible for the invention of improved paddles for steamboats, patented in 1827 and 1851. Another great uncle, Robert White Stevens, had written a standard work on shipping, *On the Storage of Ships and their Cargoes* in 1855, which eventually was to be issued in some seven editions over a 20-year period.

The young Marshall Stevens was educated at the Mansion House in Plymouth, and is believed to have entered the family shipping business around 1868. His sense of adventure and risk-taking manifested itself before the age of 20 and the year 1870 saw him caught up in the Franco-Prussian War. He broke through the lines of Prussian troops besieging Paris, in order to buy hides from the Parisians, only to find that they had all been eaten by the starving inhabitants.

Returning to England, in 1873 he married Louisa Blamey, the daughter of Philip Blamey of Cusgarne in Cornwall. About 1877, he left the family business to settle at Garston, near Liverpool, where he set himself up as an independent steamship agent in what has been described as a 'creative response' to the challenge of the steamship-dominated shipping businesses of Liverpool to the still predominantly sailing ship enterprises of the West Country. At the railway-owned port of Garston, he developed trading connections with the natural hinterland of Lancashire, Cheshire and Ireland,

12 *Marshall Stevens, the founder of the industrial estate, photographed whilst on a visit to Washington in the early 1900s.*

bringing in produce from the West Country by steamship instead of by the usual overland routes. Between 1877 and 1885, he and his later partner, a Mr. Nicholson, established steamship routes between the Mersey and the French ports of Rouen and Nantes as well as to the Channel Islands.

Stevens's interests and talents were soon to be diverted to something greater. In 1881, he was making enquiries through a firm of Manchester estate agents, Messrs Isaac Nield & Co., into acquiring land for a wharf in Manchester, with the aim of carrying freight between Manchester and Liverpool at more competitive rates. Isaac Nield & Co. were involved in the promotion of the then infant Ship Canal scheme and, after securing Stevens's interest, arranged the necessary introductions. In 1882, he attended the important initial meeting called by the industrialist, Daniel Adamson, at his Didsbury home, The Towers, at which the Ship Canal scheme began to take shape. Stevens himself subscribed £200 towards the fund established to promote the vital legislation, became a member of the Provisional Committee, and for the next three years effectively became Adamson's first lieutenant, burning many hours of midnight oil. Stevens became the Canal Company's main commercial witness at the numerous Parliamentary hearings that took place in 1883-5. He provided detailed estimates of potential traffics and revenues, and his knowledge was unrivalled. His expertise in the different carriage costs of freight by land and sea was impressive, and he was an unshakeable witness in the face of intense cross-examination from lawyers representing the many opponents of the scheme.

The Ship Canal Company finally obtained its Act on 6 August 1885. Some five days later, Stevens was appointed Provisional Manager responsible for 'organising the means of raising the capital in Manchester and surrounding districts, and to such other matters as the Directors may require'. He was paid £25 per month on a temporary arrangement from 1 August, which was increased to £35 per month some 13 months later. In the meantime, he wound up his own business at Garston.

Over the next few years, Stevens worked hard for the Canal Company, acting again as advocate and witness before yet more Parliamentary hearings, especially on the subject of excessive railway freight rates, an opinion that he formed from his relationship with the owners of Garston Docks, the London and North Western Railway Company. He addressed public meetings in favour of the scheme, and survived the resignation of Adamson, the scheme's founder. In 1891, he was appointed General Manager of the Canal Company, and over the next few years worked hard to attract traffics to the canal, which finally opened in its entirety, after delays caused by bad weather, the death of the contractor and financial difficulties in raising capital to finish the scheme, at the start of 1894. Of particular importance in this connection was a visit he made to the United States to encourage trade for a new Manchester-based steamship line that would serve American ports not already having established ties with Liverpool. Stevens also secured for the Canal Company full control over all the Port's staff, initially excluding trades unions and introducing piece work. By raising the productivity of the Port's labour force, he was able to set Manchester's dock charges at half those of the older rival. He was also instrumental in the provision in the Manchester docks of multi-floored transit sheds. Perhaps his greatest achievement during this era was the establishment of the vital railway links with the new docks and the associated railway freight rates, although the railway companies were reluctant partners for the new canal, and had to be compelled to cooperate following an appeal by Stevens to the Railway Commissioners.

Stevens's optimistic traffic predictions for the canal, made before Parliament, did not materialise in the years 1894-6. The 3 million tons of goods forecast for 1894 was not achieved until 1900, and the 4.4 million tons predicted for the second year did not occur until 1905. The initial dividend of the Company, forecast at four and a half per cent, was not paid until 1923.

Despite these initial setbacks, Stevens had established for himself a position of respect and authority within the Canal Company, and his departure was at first regretted. On 31 December 1896, he was presented with an illuminated address signed by all 361 members of the Canal Company's staff below the level of Director. J.K. Bythell paid him a glowing tribute at a shareholders' meeting in February 1897, referring to his 'knowledge, resourcefulness and versatility' and said that: '... every success that [the Canal Company] had hitherto obtained in bringing traffic to the canal was largely due to Mr. Stevens'. He and his fellow Directors 'wished him every success in his new sphere and hope that his endeavours to plant industries in Trafford Park on the banks of the Ship Canal will be entirely successful'.

Stevens was to go on and demonstrate 'knowledge, resourcefulness and versatility' in the development of Trafford Park. His relationship with his former employers would not always be as cordial.

Flotation of the Company and early works

Stevens's appointment began to bring forth tangible progress. In mid-March 1897, a prospectus was issued for the flotation of £350,000-worth of Preference shares, secured as First Mortgage Debentures at an interest rate of four per cent. The raising of this cash at this stage would have been essential to repay Hooley the money owed to him under his own debenture, and which he himself would need to contribute towards the purchase price payable to Sir Humphrey when the sale was finally completed. The Trustees for the Debenture holders were the Rt. Hon. Lord Churchill, and the banker Mackworth Praed. Hooley was now Chairman of the Company, and Marshall Stevens one of its directors. Two directors remained from the previous August agreement. These were Lord Ashburton and William Wright. The other parties to the August agreement had presumably sold on their shareholdings. The new directors, apart from Stevens, were Colonel Paget Mosley, William Nocton (a director of the Law Fire Insurance Society), and William H. Bailey, the proprietor of a Salford engineering company and a director of the Ship Canal Company. The Company's registered office was at 18 Exchange Street, Manchester, and its Secretary was George Mellors.

The conveyance of the Estate finally took place on 14 April, simultaneously with the completion of the sale from Sir Humphrey, who it is understood left the area and went to live in rented accommodation at Market Harborough. Inclusive of fixtures and fittings, the final sale price was £370,794. Hooley was to claim in his autobiography that it was the most profitable deal he had ever undertaken, making for himself a clear £640,000 after expenses. On paper, Hooley's profit would appear to have been more in the order of £235,000.

The prospectus and its plan share some common features with the Edis plan of the previous year. The centre of the Park features a 200-acre area, containing a one-mile 'straight' reserved for a racecourse or a public park, whilst Trafford Hall was to become a hotel, with adjoining golf links. A strip of land along the Ship Canal was reserved for 'dockside purposes'. Ominously, the prospectus states that:

13 *The Chester Road entrance gateway and lodges, opposite the entrance to the Manchester Botanical Gardens, later the White City. The photograph was taken during the early years of Estates Company control. A sign for Crookes' boatyard is to the right of the gateway.*

'... the site, with its invaluable wharfage rights will almost certainly be required by the Ship Canal Company, or by one of the large Railway Companies for dock, wharf and terminal premises, and at a moderate computation must by itself realise a larger sum than the amount of the whole Debenture issue ...'.

In other respects, however, the plan was vastly different. An estate tramway ran from the Old Trafford to the Barton entrances, with railways running parallel to the Bridgewater Canal for most of its length, and connecting outside the estate to the docks, and to neighbouring railways at Eccles and Chorlton cum Hardy. The plan also shows a by-pass canal across the southern corner of the estate, connecting at both ends with the Bridgewater Canal, a canal basin and branch in the Davyhulme area, and a coal barge basin and tipping dock at Barton connecting the Bridgewater and Ship Canals. A dry dock, ship building yard, tar distillation works, oil tanks and a Patent Fuel works are also shown at Barton. The rest of the estate, about 750 acres, was to be devoted to: 'iron works, seed crushing mills, matting houses, machinery works, merchants depots, cottages and similar requirements.'

Although the local press would continue at times to refer to 'Villadom' being established on the estate near the Hall, that part of the Edis plan did not appear.

The prospectus stressed the unique position of the Estate and its proximity to 'the deep waters of the Ship Canal'. The traffic using the Ship Canal is shown as growing at a rate of 40 per cent per annum and that 'by arrangement with the Ship Canal

Company, portions of the Estate will immediately be used for the storage of timber and other merchandise'.

The new company appears to have taken over the running of the Estate a few weeks before the actual sale from Sir Humphrey. In late March, the Park is reported as being open to the public on payment of a small charge. Some 2,000 pedestrians, cyclists and other vehicles visited the Estate on one particular Sunday. Unfortunately, the 'rough element' was evident, and there are reports of gates being lifted off their hinges, acts of trespass, poaching and fires being lit in the woods. An appeal was made to the public to keep to the Park's roads, otherwise the Estate would be closed. One Wednesday, there were signs of attempted burglary at the Hall, when police found a window open and a quantity of materials packed ready for removal. The fact that the Estate was devoid of its tenants was not conducive to security. This was only to be a temporary phenomenon, however; after a few months when tenants had been installed, the local press opined that the small charge levied for entrance 'kept out the rough element'.[7]

The development of the Park for industry could not of course begin until the end of the Royal Agricultural Show, which would occupy a substantial and strategically important eastern sector of the Estate until 1 September 1897. The Show itself only ran from 23 to 29 June, but the Company was bound by the terms of Sir Humphrey's agreement with Manchester Corporation.

For the Estates Company, matters could not stand still. The Park was an immense size and, until industrial concerns came forward, some income had to be generated out of the Estate as it stood in order to maintain the Park and avoid spending scarce capital on such costs.

The lake therefore was let on a five-year lease to William Crooke and Sons, who also had boating concessions at the city's Platt Fields and Boggart Hole Clough Parks.

14 *Early 1900s view of boating on Trafford Park Lake, looking south east, with the chimneys of the Hatton's Wood Brick Company in the background.*

15 *The links of the Manchester Golf Club, in front of Trafford Hall, early 1900s.*

Crookes hired out rowing boats and skiffs with sliding seats to the public, at rates of between 2d. and 6d. per hour. The firm also built boats at the site, operated 'what the butler saw'-type slot machines, and apparently controlled both swimming and fishing on certain surrounding ponds, including the nearby 'Top Lake' on the later Brooke Bond site. A new boat house was built on the eastern side of the lake, and for many years the lake became a favourite place for recreation for both workers on the estate, inhabitants of the Village, and visitors to the Park from elsewhere. Rhododendrons continued to surround the lake and one slope on the north-western side was called Bluebell Hill after the delightful annual covering of bluebells.

Shooting rights and some of the farmlands were let to local farmers. An area in the centre of the Estate was let to the War Office at a rent of £3 per acre, for the much vaunted training ground, although it does not appear to have been used as such, and was given up by 1911. Some fields

RAFFORD HALL.
Telegrams:
Trafford Hall,
Manchester.
Telephone No. 6860.

RECEPTION
ROOMS on the ground floor and Billiard Room upstairs have been furnished for the use of the General Public.

BED ROOMS and BED SITTING ROOMS with the use of the Reception Rooms, and the exclusive use of Residents' Sitting Room on the first floor are now to be let to Gentlemen only. TERMS including attendance from 21/- per week.

BREAKFAST. Plain including two eggs 1/-., with Meat or Fish 1/6.

LUNCHEON, 12-30 to 2 p.m., consisting of Joint, Vegetables, Cheese and Butter or Sweets, 1/6.

AFTERNOON TEA. Chops, Steaks, &c., see Tariff.

TABLE d'HOTE DINNERS as soon as warranted. DINNERS to order.

Manchester Golf Club Head Quarters are at the Hall.

Easter, 1899.   STABLING.

16 *Leaflet issued Easter 1899 advertising the availability of rooms in Trafford Hall.*

were used for racing purposes, although a formal racecourse was never laid out in the Park. In May 1898, a meeting of the Northern Counties Riding Club was held.

The 80 acres near the Hall was let to the Manchester Golf Club, who were also allowed use of some accommodation in the Hall. The course was some three miles in length, and for the club the move to Trafford Park saw membership rise from 70 to 320. The club was prepared to take a limited number of new members from the industries coming to the Park, at a reduced subscription. Its Secretary was C.A. Grundy, who was Mellors' assistant at the Estates Company, and who, like Stevens, had been a Ship Canal Company man.

The Gas Tramway

The sheer size of the Park, and its distance from existing public transport routes meant that the Company would have to think about transport infrastructure that would have to be provided within the Estate.[8] As early as March 1897, Marshall Stevens enquired of the Manchester Carriage & Tramways Company, the area's dominant operator, whether they would run a horse-bus service through the Park from Old Trafford to Barton. Nothing came of this, and so the Estates Company itself set about providing an estate tramway, which had featured in the Debenture prospectus as serving the same route. A contract was placed with a Mr. J. Nuttall with the stipulation that the route should be ready by the time of the Royal Agricultural Show in June. The route was to run from a point on Trafford Wharf Road, close to the recently erected grain silo on the banks of the Ship Canal, past the Showground site, and then run along the southern side of the main estate driveway leading to Trafford Hall, from where it would travel across fields to meet up with the road linking the Hall and Barton. Both road and tramway would then share the same bridge across the Bridgewater Canal, with the tramway ending just inside the Barton Lodge entrance gates.

At the same time, an agreement was made by the Estates Company with the British Gas Traction Company Ltd. for the operation of the service. The latter had recently opened a similarly operated route between Blackpool and Lytham. The Gas Traction Company placed an order for gas engined cars from the Lancaster Railway Carriage & Wagon Co.

The press reported in May that about three-hundred men were at work laying the new line, which it was hoped would be ready for operation by Whit Week.

All did not go well for the gas tramway. The delivery of the cars was late, and there was friction between the Estates Company and the Gas Traction Company. This was partly due to the fact that the former knew little about the requirements for the operation of a tramway such as this, and were happy to leave matters to their own contractor. He, in turn, appeared to be similarly ill-informed, and was building a line suitable for freight working, which purpose the line would also serve, rather than the more exacting standards required for passenger operation.

Meanwhile, the projected opening date of Friday 4 June came and went and, instead of the planned ceremonial opening, Marshall Stevens was obliged to undertake a trial inspection of the line in two goods wagons hauled by a Ship Canal Company locomotive. The tramway did not operate during the week of the Royal Agricultural Show. Eventually, the condition of the track was improved and one car was delivered, and on Friday 23 July an hourly service was started using the one tramcar. The following day, Stevens took his directors for another trial inspection in the car. He was annoyed to find on arrival that the service had been suspended at lunchtime to allow the tram driver

17 (above) *Trafford Park Road, c.1900, looking eastwards with train and gas tram. The Lancashire Dynamo and Crypto factory is on the left, whilst Kilvert's can be seen under construction on the right.*

18 (right) *Trafford Park Post Office and gas tram track, at the junction of Trafford Park Road and the future alignment of Ashburton Road, photographed in November 1901.*

to go home for dinner. After some heated exchanges, the Gas Traction Company offered to put things on a better footing. This was not to be, however, as the following Wednesday a car was de-railed, throwing two women passengers around inside the car, who were threatening to claim compensation. As a result the Gas Traction Company ceased the service altogether. An independent inspection the following month found that the tramcar had left the rails at a badly fitted set of points. Although some work was done by the Estates Company, the Gas Traction Company were still not satisfied. As neither party would give way, the service remained suspended, and was not to resume until the following year.

The first industries arrive

The Estates Company could not afford to sit back and wait for new industries to arrive in the Park. Although, in March, Stevens had claimed that 'many old established businesses are already in treaty for sites and brisk competition will ensue', this was not the case. An early suggestion was made to the Company by some manufacturers that the Company itself should consider erecting buildings for letting. The directors did not accept this suggestion, being relatively short of working capital, as we shall see later, but did think that they would be able to consider proposals for lending capital to industries able to provide adequate financial security, in addition to that provided by the buildings themselves. In the case of the Park, some of the initial industries would be started by the Directors themselves.

One of the first, the Manchester Patent Fuel Co., was established in March 1897, with Grundy, Mellors and Stevens as the original subscribers, although most of the shares were later sold to the public. The new company was allocated a site next to the Bridgewater Canal at Barton. Construction of the plant by a contractor, a Mr. Westlake, was surrounded by difficulties and the works were not operating by March 1898, the projected opening date. By February 1899, it was still not possible to manufacture the briquettes continuously, and the Company had made a loss of £905 13s. 5d. up to the end of 1898.

Another new Company was the Trafford Brick Company, established in April 1897, which leased a 40-acre site at the southern apex of the Estate at Waters Meeting Farm. Again, Stevens, Mellors and Grundy were directors, this time being joined by the contractor, Nuttall, and by Francis Ellis, Sir Humphrey's land agent, who had continued to work for the new company. The Brick Co. was to manufacture and deal in bricks, tile, terracotta, iron, steel, ironstone and also carry on the business of joiners and builders.

Both these enterprises had been mentioned in the March prospectus. Other proposals mentioned included a flour mill. Towards the end of 1897, Stevens was involved in negotiations to buy some collieries and a steamship line. None of these efforts had any immediate results.

Other firms, unconnected with the Estates Company, slowly began to arrive. Morrison Ingram & Co. (Sanitary Engineers), Bennett's (Sawmills) and Nuttall's the contractors took leases of land at the eastern end of the Estate next to Trafford Park Road, as the main driveway leading from Old Trafford to the Hall would now be called. Up to the end of June 1897, the area leased to industrial concerns amounted to less than one per cent of the entire Park, although it was claimed that the rents, when capitalised, would exceed 10 per cent of the Debenture issue.

The departure of Hooley

The slow progress of 1897 was not helped by the growing financial difficulties of the Company's Chairman, sometimes referred to by the Company at this time as 'the Vendor'. He resigned on 4 October in anticipation of his impending bankruptcy. His downfall was caused by a legal action brought against him by the M.P. for Gainsborough, Emerson Bainbridge, to whom he owed money. Due to his extravagant lifestyle and mercurial business dealings, notwithstanding his profit made at Trafford Park, Hooley simply did not possess the £80,000 awarded against him. Facing claims for £1 million, Hooley filed for bankruptcy himself in the 'most sensational bankruptcy ever known in this country'.[9]

The bankruptcy caused immediate practical difficulties for the Company and were part of the explanation why many of the elaborate infrastructure proposals of the 1897 prospectus were not carried out. Hooley was unable to supply the £100,000 promised as working capital, and provided only £25,000. The total Company shareholding of 650,000 Ordinary shares had to be reduced to 573,000 to allow for the fact that Hooley's share entitlement had to be withheld in part.

The remaining directors were also obliged to accept a higher liability for interest due to the Debenture holders, and litigation dragged on for several years as the directors tried to get redress from Hooley. After three years, a sum of £42,000 was deposited with the Company's bankers to cover the claim, but the outcome of the litigation is not known.

Hooley's position as chairman was taken by Colonel Paget Mosley.

The start of the Estate railway system

Mention has already been made of the gas tramway route, which was also intended to carry freight trains. No statutory powers to run this line were apparently applied for at this stage, although this omission would prove a slight embarrassment to the Company in a few years' time.

The omission was not to be repeated and the Company in 1897 put in a formal application to the Light Railway Commissioners for permission to build and operate the other estate lines as envisaged in the Debenture prospectus. The application did not include the connection to Eccles, but included lines to Chester Road, to the Manchester to Altrincham railway line, and to the Midland Railway at Chorlton cum Hardy. Lines within the Estate would run along what would become Westinghouse Road, and from there to Barton following the Bridgewater Canal to join the gas tram line. The application was partly successful, with the lines within the Estate and to Chester Road being approved under the West Manchester Light Railway Order 1897.

At this stage, no work was done on the lines, other than the estate tramway and the temporary connection to the Ship Canal's own lines on Trafford Wharf Road which was put in between May and July 1897. Marshall Stevens was in the meantime pressing the Canal Company to allow a more permanent connection, which they agreed in principle subject to reasonable terms being agreed. It is unlikely that any freight traffic was carried on the infant system in 1897, but it is known that 7,713 tons were carried the following year.

Barnum's circus and problems with the estate tramway again

The estate tramway finally resumed operation, this time with a full service, on 8 April 1898, after lying moribund for almost eight months. The dispute between the Estate and Gas Traction companies was resolved by a fresh agreement, brought about by the forthcoming arrival of Barnum and Bailey's Circus, which had obliged the Estates Company to give some ground in the issue. The Company agreed to alter the points to allow the safe passage of trams, and also to extend the track to the Trafford Road entrance, a point more convenient for the rapidly growing workforce of the Park. The Company would also maintain the line and car shed, and provide land near the new terminus for a temporary compressing shed. The Gas Traction Company, in return for a three-year agreement terminable on three months' notice, would operate and maintain the cars, provide and maintain the compressing shed, and agree to be bound by the decision of the Ship Canal Company's Railway Engineer on the fitness of the line for working.

The Circus itself started on Easter Monday 11 April. It was widely advertised in the press:

> The Greatest Show on earth ... The most Collosal [sic] Show ever Devised. Under Twelve Mammoth Canvas Pavilions, seating nearly 15,000 people! On its own specially constructed railway cars–each car nearly 60 feet long–arranged in four monster trains! Enlarged. Increased. Changed and Improved. Greater, Bigger, Grander than Ever! Living Curiosities and Freaks. Three herds of performing elephants. Lady Clowns. Lady Ringmaster. 100 startling circus acts and displays. Three Rings. Two stages! A Perfect World's Fair of Wonders![10]

Additional features included two menageries and 'Alar' the Human Arrow. Admission prices ranged from one shilling to 7s. 6d. for a box. Getting the show to the site near the Trafford Road entrance was a logistical feat, involving the vast trains travelling through the Canal Company's dock railway system to reach the estate. On the first Saturday, a large street parade over a mile long travelled between the Park and the City Centre. Some 11,783 attended the Easter Monday performance, and the gas tramway coped admirably.

After the circus left in May, use of the tramway declined as most of the route was still predominantly rural in character, and passengers would be few, especially in winter. The service acquired the nick name 'Lamp Oil Express', on account of the smell from the traction system, but the speed of the cars was only 6 or 12 m.p.h. A total of four cars was available to work the service, the fleet being referred to collectively as 'The Channel Fleet' on account of their heavy appearance. In operation, the tramcars emitted a chug-chugging sound, and sported a green and cream livery.

By the end of 1898, receipts from the line were so low that the Estate and Gas Traction companies were obliged to reach a fresh agreement, with the Estates Company accepting a reduced share of the takings (now only a quarter), instead of equal shares, over the winter months. This alteration was to prove insufficient for the Gas Traction Company, who in April 1899 gave three months' notice to terminate their obligations under the agreement. A series of frantic negotiations then took place between the parties to maintain the service, but the Gas Traction Company was in serious financial difficulties and could not rely on their undertakings elsewhere to support the Trafford Park operation. By July, Marshall Stevens was looking at the possibility of building an electric tramway, suggested by the firm of Lacey, Clirehugh and Sillar. A decision to proceed with an entirely new line was made but, in the meantime, Sir William Bailey managed to secure agreement from the Gas Traction Company that they would continue until the end of the year, in return for keeping 75 per cent of the line's receipts. The service in fact continued to run until 3 November when operation ceased after Salford Corporation refused to supply any more gas to the Traction Co. on account of the latter's indebtedness. Although the Estates Company were keen to settle the bill, Salford refused to accept the money as the Gas Traction Company had by then gone into voluntary liquidation.

This latest problem had only one solution for the Estates Company, namely to buy the undertaking itself, which they did for £2,000. The operation was subsequently resumed. By August 1900, under Estates Company control, a clear increase in usage of the gas tramway was evident.

Further industries in the Park

The pace of development increased slightly in 1898, with sites being taken by the Manchester & Liverpool Transport Co., the timber merchants J.W. Southern & Co., J.D. Sandars & Co. (Maltsters), James Gresham (Engineers) and W.T. Glover & Co., a cable manufacturing company established in Salford in 1869.

Glover's had become a limited Company in 1898 with a capital of £150,000, and started to expand. By 1902, the company was entirely located in Trafford Park, with a large site at the eastern end adjoining Trafford Park Road. Glover's also agreed to supply electricity to the Park, and took a site, adjacent to their works on the banks of the Bridgewater Canal, for building a power station. Manchester Corporation had initially been approached by the Estates Company with a view to electricity being supplied to the Park at the same rates as supplied within the city, but Stretford Urban District Council had objected to another local authority supplying electricity within its area.

19 *The typists' room at W.T. Glover's, the first large concern to locate in the Park, seen here in 1901.*

A large disposal of land was made in 1898 to Edmund Nuttall & Co. This was described in the press as being for the erection of 1,200 houses. The disposal was to form the nucleus of the Trafford Park 'Village'.

A similar number of sales took place in 1899, with sites going to Morrell Mills (Engineers), Kilvert's (Edible Fats), R. Baxendell & Co. (Millers), the Liverpool Warehousing Co., and the Lancashire Dynamo & Crypto Ltd. A large site near Mode Wheel Locks went to the Bagnall Oil Company. Trafford Park Road was surfaced between Trafford Road and a point that was later to become its junction with Ashburton Road.

1899 also saw some sites being sold off purely for investment purposes, principally to bring in early capital receipts, for the Estates Company was short of ready cash and capital was not available for the erection of buildings for rent. 78 acres in two parcels were sold to Grain Elevator Estate Ltd. One parcel adjoined Trafford Wharf Road near the recently erected grain elevator, whilst the other site adjoined the Bridgewater Canal. Another site, between the Bridgewater Canal and Chester Road, was sold to Throstle Nest Estates. Both these disposals were to companies controlled by some of the Estates Company's own directors. Additionally, further sites were sold to Marshall Stevens's wife, and to A.J. and F.M. Bailey, the latter being sublet to Ashworth's and the Lancashire Dynamo Co. The Estates Company, despite these moves, were obliged to seek extra capital, and in 1898 authority was given to raise a Second Debenture of up to £150,000 at an interest rate of 5 per cent. Some £53,640 of this debenture was raised in 1899; by 1902 the amount raised had risen to £75,000.

Railway Agreements with the Ship Canal Company

An important agreement was made between the Estates and Ship Canal companies on 1 November 1898. The most important feature of the agreement was the commitment on the part of the Canal Co. to carry freight between the docks and the Park, and in the reverse direction, at the rate of 6d. per ton. As such a charge already existed and operated on the dock railway system itself, the agreement effectively granted free haulage over railways within the Park at no additional expense. The concession also applied to any buildings sold or leased by the Estates Company within the Park.

The agreement related only to the haulage and provision of wagons, and did not relate to any 'terminal services' provided by the Canal Company. When the dock railway system itself was congested, the Canal Company had the right to restrict or prohibit use of their railways in respect of any traffic not imported or exported by the canal, although this restriction did not apply to any finished products made from materials brought in via the canal. Other clauses gave the Estates Company permission to connect permanently to the dock railway system, replacing the temporary connection provided near the Foreign Animals Wharf at the western end of Trafford Wharf Road. The agreement also covered the question of through rates with the main line companies, where the Canal Company promised not to oppose any application for such rates by the Estates Company, even where these routes involved passage over Canal Company lines.

The Estates Company in 1899 obtained a further Light Railway Order, the West Manchester Light Railway Order 1899, under which a separate subsidiary was established, the West Manchester Light Railway Company. The latter was authorised to make certain railways in the Park, and to take over the estate tramway. In due course, the railways built in the Park were conveyed to the new Company in 1904, which provided for the Estates Company to receive a land rental of £300 per annum, together with a rental of one shilling per annum for each additional yard of track laid. The making of the permanent connection between the dock and estate railway systems was to prove difficult, partly due to the deteriorating relations between the two companies that occurred after 1898. The problem first arose in Spring 1899 when Baxendell's, who had taken a site on the southside of Trafford Wharf Road, wanted to make a connection direct to the dock lines on the northern side of the road. The Canal Company's Board was alarmed at the prospect of a large number of similar connections crossing the road from land let or sold by the Estates Company, which adjoined the road on its southern

20 (below) *The start of work on the erection of the steel foundry within the Westinghouse works, 8 June 1901.*
21 (centre) *Substantial progress of the steel foundry is evident by 3 August.*

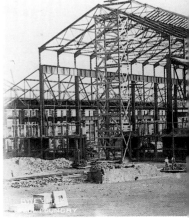

frontage. The Canal Company therefore insisted that Baxendell's make their own arrangements with the Estates Company. A protracted series of discussions followed, culminating in a second agreement between the two companies in June 1900. This provided for the Estates Company to convey to the Canal Company a strip of land next to the road. This strip contained the wall insisted upon by the late Sir Humphrey de Trafford, which the Estates Company were permitted to remove. Effectively, on the southern side of the road, another line of dock railway was to be built, with three tracks, two as running lines, with the third to act as a loop line to give direct access to traders' premises. The latter was maintainable by the Estates Company. If the arrangement was undertaken to its satisfaction, the Canal Company would in turn permit a second connection between the two systems at a point to be agreed.

The implementation of the agreement and the making of the permanent junction was fraught with difficulties. Again, contractor Nuttall was involved on the Estates Company's behalf. His temporary junction, installed in 1897, by June 1900 was causing problems for the Canal Company in that the layout obliged the Canal Company's locomotives to carry out a large amount of back-shunting on the estate tramway, causing delay and danger to the gas trams, or on the steeply graded line connecting the tramway route to Trafford Wharf Road. In addition, the demands of Park industries was now such that siding accommodation within the Park was considered insufficient by the Canal Company. So concerned were the Canal Company that on 20 June they gave notice that no traffic would be received after noon on 25 June.

This threat was effective for, in a letter to the Canal Company, George Mellors gave an undertaking that the Estates Company would instruct Nuttall to install a siding at the top of the incline. After a further flurry of correspondence, the siding was ready by 4 July, and the permanent connection was brought into use shortly after.

The arrival of Westinghouse 1899-1902

The growing industrialisation of the eastern end of the Park was well and truly established by the arrival of the Westinghouse factory. George Westinghouse had been seeking a site for a British factory for his electrical engineering business for some time,

22 (below) *The steel foundry is nearly complete by 2 September 1901.*

and had already considered a site in Wolverhampton. The approach he received from the Estates Company immediately alighted his interest in the Park.

Westinghouses's aim behind his British venture was to take advantage of the rapid progress of electrification then taking place in British industries and homes. In particular, he thought that the U.K.'s railways were about to undergo a rapid conversion to using electric motive power.

Two sites totalling 130 acres were bought; the larger, at the southern end of the Estate, was on the site of Waters Meeting Farm, previously occupied by the Trafford Brick Co., and was to be the site of the main works. The second site was on the other side of what was now to be called Westinghouse Road, and to the west of Mosley Road. From the outset, the whole works was conceived on a colossal scale.

In 1899, Westinghouse formed a British subsidiary, the British Westinghouse Electric Company, with the aid of the bankers, Rothschild's.

Preliminary work started on site in August 1900, using both local and London based contractors. Progress was relatively slow, and the following January saw a contract signed with James Stewart, a Canadian-born contractor famed for his rapid building methods in the United States. His instructions were to reduce the five-year building programme for the £1.7 million plant to 15 months. Within a week, the number of building staff rose from 250 to 2,500, then 4,000. Key posts were filled by Americans, and some 200-300 truckloads of building materials arrived daily. Automatic tools were provided and steam hoists replaced the traditional hod carriers. Bricklayers were taught to lay 1,500 to 2,000 bricks per day instead of the usual 400-500. This inspired correspondence to and a leading article in *The Times*.

The main building of the new works was some 900 feet by 440 feet. It passed over the Manchester Corporation outfall sewer leading to Davyhulme Sewage Works, which had been laid following agreement with Sir Humphrey Francis de Trafford in 1889. In the total scheme, some 11 million bricks were used, nine million feet of timber, and some 17,000 tons of steel. The Foundation Stone, containing beneath it coins of the realm, was laid on 3 August 1901 by the Lord Mayors of London and Manchester. The first building was finished within 10 months and the whole scheme within a year. The office block, virtually the only building with any ornamentation, is said to have been a virtual replica of the one at the Westinghouse works in Pittsburgh. Production started in 1902.

As well as using American building methods, designers and attitudes, Westinghouse was determined to use similar methods in the manufacturing process. From 1899, key British personnel, the future managers of the new complex, were taken to Westinghouse's base at Williamsburg, near Pittsburgh, for training. Known as the 'Holy Forty' (although the numbers were always greater), the individuals contracted with Westinghouse to work some 5,480 hours at a rate of 20 to 25 cents an hour, and then to remain with the British subsidiary at a salary of £150 to £175 per annum. Within the United States, the 'Holy Forty' were sometimes referred to as the 'British Specials'. Close to the American factory, a town for workers called 'Trafford' was erected.

The start of Trafford Park Village

The Estates Company's disposal of land for housing to Edmund Nuttall preceded the arrival of the Westinghouse works. Nuttall, however, had undertaken no work on the site. The stimulus caused by the announcement of the Westinghouse factory soon changed this. In 1899, Trafford Park Dwellings Ltd. was formed. It took over the land sold to Nuttall, and set about constructing a residential development to cater for key workers,

23 *Aerial view, taken in 1903 from a balloon, of the completed Westinghouse works, sometimes referred to as 'The Big House'. The distinctive water tower, used for the works hydraulic power system, is clearly visible.*

24 *View of the Village from Westinghouse Road. The original Ford factory is just off the left of the picture. The playing field was built on during the First World War, when the government constructed a tractor factory, which later became part of Ford's.*

particularly at the new Westinghouse works. Initially, the Dwellings Company was independent of the Estates Company, having only some common directors, but as early as 1906 the Debentures and some of the Ordinary share issue had been taken over by the Estates Company. In the same year, some 25.5 acres of land were sold to the Dwellings Company at a sale price equating to 2d. a square yard, a concessionary rate apparently applied to the earlier disposal, and considerably less than sales for industrial purposes, which could be as high as £1 per square yard.

The development of the residential area took place along a rectangular grid pattern 'surprisingly American in character', according to a press report in 1903.[11] Streets running north-south were numbered 1 to 4 and called Avenues, whilst east-west streets were numbered 1 to 12 and called Streets. It has been suggested that Stretford Council objected to the roads being named. Some reports suggest that as many as 3,000 houses were first planned, others only one thousand. By September 1903, some 549 had been completed; the final number was to be nearly seven hundred and thirty. Not all the houses were built by the Dwellings Company; some plots were sold on for building at a rate of 4d. to 18d. per square yard. Rents of houses ranged initially from 6s. 9d. to 9 shillings per week, and it was a condition of the tenancy that electricity was taken from the Trafford Power and Light Company. The smallest houses were built to the south of Fifth Street, with larger dwellings having large outrigger structures to the rear, between Fifth and Twelfth Streets. Houses on Second, and parts of Tenth and Eleventh Streets had initially no road frontage, with front gardens opening onto a footpath only. A few larger houses, for supervisory staff, were built on Fourth Avenue. Development finished about 1904.

The 'Village', as it came to be known, had its admirers and detractors. It had many of its own facilities, some provided by the Dwellings Company. Its relative isolation from other housing, the close density of its own development, and the common employment of many of its inhabitants led in time to a strong community spirit, which persisted throughout the life of the development. On the critical side, although the houses built were substantial and clean, the estate layout, with few gardens and narrow streets, meant that it was similar in many respects to the miles of terraced properties in surrounding areas, which would form the 'slum' clearance areas of later years. As early as 1901, critics were pointing out the proximity of the housing to the noise and pollution of surrounding industry, the narrowness of the streets, and lamenting the fact the opportunity had not been taken to provide something along the lines of Port Sunlight. In its early years, the turnover of tenants was high. In 1907, about 97 houses were empty, about 13.3 per cent of the total. The total population in that year was estimated at 3,060, or about 4.19 persons per house.

At first, the streets of the Village were unpaved, being lit by small electric lamps. They were brought up to a standard suitable for adoption by the local authority in 1907. A range of local shops were built, facing onto Third Avenue, the main north-south thoroughfare. Three corrugated iron churches were provided by the Dwellings Company. A Methodist Chapel was built on Third Avenue in 1901, followed by St Cuthbert's for the Church of England in 1902, and finally St Antony's on Eleventh Street for the Roman Catholics in 1904. A residential club for workmen was built at the junction of Westinghouse Road and Third Avenue: it was often used as a hostel for visiting contractors and company officers at the Westinghouse works. Games of billiards could be played and a shale tennis court was available nearby.

In 1902, the *Trafford Park Hotel* was built at the corner of Third Avenue and Ashburton Road at a cost of £13,000. A large structure of red brick and terra cotta, it contained

25   *A May Day or similar celebration, within the Trafford Park Council School, c.1927.*

26   *The children of the Village taking part in the annual Whit Walk along Third Avenue.*

a large dining room provided at the suggestion of the licensing justices. In the same year, a site of nearly three acres was sold to Stretford UDC for the erection of a corrugated iron elementary school. This was a somewhat larger site than the Council required, but the sale was subject to the condition that part of the site was laid out as a recreation ground, which was duly provided in 1908 with a playground, two bowling greens and a tennis court, between Sixth and Eighth Streets. A police station and a post office were also provided, the latter being operated by the Estates Company for a time.

On the western side of Third Avenue, the Dwellings Company arranged for the re-erection of the large glass conservatory, previously at Trafford Hall. This served as a public hall; by 1910, it was being used as a silent picture house, with a Mr. J. Boardman as the operator. Admission to the establishment was 1d. and seating was on wooden benches, which were moved out for dances at the weekends. The local brass band often played for dances. The general noise levels inside the building when in use as a cinema were described as 'appalling' and the children who attended on Saturday mornings 'not well behaved'. The pianist who accompanied the silent Charlie Chaplin, Buster Keaton and Keystone Cops films is described as 'fluent but high-spirited'. The building also had a rifle range attached to it.

Trafford Hall and the rural estate

With the exception of the Patent Fuel Works, all the industrial developments in the early years had taken place at the eastern and southern ends of the Estate. The Company therefore continued to administer the rest of the estate to earn much-needed rental income.

The Hall itself had featured in the Company's earliest announcements. Its planned use was as a hotel, but in 1898 an application for the necessary licence was thrown out by the justices. In 1899, the Company furnished the building and at Easter opened it as an unlicensed hotel, functioning as bachelors' residential chambers. Forty bedrooms on the first floor were furnished for this purpose, at charges of one to two guineas per week. The use of entertaining rooms on the ground floor was permitted, and breakfast, luncheon and teas were available, with *table d'hôte* dinners 'as soon as warranted'. Stevens intended the building to serve the needs of the rapidly growing industrial estate by accommodating prospective industrialists and early key staff involved in establishing new factories: he himself lived there at times over the years up to the First World War, despite the fact that his home was in nearby Bowdon.

In 1900, some of the timber on the Estate was cut, particularly a swathe through Warren Wood and Long Wood, which was intended to take a road and rail continuation of Westinghouse Road through to Barton. The timber was sold for making clog soles, which took place in the stables behind Trafford Hall. Between 1900 and 1902, the stables and some of the outbuildings were used as a horse mart and for stock auctions. The Estates Company were the proprietors, employing a William King as manager, with the Manchester firm of Edwin Bradshaw & Sons as auctioneers. The venture did not last long. In 1902, the Manchester Polo Club established a polo ground between the Hall and Ship Canal. This appears to have continued until about 1906.

The Estate's herd of free roaming deer, inherited from the de Traffords, had initially been allowed to remain. The increasing activity within the Park made their presence inappropriate, and the last of them was killed in 1900. Its antlers for many years hung in various offices and the Boardroom of the Estates Company.[12]

The introduction of industries to the eastern end of the Park led to the abolition of the entrance charge, last mentioned in 1897. However, at Barton, the charge was still being levied in 1904, on all except passengers for the gas trams. It is not known when this charge was abolished.

In 1906, the Estates Company arranged for the cutting of two million tons of peat from the mossland areas, particularly along the line of the proposed extension of Westinghouse Road. Negotiations were started for its sale to fuel merchants, but before they could be completed, the stockpiles were set on fire by local youths and were entirely destroyed. From time to time it was necessary for the Estates Company to clear areas of peat from sites to be developed. The peat cleared in this way for many years appeared as a series of mounds along the western boundary of the Estate where they formed a useful playground for children from the Village, who referred to the site as the 'Boggy Hills'.

The purchase of the Manchester Racecourse

The Manchester Racecourse at the time was located at New Barns, to the immediate west of the Ship Canal's No. 8 Dock. When the canal was being built, the transit sheds on the western side of No. 8 Dock had been built with a pleasing red-brick façade to appease the Racecourse's owners. It was expected by both concerns that any expansion of the Salford Docks would eventually require the Racecourse site, and an agreement was entered into in March 1893 effectively giving the Canal Company first refusal to buy the site for dock purposes. The provisions of this agreement were incorporated into the Canal Company's Surplus Lands Act of the same year.

The interest of the Estates Company in the Racecourse site started even before Stevens took up office, as the first few days of December 1896 saw Hooley and him discussing a possible take-over of the Racecourse Company, with a view to offering the land to the Canal Company. It was later stated that an offer of £400,000 had been rejected by the Racecourse Company at this time. Negotiations started again two years later, and in August 1899 the Canal Company made a similar approach, a month or two later giving formal notice that they intended to promote a Parliamentary Bill authorising compulsory acquisition if negotiations failed.

Marshall Stevens, however, was ahead of the Canal Company. On 8 November, he wrote to the Lord Mayor of Manchester, Thomas Briggs, informing him that Trafford Park Estates had agreed to buy the Racecourse Company outright, a clever legal move intended to evade the legal requirements on the Racecourse Company of both the 1893 Agreement and Act. In making his approach, Stevens clearly hoped to secure the Corporation's support, who had a majority on the Ship Canal Board, to forestall any opposition from the Ship Canal Company. He implored the Corporation to allow the Estates Company to provide for the Canal Company's requirements and to 'secure the interests of the City of Manchester without necessitating an appeal to Parliament'.

The Corporation wisely declined to become directly involved, sensing its own financial interests were being compromised, and referred the letter to the Canal Company's Board. The latter were taken aback by the activities of their former General Manager, and ordered that a copy of the Lord Mayor's reply to Stevens be sent to the Press. Only a few days before Stevens's letter, Sir William Bailey, at the time a director of both companies, had denied any accuracy of the rumoured interest of the Estates Company in the Racecourse. He did, however, undertake to check the matter with Stevens. On hearing the truth, Bailey decided to resign from the Board of the Estates Company, but rejoined a few months later after matters had died down.

In December, negotiations between the Estates and Racecourse companies were completed. The shareholding in the latter company was to be acquired for £280,000.

The racecourse could remain at its present site if an alternative could not be found, although the Estates Company would not oppose an application for the licence to be transferred elsewhere. The Estates Company would not seek to establish a competing racecourse within Trafford Park (apparently allowed under its articles of association). The Racecourse Company would in turn receive a three-year option to purchase a 130-acre site within the Park, incorporating a 'straight mile', for re-siting the racecourse. The 'Racecourse' site did indeed appear on Estates Company layout plans produced for the next few years whilst the now evident dispute with the Canal Company continued.

The Canal Company's response was to seek a legal injunction in January to prevent the sale taking place. In May 1900 they succeeded, and judgement was confirmed the following month in the Court of Appeal. The Estates Company then petitioned against the Canal Company's Bill arguing that no extension to the Manchester Docks was required. Meanwhile, the Estates Company endeavoured to negotiate a solution with their opponents. Letters sent by George Mellors to the Canal Company in January and June, offering to meet, were rejected. Three proposals for the Racecourse site were then put forward. Firstly, the Estates Company offered to lay out and operate 50 acres of docks, secondly to lease the land to the Canal Company at a low rent in perpetuity for dock purposes, and lastly to build the docks for Canal Company use charging only land rental and reasonable interest charges for the dock works. In December 1900, they made a further offer which would provide both the Canal Company and the Lancashire & Yorkshire Railway Co. with sufficient land for reasonable railway siding requirement, to the Canal Company sufficient land along the southern boundary of the Racecourse 'as may be required for the better working of the Canal Company's railways, as well as for the ... existing Salford Quay'. In return, the Estates Company would seek to lay out the remainder of the Racecourse as a dock, if necessary entering into an agreement with the Canal Company to protect each company's interests.

The Canal Company declined to give any ground in the matter: their legal advisors took the view that 'it would be inexpedient to enter into any negotiations or discussion ... litigation of a most important character is pending'.

The Racecourse Company itself became embroiled in the dispute, and in July 1900 asked the Canal Company whether an arbitrator was appropriate. In September, the Racecourse Company submitted a claim for £1 million, a figure said to have been suggested by three firms of eminent surveyors in London, Liverpool and Manchester. By November, both parties had agreed to the appointment of Robert Vigers as arbitrator. In December, the Racecourse Company asked for the arbitration to be deferred, pending the outcome of the Estates Company's petition against the Canal Company's Bill. On 15 December, the Estates Company submitted its own claim for £1 million, which was hastily rejected by the Canal Company; they were now facing compulsory purchase, and the compensation due to the Racecourse Company could not be on commercial lines.

Eventually, the Estates Company offered to withdraw their petition, effectively ending their hopes of acquiring the Racecourse site. They demanded in return, and received, a safeguarding clause in the Canal Company's Act, to the effect that the Canal Company would not use any part of the racecourse site except for dock purposes, and not sell any of it except to railway companies.

The arbitration dragged on, with dates for the hearing being postponed four times to 11 March 1901. The final award, made on 19 April, was for £262,500. An application for an appeal was made in April, but was not allowed.

At the Estates Company's Annual General Meeting, held in October 1901, the directors were forced to admit that the entire episode had cost the shareholders a shilling a share. They took a brave view that this expenditure had been worthwhile, and that land prices in the Park had been maintained by preventing the development of a competing site on the opposite bank of the Ship Canal.

Closer examination suggests that this was a reasonable view. The objective of the Estates Company's interests, stated in the 1900 Directors Reports, had been 'to place such a valuable site out of competition with Trafford Park'. In this respect, they had succeeded and had in the process forced the hand of the Canal Company into building another dock, No. 9, perhaps ahead of requirements. The Canal Company duly took possession of the Racecourse site in 1902, the racecourse itself being re-established at its former site at Castle Irwell, and the new dock was finished by 1905 at a cost of over half a million pounds.

The Canal Company faced a difficult situation. If the racecourse had fallen into other hands, the Canal Company would have been at the mercy of the Estates Company if and when further land was required for dock expansion. They feared being hemmed in, and reference would be made by the Canal Company to this pincer-like movement 'to throttle the Ship Canal in the future'.[13] More immediately, they saw it as an attempt to force them to buy land in Trafford Park at a high price, an offer repeatedly made by the Estates Company, and which it will be recalled had been advertised quite prominently in the 1897 Debenture prospectus.

On a more sinister note, it was apparent that by now personal animosity was building up between Stevens and his old colleagues in the Canal Company. Although, as yet, neither Company was profitable for its shareholders, the Canal Company clearly thought that the Estates Company were trying to gain at their expense. Stevens's own suggestions, made during the dispute, that his own company should become a public dock operator, and that the dock and terminal functions of the canal should be transferred from the Canal Company to others, including the Corporation, would be viewed as particularly aggressive and threatening.

The dispute itself set in course a few years of strained relations between the companies, and also between the Estates Company and the Corporation.

The development of the tramway system

After it had taken over the gas trams in November 1899, it quickly became obvious to the Estates Company that the transport systems both within and surrounding the Park would need to be vastly improved to meet the growing needs of the Estate's new industries and its labour force. As a temporary measure, in February 1900, the Estates Company bought three horse buses, and started a service between Pendlebury and Trafford Bar, connecting en route with the gas trams and at Trafford Bar with the horse-tram routes into Manchester. The service was immediately successful, and ran until June 1901, when it was largely replaced by a horse-tram service provided by Salford Corporation.

The Estates Company's desire to start an electric tramway service within the Park was to be a long drawn-out affair. Initial approaches were made to the Westinghouse Company, to Manchester and Salford Corporations, and to the South Lancashire Tramways Company, all without success. The interest of the two local authorities was diverted at the time to the rapid electrification and expansion of their newly acquired horse-tramway systems. In the case of the Park, the interests of the third local authority,

Stretford Urban District Council, would also come into play. Their main interests were to secure total control over any tramways operated by others within their area, whilst resisting attempts by Manchester to take them over, and at the same time to expand their degree of control over the still largely private fiefdom of the Park.

Faced with lack of progress, the Estates Company decided in September 1902 to invest in their own electric tramway. An agreement was drawn up with Lacy, Clirehugh and Sillar, and the work was put out to tender. Edmund Nuttall was given the job, and work began on the loop line, which began at the Old Trafford entrance, and then proceeded via Trafford Park Road, Ashburton Road to Third Avenue, before returning by Westinghouse Road. Unlike the gas tramway, which ran at the side of the road on the same track as the freight trains, the electric tramway ran on its own track in the centre of the road. The total route length was just over two and a half miles. Five double-deck tramcars were ordered from the British Electric Car Company, newly established in the Park, and a tram shed was built on Westinghouse Road, next to the Car Company's works. The Car Company would maintain the Estates Company's vehicles in return for the right to hold trial runs of new vehicles along the new route.

At first, it appears that agreement with the Manchester and Salford Corporations over running powers and connections had been provisionally agreed, but by 14 July 1903, when the new line opened, it was apparent that the Estates Company would have to operate their system in isolation. This was because Stretford had refused to allow a junction between the three systems at Trafford Road.

The politics of the situation now became very complex. It appears that, whilst the tramway was under construction, the Estates Company were considering selling it to Manchester Corporation and it was suggested that the Corporation apply for Parliamentary powers to operate the line and safeguard the Estates Company's interests; in other words, to allow the Estate to develop in the way that by now had become established. The sale price would be costs plus 10 per cent. Salford Corporation were to be permitted to install a junction at Trafford Road, and both the Company and the Corporation were to use all 'reasonable endeavours' to secure the incorporation of the Park into the City of Manchester, on terms no less favourable as provided for in an agreement between the Company and the City dated 26 November 1901.

Almost at the same time, the Company had offered to sell the tramway to Stretford for £25,000, and the latter wanted to know whether Manchester would take a lease of the tramway if Stretford decided to buy.

As part of his plans to move things forward, in January 1904 Marshall Stevens announced the deposition of the Estates Company's Trafford Park Bill, which included a clause seeking powers to make the tramway junction on Trafford Road. The Corporation were initially unmoved by this, being opposed to some of the Bill's other sections. At the time, they thought that the Estates Company were trying to sell the tramway to Stretford, and they were unwilling to enter into any arrangements with the Company whilst such discussions were ongoing. Eventually, the intentions of all three parties became clear, and by the time the Trafford Park Bill came before the House of Lords Committee on 12 May, the matter had been settled between the Company and the three local authorities. This provided for running powers to be exercised by both Manchester and Salford within the Park, with at least a 10-minute frequency on existing lines, and 15 minutes on other routes. Fares would be fixed by the Company, which would receive the net profits. The double junction on Trafford Road would be laid by Manchester for Stretford, and both Corporations would, if required, take over the Company's rolling stock and depot, at prices to be fixed by arbitration if necessary.

Manchester Corporation proceeded to lay its part of the double junction in August 1904, completing the work on 9 September. The Estates Company were charged £466 14s., being the cost of the work within the Park proper. The junction with the Salford line was more problematical, as it was necessary to get the Ship Canal Co. to construct the lines on the Trafford Road swing bridge, as contractors to Salford Corporation. This took some time to arrange, and in fact was not to be completed until 23 October 1905. Manchester in the meantime refrained from running their trams in the Park, partly because Salford were unable to do so, but also quoting some doubt over the legal status of the lines within the Park.

The Estates Company's patience was not infinite, and in January 1905 they commenced legal proceedings against both Corporations, alleging breach of the agreement made the previous May. The Estates Company's own service continued to run. Eventually, settlement was reached and both Corporations' trams started on Monday 30 October 1905, each service having a 15-minute frequency, or every seven and a half minutes within the Park. The Estates Company's own services then ceased. The Company's tramcars, now seven in number, were bought by Salford Corporation for £3,395, and Manchester bought the car shed. The staff were taken on by the local authorities, although the Estates Company retained its own inspectors to ensure that the company received its correct share of the takings.

The introduction of through running proved to be long overdue for both residents and workers of the Park, who now no longer had to change vehicles at Old Trafford. Tramway usage went up considerably.

The gas tramway had continued to run after the introduction of the electric cars in 1903, although the route had been shortened to run from Barton only to the junction of Ashburton Road, where it met the electric route. At the latter location, a waiting hut was erected. It bore a large sign saying, 'Change here for the Lake, the Hall and Barton'.

The gas trams were unaffected by the take-over of the electric cars in 1905, but after this date their standard of maintenance declined. In 1907, the Company reported a loss in operating them. At times, the trams were unable to surmount the incline over the Bridgewater Canal near Barton. To overcome this, the terminus was moved to the eastern side of the bridge. In December 1907, the Company decided to replace the gas cars with a steam train service for workers, running in the mornings and evenings only.

27 *Jacobs Biscuits factory on Elevator Road, first built in 1905. The firm left the Park during the 1930s.*

In February 1908, an order was placed for a standard saddle tank locomotive from the Leeds builders, Hudswell Clarke, at a cost of £900. At the same time, two second-hand four-wheeled passenger coaches were purchased from the Cheshire Lines Committee.

The new locomotive, 'Sir William Bailey', arrived in April 1908 and was put to immediate use pulling freight trains, whilst the two passenger coaches were modified slightly. The gas trams, of which only two were now operational made their final run on Sunday 1 May, and the following day the workmen's train started on the same route. Unlike the gas trams, only a rush hour service was provided, with two journeys in the morning and one in the evening. The gas trams, equipment and depot were auctioned by Edwin Bradshaw's on 3 June, the auction fetching £279 2s. 11d.

The Estates Company had operated a horsebus in 1904-7 running from Trafford Hall to either Third Avenue, or Trafford Road, being an adjunct to the 'gentlemen's quarters' in the Hall. Residents could avail themselves of it at any time of the day or night, and at times it would run to and from the main Manchester railway stations. It was replaced by a motor car in 1907.

Further expansion of the railway system

The arrival of further industries in the Park brought demands for the expansion of the estate railway system. The building of the lines on the south side of Trafford Wharf Road in 1900-1 has already been mentioned. 1900 also saw the completion of the permanent connection between the Estate and Ship Canal Company systems at what was to be known as Junction 'A', and its continuation across Trafford Park Road down to the end of Westinghouse Road, to serve the new Westinghouse factory and others nearby. Westinghouse also provided their own railway connection to the Cheshire Lines Committee's line, by means of a bridge across the Bridgewater Canal.

Near to this bridge a second bridge was built, making a direct connection between the estates system and the Cheshire Lines. Known as Bridgewater Junction, it was brought into use in May 1904.

The Estates Company had in 1903 obtained a fresh Light Railway Order, which authorised the building of the electric tramway, a new line along Ashburton Road, and two new lines across the Bridgewater Canal outside the estate, neither of which was to be built. The formal hearing into the application, held in March, had seen objections raised by Stretford UDC. Their objections centred on the status of the Park's roads, which the authority were either seeking to adopt as public highways, or expected to be called upon to take over as such. The Company, on the other hand, were opposed to what they saw as unnecessary interference in their running and development of the Estate. The Board of Trade ruled against Stretford in this instance. A further Light Railway Order was obtained in 1906.

By 1906, a short length of line had been laid at the Barton end of what was proposed to be the extension of Westinghouse Road. In 1908, a longer new line was built, initially to serve the new Taylor Bros steelworks at the western edge of the estate. This left the Trafford Park Road line, opposite the Hatton's Wood brick works, joining up with Ashburton Road. Both new road and railway joined up with the estate tramway for the approach to Barton, which by now was developing into a separate industrial area of its own, with several oil companies grouped around the oil wharf. In the same year, a short line was laid off Trafford Park Road to serve The Hives, built on Mosley Road.

Back in 1902, a new agreement had been entered into between the Estate and Ship Canal companies in respect of the carriage of goods between the docks and the Park.

The Canal Company by now were having doubts over the 6d. per ton charge entered into in 1898, which was being argued by the Estates Company as applying in perpetuity. A dispute arose between the parties as to whether the charge included such matters as storage in railway wagons, loading, unloading, sheeting or unsheeting or other services not technically 'haulage'. Marshall Stevens urged the traders of the Park not to pay the additional charges, and the Canal Company had to resort to litigation. In this they were successful, and the new agreement provided for reasonable charges to be levied for these services.

A further railway agreement was entered into in March 1906 between the Trafford Park Company, the Canal Company, the Great Northern, Great Central and Midland Railway Companies. This effectively gave the main line companies running powers over all the lines on the estate system, with the Canal Company acting as their agents. The main line companies would pay an annual sum (called the 'commuted sum') of £2,200 to the Trafford Park Company, together with tolls of 1d., 2d. or 3d. per ton, dependent on the precise class of traffic carried or the part of the estate where the freight either originated or was to be delivered. The Ship Canal Company in return received a working allowance in respect of the services they provided.

The Trafford Park Act 1904

The Estates Company made their boldest move yet in their struggle with the Ship Canal and the Manchester and Stretford local authorities, when they deposited their own private Bill before Parliament in November 1903. The bill's contents were ambitious and wide. Powers were sought to build a large public dock and two public wharves to be operated by a statutory company, a subsidiary of the Estates Company, which would also take over the estate roads and the powers of the West Manchester Light Railway Company. Other sections dealt with the Trafford Road tramway junction, transit sheds and warehouses, and sought protection for the status of the Park's roads and a contribution towards their upkeep from the Stretford local authority. Also controversial was a section dealing with the apportionment of the Canal Company's charges relating to the new dock undertaking.

As in the Racecourse dispute, Marshall Stevens offered to meet the Ship Canal directors to explain the proposals. He laid great stress on his object of preserving the Park from the encroachments of the local authority, and in particular to protect the Company's freedom to build railways and other facilities across the Park's roads. The Canal Company's immediate response was to appoint a Sub Committee to look into the proposal. After publication of the Bill, Stevens wrote again in December, this time also to the Lord Mayor, anxiously trying to open a dialogue. The Canal Company decided to oppose the Bill and, whilst the Lord Mayor sent a non-committal reply, the Corporation were of like minds. Both parties remained quiet for a while, but on 6 January 1904, in a statement to the Press, Councillor Southern made clear the Corporation's (and therefore the Canal Company's) opposition.

The Bill was formally read in the Lords on 8 February 1904. Its promoters were Colonel Mosley, Lord Ashburton, Mackworth Praed, Joseph Lyons, Sir William Bailey, Marshall Stevens and the Estates Company. Petitioners against the Bill were headed by the Canal Company, Manchester Corporation, Stretford UDC, Lancashire County Council, Salford Corporation, Barton upon Irwell UDC (which governed the western part of the Park), a number of traders, and, rather surprisingly, the Westinghouse Company.

The Estates Company, sensing the battle ahead, made offers of compromise. An early promise was to charge the same dock rates in the new installations as the Canal Company and 'to do anything in reason ... to meet the Canal Company'. On 21 March, Colonel Mosley wrote to J.K. Bythell formally withdrawing the dock provisions from the Bill, but retaining the two wharves. The Canal Company remained opposed to the Bill. Later, Mosley offered to deal only with Trafford Park goods at the wharves, and Marshall Stevens offered to handle restricted classes of traffic for 10 years until the new No. 9 dock site was fully used.

Matters came to a head on 12 May when the Bill was heard before a Select Committee of the Lords, chaired by Lord Glanusk. The Estates Company called an impressive number of witnesses to support the wharf proposals, one of which would have been a coal transhipment point at Barton with the Bridgewater Canal. Colliery owners from South Yorkshire, the Leeds & Liverpool Canal Company and a number of steamship owners spoke in favour. Other colliery owners, however, from the Chatterley Whitfield Collieries, and Richard Evans & Co., spoke against the coal wharf proposal, citing technical drawbacks and casting doubt on the proposed charging, particularly when compared with existing installations at Garston and Partington.

The Estates Company in support of the coal wharf placed great weight on the rights reserved to Sir Humphrey de Trafford in 1885 to have private wharves on the Ship Canal, and also quoted examples of other public docks on the Ship Canal not operated by the Canal Company. However, it appears to have been forgotten that the rights originally granted had been watered down considerably by the revised agreement with Sir Humphrey Francis de Trafford in 1888. The Canal Company were able to demonstrate that the two wharves could not be built without the effective compulsory acquisition of land off themselves, the cost of which had not been allowed for in the Bill. The crucial strip of land was at the top of the slope, originally reserved to Sir Humphrey, but later sold by his son. Finally, the Canal Company were able to show that the Estates Company's claims that additional width had been excavated on the southern bank of the canal, thereby aiding the docking of ships at wharves, a claim made in the 1897 Debenture prospectus, was simply untrue.

The hearings over the wharfage content of the Bill took place over four days. Considerable antagonism was present between the parties. Marshall Stevens referred to the 'considerable ill feeling in the matter' (from the Corporation). He himself was described as 'the active organiser of the scheme' and the Estates Company being 'operated by an ambitious and clever Managing Director'.

For the Canal Company, J.K. Bythell stated, 'the allegations as to the unfriendly nature of the Company are quite unfounded. The Company have ... given every possibility to the Estates Company and have greatly aided the development of the property.'

Specific instances were quoted of the haulage rates, the use of Trafford Wharf Road, the grain conveyors, lard pipeline, and the oil pipeline to Barton Wharf. The Canal Company saw the Bill's proposals as a threat and alleged that the proposed statutory company 'would be a mere dummy'. Finally, they stated that '[the proposals] would be of no advantage to the promoters except ... compelling the Canal Company to take over the proposed dock and wharves after completion'. Reference was made to the earlier racecourse dispute.

Having heard several thousand questions in cross-examination, their Lordships decided that in respect of the wharf proposals, the preamble to the Bill had not been proved. Consideration then moved on to the road and railway proposals of the Bill.

This time, it was Stretford UDC who led the opposition, describing the contents as 'unnecessary and pernicious' and 'an evasion of statutory requirements'. Complaints were made that the estate tramway had been built without statutory authority, and that the tramway junction should not be built unless the estate tramway was Council-owned. Stretford were less successful than the Canal Company and the Corporation. They succeeded in getting the provisions requiring them to contribute to the maintenance of the Park's roads removed, but they had to be satisfied with 21 days' notice if the Company wanted to alter any roads that had been adopted by the Council, with deemed approval if no clearance was received from the Council in that time period. A clause was also inserted that railway wagons were not to stand for more than five minutes on rails in or over carriageways. Previous disagreements over an attempt by Stretford in 1902 to take over part of Trafford Park Road were described, and Marshall Stevens laid great stress on the contribution to Stretford's rateable values that the Park offered, compared to the paucity of services received from the Council in return. Echoing a theme he would return to in later years, he stated 'it is not the case in Trafford Park that representation follows taxation at all'.

The remaining sections of the now slimmed-down Bill were considered by a House of Commons Select Committee in July, and the Act gained its Royal Assent on 15 August 1904. The Estates Company gained a new subsidiary, The Trafford Park Company, which assumed responsibilities for the Estate's roads and railways. The new company had an authorised share capital of £124,000.

'Hives' and 'Safes'

The strained relations between the Estates and Canal companies did not prevent them working together when it benefited both commercially. Certainly, in the early years, although neither company made profits, it would have been easier for the Estates Company to raise capital for new facilities, especially when the Canal Company was heavily committed in the massive investment involved in building the No. 9 Dock on the racecourse site.

The first such collaboration started the Estates Company's progress towards becoming a developer and landlord of buildings, rather than mere estate infrastructure. In 1902, an agreement was reached for the

28 *Early view of Mosley Road 'Hives', complete with loading platforms. The view is looking northwards, with Mosley Road to the right of the buildings.*

leasing of a shed between Westinghouse and Trafford Park Roads, previously used by Manchester Timber Importers, to the Canal Company for timber storage, in effect an extension of the timber facilities of the docksides. The Estates Company would receive a rent equal to 75 per cent of the rents payable by traders for timber storage, after rates and the Estates Company's railway expenses had been deducted. The agreement was terminable on six months' notice, and clearly suited both parties as a 21-year lease was arranged in 1906, after the Estates Company had replaced the original structure.

The following year saw the Estates Company go one stage further, and become a developer of a commercial building. The Canal Company agreed to lease a large cotton

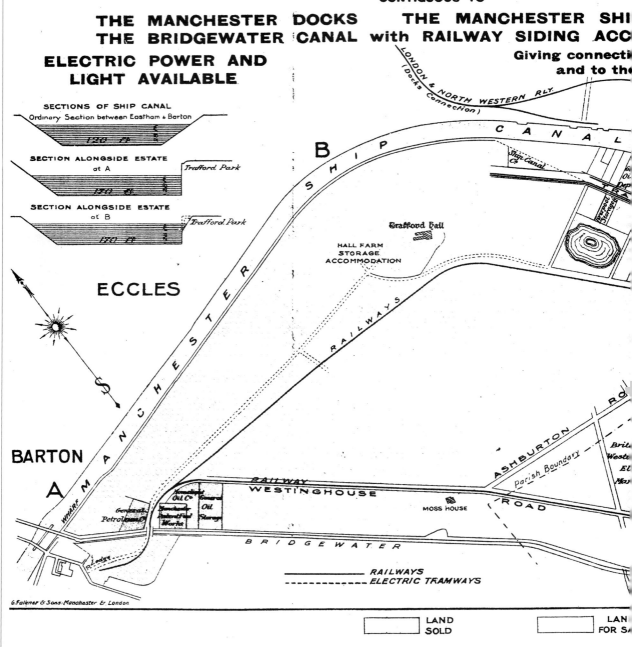

TRAFFORD PARK MANCHESTER

Land to be Leased or S

CONTIGUOUS TO

THE MANCHESTER DOCKS   **THE MANCHESTER SHI**
THE BRIDGEWATER CANAL with **RAILWAY SIDING ACC**

ELECTRIC POWER AND   Giving connecti
LIGHT AVAILABLE   and to the

SECTIONS OF SHIP CANAL
Ordinary Section between Eastham & Barton

SECTION ALONGSIDE ESTATE
at A   Trafford Park

SECTION ALONGSIDE ESTATE
at B   Trafford Park

ECCLES

BARTON

LONDON & NORTH WESTERN RLY.
(Docks Connection)

SHIP CANAL

Ship Canal

B

Trafford Hall

HALL FARM
STORAGE
ACCOMMODATION

RAILWAYS

MANCHESTER

WHARF

A

General
Petroleum

Oil Co.

Manchester
Fuel
Works

General
Oil
Storage

RAILWAY
WESTINGHOUSE

ASHBURTON

Parish Boundary

ROAD

ROAD

MOSS HOUSE

BRIDGEWATER

G.Falkner & Sons Manchester & London

————— RAILWAYS
- - - - - - ELECTRIC TRAMWAYS

☐ LAND
SOLD

☐ LAN
FOR SA

29   *Layout plan, March 1906, issued by Trafford Park Estates Ltd. Westinghouse Road as shown was not built in its entirety.*

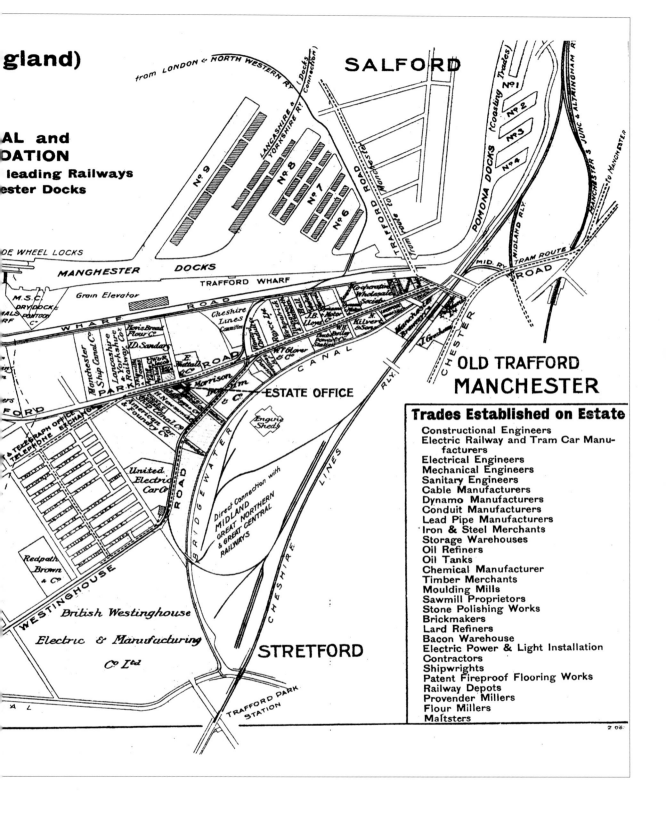

gland)

**AL and
DATION**
leading Railways
ester Docks

SALFORD

from LONDON & NORTH WESTERN RY (Docks Connection)

LANCASHIRE & YORKSHIRE RY

No 9
No 8
No 7
No 6

POMONA DOCKS (Coasting Trades)
No 1
No 2
No 3
No 4

TRAFFORD ROAD
Tram route to Manchester

MANCHESTER'S JUNC & ALTRINGHAM RY
to Manchester

MIDLAND RLY.

DE WHEEL LOCKS

MANCHESTER DOCKS

TRAFFORD WHARF

Grain Elevator

MID. RY.
TRAM ROUTE

M.S.C. DRY DOCK
MALS PONTOON
RF Co

WHARF ROAD

Cheshire Lines Committee

ROAD

CHESTER ROAD

OLD TRAFFORD
MANCHESTER

Manchester Ship Canal Co
Lancashire & Yorks Co
P.K. Railway Co

Floris Bread Flour Co
J.D. Sanday

American Car & Foundry Co

Morrison Ingram & Co

ESTATE OFFICE

Co-operative Wholesale Society

J.B. Lloyd & Co

Kilvert & Sons

W.T. Glover & Co

CANAL

BRIDGEWATER CANAL ROAD

TELEGRAPH OFFICE
TELEPHONE EXCHANGE

United Electric Car Co

Engine Sheds

Direct Connection with
MIDLAND
GREAT NORTHERN
& GREAT CENTRAL
RAILWAYS

CHESHIRE LINES

RLY.

Redpath Brown & Co

WESTINGHOUSE ROAD

British Westinghouse

Electric & Manufacturing

Co Ltd

STRETFORD

TRAFFORD PARK STATION

Trades Established on Estate

Constructional Engineers
Electric Railway and Tram Car Manu-
facturers
Electrical Engineers
Mechanical Engineers
Sanitary Engineers
Cable Manufacturers
Dynamo Manufacturers
Conduit Manufacturers
Lead Pipe Manufacturers
Iron & Steel Merchants
Storage Warehouses
Oil Refiners
Oil Tanks
Chemical Manufacturer
Timber Merchants
Moulding Mills
Sawmill Proprietors
Stone Polishing Works
Brickmakers
Lard Refiners
Bacon Warehouse
Electric Power & Light Installation
Contractors
Shipwrights
Patent Fireproof Flooring Works
Railway Depots
Provender Millers
Flour Millers
Maltsters

2 06

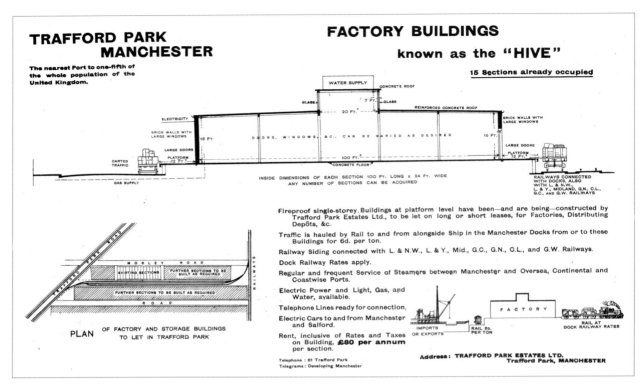

30 *Extract from an advertising leaflet for the 'Hives' and 'E' Safes, issued in January 1910.*

warehouse between Trafford Park and Trafford Wharf Roads, to be built by the Estates Company. The building was to be 200 feet by 600 feet and was required to help the Canal Company move cotton away from the docks within two weeks of unloading. The building was let on a long lease, with a rent based on a percentage of the net building cost, and a ground rent rising to one shilling per square yard after three years.

In 1908, the Estates Company went further still, building speculatively for the first time. A series of 19 small 'Hives' were built on Mosley Road. Built in a period of relative trade depression, these were contained in a long single building, 100 feet deep, capable of being divided into 25-foot-wide sections. Each Hive had a front access to Mosley Road, and rear access to a railway line, each end having platforms four feet above road and rail level to ease loading. The dividing walls between units were of lightweight construction so that units could be easily subdivided and amalgamated. The Hives were originally targeted at patentees and other small enterprises; the Company circulated some 8,000 patentees in the hope of attracting tenants, pointing out that new legislation only protected patents actually taken out in the U.K. In practice, the availability of the Hives helped to establish new businesses in the Park, with their initial low rents of £80 per annum, or to bring in larger enterprises, keen to test the locality, before moving to larger premises elsewhere in the Park. The tea firm of Brooke Bond arrived in this way in 1918, before moving four years later to a purpose-built factory.

For the Estates Company the Hives were a success and, although the rate of return would have been lower than from a larger building let to a single occupier, the availability of 'seedbed' or 'nursery' factory units, to use today's parlance, was a useful

addition to the estate. Certainly, they confirmed to the Estates Company the wisdom
of developing buildings. In the same year,
a set of large reinforced concrete warehouses known as 'E' Safes were built on
Third Avenue. Having a total cubic capacity of 778,000 cubic feet, they were designed
to encourage import traffic.

1911 saw the Estates Company begin
the erection of nine further safes, known as
the 'A' Safes, on a site between
Westinghouse Road and the Bridgewater
Canal. Discussions started with the Canal
Company the previous year, although the
precise agreement was not completed until
July 1912. This was to run for a period of

31 *Port of Manchester Warehouse Ltd.'s 'A' cotton Safes,
Westinghouse Road, showing overhead gantry cranes to assist
loading of goods delivered by road, rail or canal.*

five years, subject to three months' notice of termination by the Estates Company.
Under the agreement, the Canal Company was not to store cotton in the docks area
when space was available from the Estates Company. The latter were to accept such
cotton, and agreed not to use the buildings for any other goods in the first two years,
but could let any one Safe for the storage of cotton. Storage rates would be agreed
between the parties, and the Estates Company was allowed the preference of American
over Egyptian cotton.

The Safes were clearly another novel idea for the Estates Company, now actually
involved in the operation of warehouses. In their design, the Safes had noteworthy
features, which the Estates Company marketed with great frequency. Capable of holding some 50,000 cotton bales, the buildings had sprinkler systems fed by the mains, by
water tanks and by electric pumps from the Bridgewater Canal. Additional 'monitor'
water jets and hand jets were available. Electrically operated cranes working from
overhead gantries could load and unload goods direct from road or rail vehicles. The
buildings also had special facilities for sampling and weighing. It was claimed by the
Company that the design, the brainchild of Marshall Stevens, was later copied at New
Orleans.

The chief advantage of the Safes to traders, apart from the efficiency of operation,
was that insurance premiums on the fireproof buildings were a quarter of such costs
elsewhere. For the cotton industry the Ship Canal Company's warehouse of 1903 and
the 'A' Safes were to be virtually the only instance of Lancashire's traditional staple
industry making any use of the Park.

Estate development 1900-13

There were few disposals of land in 1900, the main transaction being the sale of more
land to Grain Elevator Estate Ltd., this time between the Bridgewater Canal and the
developing Village area.

The following year saw a large area on Trafford Park Road allocated to the Hattons
Wood Brick Company. A large shed was also erected on Trafford Park Road by the
Lancashire & Yorkshire Railway Co., and a second disposal took place at Barton, to the
Curtis Pure Oil Company. The same year saw the Estates Company establish its own
Works Department, to deal with construction and maintenance. This was first located

32 *The 'Trophy Arch' at the entrance to Trafford Park Road erected in July 1905, when King Edward VII and Queen Alexandra opened the new No.9 Dock.*

at stables at Heatons Wharf on the Bridgewater Canal, near the estate's eastern entrance. 1901 saw the arrival of a post office, at the junction of Trafford Park Road and Ashburton Road, W.H. Bailey & Co., and the British Electric Car Co., a newly established tramcar manufacturer, amongst others.

In 1902, the Caucasian Oil Company, a Russian-owned firm, was on site at Barton, and a wharf was constructed on the Ship Canal to allow discharge of oil to serve the growing township of oil storage tanks that was now in the Barton area. The Estates Company also suggested to the Ship Canal that a larger dock be formed in the old bed of the River Irwell, but the Canal Company were opposed to the idea.

Royce Ltd. took over a site on Trafford Park Road in 1902 for the manufacture of cranes. It was controlled by Henry Royce, who in 1904 cooperated with Charles Rolls in building a motor car in nearby Hulme, which led to the formation of Rolls Royce Motors Ltd. in 1906.[14] The Trafford Park Power & Light Co. opened its power station on the banks of the Bridgewater Canal. Pickfords were another firm that arrived.

In 1903, sites were sold to the Cooperative Wholesale Society and Hovis Ltd., both of whom had chosen Trafford Park in preference to sites elsewhere. Marshall Stevens had been trying to secure a flour mill for some time, quoting the Park's facilities, particularly the grain elevator on Trafford Wharf Road. Both the Hovis mill and a later one for John Greenwood & Sons, built in 1909, were connected to the Grain Elevator by underground conveyor belts. The one to the Hovis mill was half paid for by the Canal Company.

In 1904, Ashburton Road was built between Trafford Park Road and Third Avenue. Important disposals took place to Redpath Brown & Co., construction engineers, and to the American Car & Foundry Co., who took a site on a temporary basis for the building of carriages for the London Underground.

The following year, the Estates Company itself moved to the Park. Previously, it had been located at 18 Exchange Street in Manchester. The new premises were a former dwellinghouse, previously owned and built by Bennetts Ltd. on Trafford Park Road. The Works Department also moved to the new building, which was to remain the Company's head office until 1992. Trafford Park Road was made up from Third Avenue to the lake, and a sewer was laid from the Bridgewater Canal to Westinghouse Road via the line of Mosley Road South.

On 13 July 1905, King Edward VII and Queen Alexandra paid a visit to Manchester, on their return from a colonial tour, formally to open the new No. 9 Dock. The route took them along Trafford Road, where the Estates Company, in collaboration with some 50 firms, erected a large 'Trophy Arch'. This was made up of materials used and products made within the Park. The arch was topped by a steamer and decorated with steamship and railway company flags. Below the steamship, a large banner was draped proclaiming, 'Wake up England, Trafford Park is awake'.

The following year, Third Avenue North was built, and Westinghouse Road was made up as far as Mosley Road.

In 1907, a promotional leaflet was produced by the Company. This detailed the trades present in the Park, which included seven engineering firms, five contractors, eight timber merchants, three sawmills plus another 'in preparation', two flour mills, one provender mill (and another under construction), one matting house (and another under construction), and two railway and tramway works. The oil trade had a capacity of 65 million gallons, with six miles of pipeline laid. Under production were lubricating oil, electric cables, conduits, lard, gears, lead pipes, glass bottles, etc. Also present were

33 *Westinghouse Road and estate railway viewed from the roof of 'A' Safes. The Southern Cotton Oil Co.'s factory is on the right. This stretch of Westinghouse Road was recently renamed John Gilbert Way.*

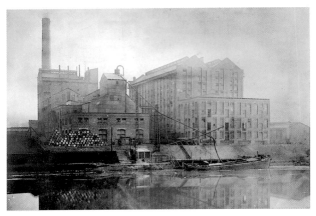

34   An early view of Nicholls Nagle factory, viewed from across the Ship Canal. Sir Humphrey de Trafford's 9 ft.-sandstone wall can be seen on the left, and has been partly removed to allow the berthing of grain barges.

an iron merchant's depot, railway depot, bacon curing factory, biscuit distribution depot, enamelling and metal refining works, as well as various service industries in the Village area. A new arrival that year was the large steelworks of Taylor Bros, who took a large area on the western side of the Park, adjacent to the Bridgewater Canal. This particular disposal necessitated the abandonment of the intention to extend Westinghouse road to Barton, and a diversion of the planned extension of Ashburton Road was made in 1908, linking with the existing carriage drive from the Hall to Barton.

Important arrivals in 1909 included Shell Mex and B.P. Ltd., the Lancashire Wire Company, the Rubber Regenerating Co., and John Greenwood and Sons. A short road, called Dynamo Road, which was laid in 1903 between Trafford Wharf and Trafford Park Roads, was abandoned. Mosley Road, between Trafford Park Road to Ashburton Road, was completed in 1910, along with Fraser Road. In 1911, Nicholls Nagle & Co., glucose manufacturers, arrived, taking a site on the banks of the Ship Canal to the north of the Hall. In the same year, other arrivals included Ford's (see later), the Southern Cotton Oil Co. and Textilose, the latter being manufacturers of yarn and twines, being the only instance of a textile related company to take space in the Park.

In 1912, sites were sold to the British Reinforced Concrete Company, Brothers Chemicals, the Carborundum Company and Turners Asbestos Cement Ltd.

A year later, 120 acres next to the Ship Canal were sold to Arthur Guinness & Co., at a price of £1,500 per acre. The disposal included Trafford Hall, which Guinness intended to use as offices, as by now its use as residential quarters had ceased and the golf course had moved out of Trafford Park in 1912. At the time, the Guinness Company's plans necessitated a long site to suit their manufacturing process, and as a result part of the recently built section of Ashburton Road was diverted to join up with the small section of the Westinghouse Road extension which had been started at Barton. Another result of the disposal appears to have been the termination of the estate tramway route at the Hall, and the abandonment of the stretch leading from there to Barton, which was replaced by a new line along Ashburton Road. The purchasers, before committing themselves to buy the site, had sunk two artesian wells to test the underground water supply. After the sale had taken place, they made a start by building a private wharf on the Ship Canal, but the First World War prevented any further work, and development was not recommenced after the War when the Company's aspirations were met in London and elsewhere.

The period 1900-14 saw the Estates Company gradually moving towards profitability, and by 1909 a dividend of half a per cent was being paid to the Ordinary shareholders. Rents received by the Company rose from £11,716 in 1900 to £41,068 in 1913. This growth, comprising as it did property rentals, ground and 'Chief '[15] rents, may be misleading, as it does not take into account allowance for capital receipts for freehold and long leasehold sales. The capitalisation of the Company rose steadily. In 1900 it stood at £575,000 Ordinary shares, with £350,000 first Debentures and £53,640 Second Debentures. By 1906, the Second Debentures had risen to £103,250. On 22 November 1906, authority was obtained to raise £600,000 of fresh debentures at 4 per cent and pay off the First and Second Debentures. In the same year, some Debentures and Ordinary shares of the Dwellings Company were taken over, and a share exchange took place in 1907. An interest was also acquired in Grain Elevator Estate, the other associated company, Throstle Nest Estates having been taken over c.1904. By 1913, the Company's Ordinary Capital was £611,730, Debenture Capital £550,000 and an annual dividend of two and a half per cent was being paid.

The Borough of Trafford Park proposal 1907

The Estates Company's relations with Stretford UDC were consistently plagued by the differing views each held towards the provision of public services within the Park. The local authority took the view that the Estate's roads ought to be dealt with like any other adopted roads, and not be subject to any special requirements as to railways and other rights. The Company naturally wanted the freedom to develop the Estate without interference, but to be able to benefit from public services paid for out of rate contributions from the rapidly growing area.

In 1901, Manchester Corporation approached Stretford over possible amalgamation, arguing that Stretford's growth was largely due to Trafford Park, itself largely due to the City-funded Ship Canal. As part of the approach, the Corporation talked to the Estates Company, who welcomed the idea, but only on the basis that, if Manchester were successful, the existing position in respect of the Park's roads would be maintained. Both Lancashire County Council, also responsible for the area, and Stretford were opposed to the suggested amalgamation, and the idea was rejected by Government after a formal Inquiry.

Stretford UDC were the first to bring the roads issue out into the open. In December 1902, they erected a notice at the eastern end of Trafford Park Road declaring it

35 *The scene looking towards Barton, c.1912 with the area's development as an oil storage centre clearly evident. Rails for extensions of the estate railway lie in the foreground.*

36 *Contractor's men and Carborundum officials outside the newly completed office building, August 1913. The building still stands at the factory's main entrance, having been extended many times since.*

a public highway. The Estates Company decided to take no action. Both the Estates Company and the Council obtained their own Private Acts in 1904, and both statutes contained sections specific to the Park's roadways.

In 1906, complaints were made in the press about the condition of Trafford Park Road. Stretford decided to move and issued the frontagers with formal notices in May, obliging them to pay for the making up of the road. Both the Estates Company and the frontagers objected, referring the matter to arbitration, where it was ruled that the UDC's standard of construction, using Welsh Granite sets, was unnecessary. The road, however, was improved and handed over to the UDC in 1909. In 1910, it was re-paved by the Council, and the Estates Company quietly rejoiced at the first work done to an estate road paid for out of rate contributions.

In 1907, a dispute arose over the eastern end of Westinghouse Road. The Council wished the Estates Company to pave the area between the railway tracks that lay in the centre of the road, and quoted the requirements of their own Act obtained in 1904. The Company in turn argued that the road existed before the passing of that Act, which therefore did not apply. After a court hearing lasting several days, judgement was given to the UDC. No work was done, however, and the rail area remained unpaved for several decades until the matter was settled amicably.

In the same year, the Company in conjunction with Park traders presented a petition to Lancashire County Council, demanding that Trafford Park be created an urban district in its own right, under the provisions of the Local Government Acts. The petition urged that, 'in order not to impede the continued development of the area for commercial purposes on hitherto adopted lines, which comprise the necessary provision of goods, manufacturing or other industrial facilities for manufacturing, your petitioners are unanimously of the opinion that Trafford Park should have independent self government'.

The application was heard by the County Council's Parliamentary Committee in June 1907. The petitioners argued that Stretford in particular was failing in its duties towards the area, having expended little despite the rate contributions. Local representation for the Park was inadequate, and the Park had little in common with other parts of the Urban District, which would still be, in rateable value terms, the largest district in Lancashire if separation were to be allowed. For the Councils, it was argued that the reasons why so little money had been spent in the Park was because the Estates Company wished to keep them out of its private fiefdom.

The County Council ruled against the application, saying that, for it to have succeeded, serious maladministration in the existing arrangements would have had to have been proved. All that had been demonstrated was that a good deal of friction existed between the parties. Some recognition of the petition was, however, granted in December, when a separate municipal ward was created, the Park Ward, out of two existing Stretford wards, after a further petition from the Trafford Park Ratepayers Association. However, this did not relate to the Barton upon Irwell part of the Park and, to the dismay of the Association, included other areas of Stretford.

In his evidence in support of the Trafford Park Act, Marshall Stevens had declared that, 'In the case of Trafford Park, taxation does not follow representation at all'. It was a theme that both he and his son would repeat from time to time, but the solution to the wider issue would not arrive within the lifetime of either man.

Manchester's first Aerodrome

In December 1909, the Estates Company received an enquiry from the A.V. Roe Company concerning a site for an aerodrome. A site of 91 acres was identified between the new Ashburton Road, the Mosley Road Hives, and the Golf Course. By mid-1910, the interest had been taken over by the Manchester Aero Club.

Officials of the Royal Aeronautical Club inspected the site in October and approved it as an official landing place for the 1911 *Daily Mail* Round Britain Air Race. On 19 December, a new Company, Manchester Aerodrome Ltd., was formed under the auspices of the Manchester Aero Club, at a meeting at the city's *Midland Hotel*, with a share capital of £1,000. A quarterly tenancy of the land was arranged with the Estates Company with effect from 25 March 1911 at a rent of £150 per annum. The rent was expected to be covered by letting out the land for grazing when not needed for flying, and by fees from subscribers who would erect hangars on the site for their own aircraft. Work to prepare the ground started early in 1911, when previous estate fencing and trees were removed and the ground was levelled. Proposals were made for an airship, the 'City of Cardiff', to fly from the Park. However the airship's owners demanded that the aerodrome company build a hangar, which the latter were unable to provide.

The first use of Trafford Park for aviation appears to have been on 7 July 1911, when Henry Melly and with a passenger flew in from Liverpool, landing on the adjacent golf course, where he was met by a reporter from *The Manchester Guardian*, and by Alliot Verdon Roe, who had arranged for white sheets to mark the landing area. The party lunched at Trafford Hall, before Melly returned to Liverpool.

37 *On 25 July 1911, the leader and ultimate winner of the* Daily Mail *'Circuit of Britain' race, Lt. Jean Conneau of the French Navy, landed at Trafford Park in his Bleriot XI monoplane after flying from Settle. The damaged Melly aircraft is waiting to be taken away on the right, and in the background the Westinghouse water tower can just be discerned.*

The golf club (which in 1912 was to move to a new site at Hopwood, north of Manchester) was used again on 25 July. Trafford Park was a staging post for the 1,010 mile circuit of Britain which had started from Brooklands three days earlier. A prize of £10,000 was available to the winner donated by the owners of the *Daily Mail.* Large numbers of spectators assembled early on the day, and Melly was engaged to give a number of five-minute demonstration flights in a Bleriot aeroplane. Unfortunately, on his first flight, he suffered an accident, although neither he nor his passenger was injured. Unusually for him, Melly had failed to have his aircraft tied down whilst the propeller was swung, and the engine had been allowed to warm up. The aircraft quickly bounded over the grass, took to the air, and then swerved sharply to the right, narrowly missing both spectators and parked motor cars, although some windows in a landauette were broken. The aircraft finally came to rest in an upright position on some iron railings. Subsequently, complaints would be levied about the lack of organisation and the absence of any control over the spectators. During the day, only two contestants, both Frenchmen, arrived at Trafford Park, with two more following on 29 July and 2 August. The latter, Samuel Cody, had first landed near the Westinghouse works before continuing to the Aerodrome.

The Aero Club tried to form a flying school in the Park in February 1912, but its protégé, the Aerodrome Company, was in serious financial difficulties by autumn of that year. No subscribers had come forward to build hangars on the site. In December, the tenancy of the Aerodrome site was given up by the Company, which itself was wound up by voluntary liquidation in late 1913. At the time, the Secretary of the Aero Club publicly voiced his criticisms of the apparent lack of public interest in aviation.

The aerodrome continued to be used for a time. In Whit week 1913, the Aero Club arranged for George Lee Temple to make a number of exhibition flights using a Caudron biplane, although his demonstration was limited by windy weather which persisted throughout the holiday period. Admission to the event was 6d.

On 20 June 1914, the Park was again used for a major air race, this time from London to Manchester and back. A total of four aircraft reached the site, the first being piloted by Louis Strange, having been guided by the Westinghouse water tower and two large arrows of white cloth pegged to the ground within the aerodrome site. Strange was greeted by the Lord Mayor, who climbed onto his Bleriot plane's fuselage to shake his hand. Strange was about to take off for the return leg of the race when his propeller broke, and he was unable to continue. On this day, admission prices to the aerodrome were 2s. 6d. and 1s., with children under 10 years half price, 2s. 6d. for motor cars, 4d. for motor cycles and 2d. for bicycles.

The aerodrome continued to be used into the early years of the First World War (see next chapter), and there are reports of its use as late as 1918.

The establishment of Ford's

The American motor car company, Ford, established a U.K. subsidiary in March 1911, and in the following months, through a number of publicity stunts, including the driving of a Model T vehicle up Ben Nevis, achieved a boost for American cars, dispelling their 'cheap and nasty' image in the process. To meet the increased demand that followed,

38 *View of the chassis erecting section at the Ford factory, showing the traditional methods in use prior to the introduction of the assembly line in 1914.*

39   *The Indian summer immediately prior to the outbreak of the First World War is well illustrated by this view of a garden party for Estates Company employees at Trafford Hall, 21 July 1914. The older Elizabethan part of the Hall is on the left.*

production in the U.K. was necessary, and on 23 October 1911 the Ford factory at Trafford Park opened, using the premises of the former tramcar manufacturer, the British Electric Car Company, on Westinghouse Road. The operation was intended to be an assembly plant for the 'Model T', using parts imported from the U.S.A.

Initially, assembly of the cars was on traditional lines and vehicles were built on the spot. The factory had an initial capacity of 7,500 cars per annum, but in the first year only 1,485 cars were built, rising to 6,139 in 1913. In 1912, Marshall Stevens managed to persuade Ford's that it was more economical to use components made locally, and the Estates Company established Trafford Park Woodworkers to make car bodies in the premises of the former coachmakers, Scotts, whose factory on Trafford Park Road had been built in 1907. The ambitions of the English Ford subsidiary under the dynamic managerial style of Percival Perry were, however, much greater, and in 1913 the Estates Company were obliged to sell the Woodworkers Company to Ford. Over the summer of 1914, the factory went over to full production-line methods, almost simultaneously as similar methods were being introduced by Ford at Detroit. Cars would now be built on a continuously moving conveyor, which could move at different speeds. At each 'station' individual employees or small groups would add single components or perform specific assembly tasks, each of which would be allowed a specific time for completion. Depending on the speed of the conveyor, completed chassis came off the production line at rates of 7-21 per hour.

Even before the introduction of the assembly line, the factory had already established its own way of working, on largely American lines. Wages were high, encouraging many local people to want to work at 'The Fords', and upsetting many of the surrounding engineering companies who lost labour as a result. Working conditions were strict, and staff wore a one-piece uniform containing the Ford emblem in red on the back. In the early years, neither trades unions nor trade union membership were permitted.

The factory assembled vehicles other than the Model T, with touring and saloon cars being produced as well as small vans, both open and enclosed. The full benefits of assembly line production methods were to be seen in the years after the First World War, when production increased from 8,000 cars in 1919 to 26,000 in 1920.

Notes

1. *Manchester City News* article.
2. *Sunday Express*, 22 September 1929.
3. ibid.
4. *Manchester Weekly Times.*
5. Hooley's account conflicts with the evidence of the Corporation's activities as detailed in the previous chapter. The Corporation made no offers in 1896.
6. ibid.
7. *Manchester City News*, 24 July 1897.
8. For much of the information about tramways in the Park, I am indebted to the works by Edward Gray and Arthur Kirby.
9. From *Hooley's Confessions.*
10. Newspaper advertisement quoted in E. Gray's *Trafford Park Tramways* (1964).
11. *Manchester City News*, 5 September 1903.
12. They were finally stolen from the Estates Company's new offices at Ashburton Road shortly after the Company moved in late 1992.
13. See later sections dealing with the 1904 Trafford Park Act.
14. Royce Ltd. later amalgamated with Morris Cranes of Loughborough and left the Park in the early 1930s. Their site was taken over by the Knowsley Cast Metal Co. An old Royce Ltd. logo was still visible on one of the buildings until it was demolished in 1994.
15. Chief Rents are peculiar to Manchester, Liverpool and Bristol. They apply where a freehold is sold but part of the purchase price is reserved to the Vendor through the payment of an annual (usually fixed) payment.

Chapter III

Further Development of the Estate
1914-1939

The First World War

The First World War saw a further phase in the development of Trafford Park. During every year of the war, numerous disposals took place, important sites including the Superheater Company (1914), Edward Wood & Co. (1916), Harley Davidson Motor Co. (1916) and Brooke Bond & Co. (1918). Existing occupiers also expanded their sites including Taylors, Redpath Brown, Trussed Concrete (all in 1914). The Estates Company invested in both infrastructure and buildings on a large scale. Ashburton Road was extended together with its railway from Taylors to Barton in 1914, and Trafford Park Road was extended from Trafford Hall to the new Nicholls Nagle factory in the same year. The northern section of Mellors Road was built, and an embankment was thrown up at Barton to enable a new bridge to be built over the Bridgewater Canal to replace the old carriage drive cum tramway bridge. A dispute with the Ship Canal Company, the owners of the Bridgewater Canal, prevented the latter scheme from being undertaken. Further roads were built in 1915 (Trinity Road) and 1918 (Richmond Road and the western extension of Westinghouse Road). The total length of the estate railway extended to 16.25 miles by 1918, including 'Gallipoli sidings', laid out in 1916 on part of the Hatton's Wood Brickworks site. The Trafford Park Company itself bought two additional steam locomotives, named 'Sir Joseph Lyons' and 'Lord Ashburton', in 1916 to cope with extra traffic generated by the war effort, particularly between factories within the Estate. By 1917, the company owned five steam locomotives, 10 steam cranes and 400 wagons.

The Estates Company and its Port of Manchester Warehouses associate engaged in a vast building programme, much for use by the Ministry of Munitions. In this way, steel, leather, army clothing, silk, and other army and navy materials, including armaments, were stored, sometimes in the open. The Mosley Road 'Hives' were extended in 1914. In 1915, 'L' Warehouse was built with a cubic capacity of 1.26 million cubic feet, reputedly within a period of six weeks whilst a ship carrying 15,000 tons of grain destined for the building was en route from Australia. Also built that year were the 'J', 'K' and 'P' warehouses, the latter being built to house the

40 *Recruits from the Westinghouse factory parading along Westinghouse Road, August 1914.*

41 *Marshall Stevens, Estate Company officials and contractor's men celebrating the completion of 'P' or Petrograd warehouse in 1915. The slogan is 'Prosperity to Petrograd'.*

collection and dispatch of war stores to Russia destined for the Petrograd Boot Company. In 1916, 'C', 'F', 'M', 'N', 'B' and 'D' warehouses were built, with a total capacity of over 9.5 million cubic feet. Seven more such warehouses were built in 1917, with a capacity of over four million cubic feet, and finally 'V' and 'T1' warehouses in 1918. The government allowed the Estates Company to offset the costs of these huge buildings over very short periods for taxation purposes.

The Ministry of Munitions also used vacant sites for the storage of sulphur and pitch. The former required the constant attention of the Eccles Fire Brigade. 'G' warehouse, still containing both pitch and ammunition, caught fire in 1919 and was destroyed. The aerodrome site on Ashburton Road also saw some use. A.V. Roe & Co. Ltd. built a shed and tested a number of aircraft. Another was built by the Central Aviation Company.

Trafford Hall was used as a military hospital, called the 'Trafford Hall Auxiliary Military Hospital'. Run by the Red Cross, and having a capacity of 125 beds, it was partly financed by the Estates Company, Guinness, and other firms on the Estate.

Many of the firms on the Estate at the outbreak of war were turned over to war production. The Ford works was placed under government control, and partly turned over to munitions manufacture. In 1915 Ford's started building military ambulances out of wood and canvas. Capable of holding four sitting or two stretcher patients, ambulance production had reached 100 per day when the war ended. The works was extended at the time and two factories were also built by the Ministry of Munitions for tractor production next to the works in 1916 and 1918, although the war had ended by the time that production was due to start.

At the Westinghouse works, some 500 men enlisted for service in the forces at the outbreak of war, and by the end of 1914 a third of the workforce had volunteered. Men and women of lesser skill took their places, but so serious was the loss of skills that the

War Office began to refuse to allow workers to leave the factory for the forces. During the course of the conflict overall numbers employed rose from 5,200 to 8,000, with women workers increasing from 620 to 2,500.

The factory itself produced parts for field guns, engines for tanks and submarines, mines and mine-sweeping 'paravanes', marine turbines, narrow-gauge petrol railway locomotives, shells, bombs, and fuses. The works successfully adapted a German magneto from a crashed Zeppelin for use in aircraft engines. It was named the 'Bosch Magneto'.

Port of Manchester Warehouses Ltd.

In 1914, a new company was formed by the Estates Company to take over and run its warehousing operations. The directors of the new venture included Marshall Stevens, T.G.

42   *Visit of King George V to the Westinghouse factory, May 1917, who toured the works after 'clocking in' like other workers.*

Mellors, Edmund Nuttall and Sir Walter Royce. Captain W.C. Bacon of the Ship Canal Company and R.B. Stoker of Manchester Liners were also directors.

The 'Safes' already erected, 'A', 'D' and 'E', were all sold to the new company, and all the warehouses built during the First World War came under the control of Port of Manchester Warehouses Ltd. The 'Safes' agreement of 1912 with the Canal Co. was terminated in June 1914 to hand over the Cotton Safes to the new company.

'D' Safes on Mosley Road, started by the Estates Company in January 1914, were completed in June. The building was used temporarily to store cotton, and then put to its intended use of tobacco storage. On 17 July, the building and its entire contents caught fire and were completely destroyed. Work started on a replacement building only two days later on an adjoining site, and by the middle of October a third of the new building was ready for occupation.

The war period saw the new company develop at great speed, and in due course it became the largest warehousing operation of the time in the U.K. In 1919 a new head office building for it was completed on Ashburton Road. By 1925, it controlled no less than 44 warehouses capable of holding 100,000 bales of cotton, 40,000 barrels of wines and spirits, 10,000 'tierces' of tobacco leaf, 20,000 tons of sugar, 15,000 tons of miscellaneous products and 35,000 chests of tea.

The new company brought sophistication into the provision of warehousing, and used mechanical handling devices to great effect, including electric stackers, monorail cranes, conveyors, presses etc. Access to all warehouses was possible by both road and rail. To celebrate its success, and to advertise its facilities, the Company commissioned, in 1921, the artist W. Heath Robinson to supply illustrations for a publicity book entitled *Then and Now*. Photographs of the company's operations are shown and compared with rather improbable looking devices devised by the artist in his usual fashion. The book cost one shilling and the drawings by Robinson were said to be a slight satire on a recent work by H.G. Wells.

In June 1920, Marshall Stevens wrote to the Canal Company, offering to sell Port of Manchester Warehouses Ltd., the estate railway system and the newly established

Cold Storage Company. The price for the warehousing and cold storage companies was to be the updated building and land costs, plus a share of the profits to be payable annually. For the railway, the price would be the updated building and land costs, plus the value of the equipment. The railway sale would be subject to the 6d. haulage rates rising to one shilling per ton. The Canal Company were to accept an obligation to extend the railway to undeveloped sites, and to accept the Estates Company's obligations over the construction of the new Barton Power Station by Manchester Corporation.

These terms must have been too high for the Ship Canal, whose Board declined the offer.

Trafford Park Cold Storage Ltd.

Proposals were made in 1917 for the erection of a large cold storage building on Mosley Road. This followed an agreement between the Estates Company and the Ministry of Food under which the Company undertook to provide 10,000 tons of storage capacity, with the Ministry providing a loan of £45,475 for refrigeration equipment and insulation. A new company was formed in 1918 to operate the facility. It had an Ordinary capital of £50,000 and £50,000 worth of Debentures, the latter being guaranteed by the Estates Company.

The new building was not in fact finished until 1919, but it was a huge building, with over 1.5 million cubic feet capacity. At the time, it was claimed to be the largest such building in the area, and the third largest cold storage facility in the country. Like the Safes and warehouses, the cold store was equipped with modern handling machinery. The insulated buildings could maintain a constant temperature of 15-16 degrees fahrenheit, and used a compressed ammonia circulating system. In addition, cold air within the

43 *Exterior of the Trafford Park Cold Storage building, Mosley Road, showing the elaborate electric gantry crane systems used in the inter-war years, railway wagons and a Port of Manchester Road Services insulated van.*

44 *Crookes boatyard on the banks of Trafford Park Lake, c.1920, with the Carborundum works in the background.*

building was distributed by ducts from batteries of coolers at a temperature of five degrees. When the air inside had risen in temperature, it was drawn off to pass over large batteries of brine-cooled pipes.

The building was similar to the Safes in that the flat roof was used as an operating platform, pierced with hatchways. Overhead, a large steel gantry acted as the track for an electric travelling crane. Frozen material could be delivered to any part of the building on slings carried by the cranes. Storage would be segregated according to grade and quality. Up to 500 tons could be moved in or out of the building daily. In 1925, the firm claimed that up to 25,000 carcasses of single-grade mutton could be moved within an eight-hour period. Other electric equipment for stacking and storage was also provided.

Magnificent though the new building was, it was finished too late to be used in the First World War, and the expected supplies of beef and mutton from Australia did not arrive in sufficient quantities in the early years of the venture. The Estates Company would be drawn into creating separate companies in the 1920s to encourage business for the Cold Storage Company. Success was not to be established until the end of the decade.

In 1922, the Cold Storage Company erected a separate building on Mellors Road, known as the 'Cool Store'. This was a smaller building, only 1,060,000 cubic feet. It was intended for foodstuffs that did not require refrigeration, and in its early years handled chilled beef, eggs, dairy produce, and fruit. Its cooling system was a series of direct expansion pipes suspended from the roof, with coils distributed around the walls and the central stanchions of the building.

The Cool Store enjoyed moderate success in the 1920s and 1930s, but by the end of the Second World War it had been passed to Port of Manchester Warehouses for use as a tobacco warehouse.

Expansion Westwards and the Barton Dock area

In the 1897 sale, Sir Humphrey de Trafford sold only a small parcel of land on the western side of the Bridgewater Canal, around the Barton entrance lodge and driveway. Sir Humphrey retained ownership of about 1,300 acres on the western side of the canal, although control passed to family trustees in 1904. For the Estates Company, given the location of the Park next to the immovable Ship Canal and Docks, and an ever more urbanised Stretford to the east, the logical step would be to expand westwards when development of the Estate was complete.

A start was made in 1916, when the small Lostock Farm, not in de Trafford ownership, was bought, ostensibly for a staff housing scheme. The Company's true intentions were demonstrated the following year when an application was made to the Light Railway Commissioners for the Barton and Stretford Railway, which would have linked the Estate railway at Barton with the Cheshire Lines Committee's tracks near Water's

Meeting Junction on the Bridgewater Canal. The de Trafford Trustees had proposed a similar scheme in 1916, which was opposed by the Canal Company if it were to connect to the Estates Company's lines. In turn, the Estates Company opposed the Trustees' line. A complicated series of manoeuvrings took place over the next four years between the parties to determine who would buy the de Trafford land, and on what terms. The obtaining of the necessary Light Railway Order, so essential for the development of the land for industry, would be a useful bargaining tool in such negotiations.

The Estates Company's application was rejected in April 1917. The Company then pledged its support to the de Trafford application, which was obtained in 1919. This support, however, did not bring the desired result, and negotiations, carried out for the Estates Company by Dunlop Lightfoot and Wallis, were not successful. Instead, in 1920, the Trustees agreed to sell 1,000 acres to the Canal Company, with an option to purchase the rest later. The land was sold for industrial development, on a rising rent basis, starting at £8,000 per annum, and rising to £25,000 per annum after 15 years. Although an initial disposal took place in 1921 to D. Anderson & Co., development of the site was slow, in spite of a significant disposal at the eastern end took place in the late 1930s when the Kelloggs factory was built south of the Westinghouse works.

The Estates Company decided to make the best it could in the circumstances, and agreed to exchange most of the Lostock Farm land, which divided the ex-de Trafford ownership, for a small area of land at Barton to the south of the Company's holdings, which was added to the Estate. The remaining part of Lostock Farm was retained for the route of the proposed Lostock Light Railway. This was a passenger tramway proposal, first submitted in 1915, designed to extend the existing electric tramway in the Park in the Davyhulme and Urmston direction.

Fearing a repetition of the Racecourse dispute, the Estates Company in 1922 resurrected their 1904 dock proposals, and drew up plans for a 50-acre dock in the Park proper. They offered to sell it to the Canal Company in exchange for land of equal value recently acquired by the Canal Company at Barton. The Canal Company declined the offer. The proposal surfaced again two years later, when the Canal Company were offered the site 'on reasonable terms'. They saw no reason to act.

At about the same time, the Estates Company purchased a half share in Dumplington Estates Ltd., a company set up in 1923 with a capital of £15,000 to administer 38 acres of land to the west of Barton, which Taylor Bros had bought in 1918 from the de Trafford Trustees, with the intention of building a 'garden village' of staff housing. This particular acquisition was to prove fortuitous, because not only had Taylors abandoned their housing plans, but the site formed another 'salient', effectively splitting the Canal Company's 1921 purchase, and therefore hindering any plans to serve it with a Ship Canal frontage.

The two Companies came to an agreement in 1929, when the Canal Company acquired Dumplington Estates in return for granting the Estates Company more land to the south of Barton, which became known as the Trafford Park Extension.

As part of the agreement, provision was made for rail traffic from the area to the west of the Bridgewater Canal via a new junction between the Estates Company and Ship Canal systems, known as 'Junction C', free of tolls up to a total of 300,000 tons per annum. The Estates Company received in return an undertaking from the Canal Company that any traffic conveyed from the Trafford Park Extension would be carried at the same haulage rates as contained in the 1898 agreement.

The Canal Company's records at this time refer to the potential of the ex de Trafford land for dock purposes, and it has been known since as the Barton Dock

45 *View of the junction of Trafford Park Road and Mosley Road in the early 1920s. On the right is Davidsons motor body works and Brooke Bond Ltd.*

Estate. No docks were ever built, although developments did continue around Barton Dock Road during the Second World War and thereafter. The western end between Containerbase and the Ship Canal, including the former Dumplington Estates area, remains largely undeveloped to this day. The past few years have seen mammoth legal and planning battles between the Canal Company, local authorities and other interested parties over its proposed development as a large regional shopping facility, to be called 'The Trafford Centre'. This was resolved on 24 May 1995 when the House of Lords finally ruled in the scheme's favour.

Marshall Stevens and Politics 1918-22

In December 1918, Marshall Stevens was elected M.P. for the Eccles constituency. He was a Conservative, first having become involved with the party in his days of campaigning for the Ship Canal, and stood under the 'Coalition Unionist' ticket of Lloyd George. Stevens had also been treasurer of the Eccles Conservative Club and later its president.

During his campaign, Stevens made much of his business experience, and one of his slogans was, 'An A1 British Empire with an A1 British people'. He also returned to an old theme of his, namely the excessive hold of the Port of Liverpool on shipping interests, and the adverse effects this had on the Port of Manchester. His Liberal opponent, Richard Holt, the owner of a shipping firm, was attacked mercilessly in pamphlets, one of which contains a short but dismissive reply from Holt.

Stevens won the seat, by 15,821 votes to 3,408, reputedly the largest majority ever achieved in the constituency. After the election results were announced, Stevens was paraded through the streets to the Conservative Club, where he was presented with a large Eccles Cake inscribed 'Marshall Stevens takes the Cake'.

His tenure as an M.P. lasted only one term. In November 1922, he was defeated by John Buckle, who became the town's first Labour M.P., winning a majority of 803 votes, although Stevens's vote had held up reasonably well. He had stood for law and order, but miners from the Pendlebury area supported Buckle. In 1923, Stevens stood again and lost. This time, his share of the vote dropped from 49 per cent to 30 per cent. Stevens did not stand for office again.

Railways and Transport within the Park

The length of the Estate railway system continued to grow in the 1920s and 1930s, virtually doubling by the early years of the Second World War. Important additional routes included a line between Redpath Brown's and Praed Road, called the 'Electron route' (opened in 1919), a link from Westinghouse Road to Trafford Park Road adjacent to the Estates Company's offices (opened in 1920), further extensions along Westinghouse Road to the British Alizarine factory (opened in 1921), an extension of the Ashburton Road line across the Bridgewater Canal to Barton Power Station (1921), an extension

46   *Office staff, Model T Ford and Estates Company locomotive* Lord Ashburton *outside Port of Manchester Warehouses Ltd.'s new offices on Ashburton Road, early 1920s. Note the use of Estates Company logo on the locomotive.*

across Redcliffe Road to the Dumplington Estate (1922) and between Tenax Road and Ashburton Road (by 1929).

In addition, many other lines were doubled over this period, including the line across the Bridgewater Canal leading to Bridgewater Junction, necessitating a new bridge over the canal, which was finished in October 1932. Gallipoli Sidings, to the north of Trafford Park Road, were substantially extended in 1922 at a cost of £85,000, following an agreement between the Estates Company, Canal Company and the L.N.W.R. in February. The resultant facility, containing some seven miles of track length and capable of holding 1,600 wagons, became known as 'B Sidings'. The agreement provided for the Canal Company to convey traffic via the dock railway system to the L.N.W.R. at New Barns Junction in Salford.

Over the same period, the annual tonnage carried on the Estate railway system increased from 1,742,400 tons to 2,140,449 tons. In the 1930s, the Company claimed that some three per cent of the entire U.K. rail freight had travelled over Trafford Park rails at some point in its journey.

With the increase in motor traffic over the same period, it was necessary to minimise conflicts at level crossings. In December 1927, the first electric 'Danger' signs were erected at crossings. By 1940, a number of crossing keepers were employed, whilst other crossings were controlled by 'robot signals'. In 1919, the Company adopted a set of formal regulations to govern safety of the system. Traffic was to be worked by the shortest route, an overall speed limit of 10 m.p.h. was applied along with a system of engine whistles, and trains were not to exceed 30 wagons in length except when locomotives were in short supply. Formal Bye-Laws, obtained in 1936, contained further safety provisions.

Throughout the First World War, the main-line railway companies had effectively been under Government control. The gradual ending of this control, and ideas for railway nationalisation, eventually resulted in the 1923 Grouping, out of which emerged four main-line companies. As a result, the Trafford Park Company sought a new Act of Parliament to replace the railway powers contained in the 1904 Trafford Park Act, and to increase the capitalisation of the statutory company responsible for the estate railways.

The Parliamentary hearings saw few of the fireworks of the 1904 Act, although the Canal Company opposed the Estates Company again. The Bill also sought running powers over the Ship Canal's own railways, and to tear up the 1906 agreement under which the Trafford Park Company received tolls in respect of traffic passing to and from the main line companies. Neither of these provisions survived into the Act. Powers were also sought to run trolley buses in the Park. Arguments did ensue at Committee stage about the status of Ashburton Road, and the Company were obliged to upgrade it to a width of 30 feet, and to provide a kerb between the railway lines and the roadway.

The slimmed-down Act duly passed onto the statute books and the existing status of the estate's railways was confirmed. Prior to the Act, the Company was obliged to make agreements with the Canal Company in February and March. These effectively ended the limited haulage that had been undertaken directly by the Trafford Park Company, mainly point to point traffic within the Park which had been developing during the First World War. Also ended was the passenger train service run by the Company since the demise of the gas trams in 1908. The 1922 Act only provided for the estate system to carry freight. The Trafford Park Company passed all its steam locomotives and most of its wagon fleet to the Ship Canal Company, retaining only a few wagons and a steam crane for maintenance.[1]

To replace the 'Barton Mail', the Company bought three open-top AEC buses. These first ran on 21 March 1922, running an hourly service from 6.30 a.m. to 5.30 p.m., or 12.30 p.m. on Saturdays. The route ran from the *Trafford Park Hotel* to Patricroft Bridge, and a 15-minute frequency operated between the Hotel and Barton (Twining Road) at rush hours. At weekends, the buses were offered for private hire, and at slack times one stood at Patricroft station advertising day excursions to seaside resorts. By October, it was reported that the service was operating at a considerable loss, and after a delay it was taken over by the Lancashire United Transport Co. from 29 June 1925.

The electric tramway, running in its loop through the Village, continued in operation with the two local authorities. By 1920, it too was running at a loss, and the fare was increased to 1°d. By 1921 the tram tracks were showing signs of wear. The lines were re-laid by the Estates Company at a cost of £50,000 between August 1923 and February 1924. At the same time, single-track extensions were built along Ashburton Road and Westinghouse Road, the former for a considerable distance, in anticipation of the implementation of the Company's Lostock Light Railway Order, obtained in 1919. Despite apparent agreement with the local authorities, nothing was done and the

Ashburton Road line lay disused, although the Westinghouse Road line was used for storing extra rush-hour tramcars.

In 1924, it was reported that Stretford UDC were again negotiating to purchase the tramway. Negotiations also took place over many years with Manchester and Salford for continuance of the existing services. These were finally completed in 1933, the agreement of that year being replaced in 1934 by a lease of the system to Manchester Corporation for a term of 10 years at a fixed rent. With the agreement of the Company, the Corporation considered the replacement of the trams with buses. By March 1938, Manchester's regular tram service had been replaced by buses, and Salford followed in July 1939.

Over the years, the Company fought battles with both the L.M.S.R. (as successors to the L.N.W.R.) and the Cheshire Lines Committee over the tolls receivable by the Trafford Park Company. Increases were agreed in 1927 and 1937. Port of Manchester Warehouses also engaged the main-line companies in litigation from time to time, seeking reduced charges for particular goods. Two cases in 1922 were lost, as was another in 1924, against the L.M.S.R. for quoting a low rate for sugar passing from Manchester to Liverpool.

Westinghouse becomes Metropolitan-Vickers

Although successfully established in the Park as a building project, the giant Westinghouse factory failed to meet its capacity in the early years, and no ordinary dividend was paid. Not only did the U.K.'s railways fail to engage in large-scale electrification, but other demands, such as from the area's textile industry, did not materialise in any quantity. Alternative sources of power, such as steam and gas engines, remained popular with local industry.

George Westinghouse relinquished control and severed all connections with the U.K. company in September 1909, but it remained in American hands. During the First World War it was felt that this ownership was not in the company's best interests, and by 1916 negotiations had started with a view to buying out the American control. In May 1917, a British-owned holding company was formed to buy out the American shareholders, with funds provided by the Metropolitan Carriage Wagon and Finance Company. In early 1918, the authorised capital of the holding company was increased from £1.395 million to £5 million, and shortly thereafter the remaining American directors resigned. The Metropolitan Company and its Westinghouse subsidiary were in turn bought out by the Vickers Company in early 1919, and in September 1919 the name Metropolitan-Vickers Electrical Co. Ltd., often colloquially shortened to 'Metrovicks', first appeared. It was also the first year that a dividend was paid to ordinary shareholders.

A further change took place in the Company's structure in 1927, when Vickers itself was taken over by the International General Electric Company. In 1928, the companies owned by GEC were reorganised, and the Trafford Park factory came under the ownership of Associated Electrical Industries Ltd., or AEI. The name Metropolitan-Vickers continued to be used for trading purposes.

Throughout the 1920s and 1930s the firm steadily grew. As a trainer of staff, its reputation was unrivalled, with places at its Apprentice Training School, located on Moss Road, being heavily sought after. As the largest employer within the Park, its factory gates attracted political demonstrations, the most common being for the Communists or the Mosleyites. At one of the former events, in March 1930, the young

Edmund Frow, later to become renowned in the Manchester area as a labour historian, exhorted the demonstrators to: 'Come to my assistance, comrades! Shoot for it comrades as they have done in Russia. Three cheers for machine guns. Down with the Labour Government'.

Frow was arrested, fined 40 shillings and imprisoned for a month.

Within the works itself, the firm became famous for its good labour relations. It saw the establishment of Britain's first Works Committee in 1917, which was largely credited with the fact that the factory lost only one day's production during the General Strike of 1926. The Works Committee became the breeding ground for many names that went on to rise to prominent national positions in the labour and trades union movements. One such was Hugh Scanlon, who went on to become leader of the engineering workers' union.

Manchester's First Radio Station

Although the Metropolitan-Vickers Company severed its American connections, some contact was maintained, because one of the Company's engineers was sent in 1920 to experience the broadcasts of Station KDKA, run by the American Westinghouse Company in East Pittsburgh. The results of this visit persuaded Metrovicks to enter the broadcasting field. In March 1921, the Company's head of research, A.D.M. Fleming, applied to the Postmaster-General for a licence to establish two broadcasting stations, one in Manchester and one at the Slough base of the Radio Communications Company, who were to supply the equipment for the Manchester studio, and cooperate in the development of the new medium.

After some trials in Fleming's own home at Hale, a studio was set up in the small conference room in the Metrovicks research building. The studio was equipped with a marquee-like structure of sail-cloth on a wooden frame designed to create good sound conditions. Added to this, heavy curtaining was used on the walls and ceiling, and a half-inch thickness of felt covered the floor. A 'Control Box' was fitted inside the studio, and a cage-like aerial was slung between the top of the building and the nearby works water tower. The transmission equipment was housed in spare space under a stairwell.

The first experimental broadcast took place on 17 May 1922, when an extract of a speech by a Mr. McKenna, reported five days earlier in *The Times*, was read. Three musical items and a further newspaper extract were also broadcast, on differing wavelengths. Careful monitoring of the broadcasts was undertaken. All the work at this stage, by both technicians and performers, was undertaken *gratis*, with Metrovick staff working outside their normal hours. Many works staff took part as performers. From 22 July, the broadcasts were undertaken on a weekly basis, and more frequently later. In October, the transmission equipment was substantially upgraded in power.

In December 1922, a licence was granted to the British Broadcasting Company, itself formed from six large firms, one of whom was Metropolitan-Vickers. The first official broadcast of the new Company from London was on 14 November 1922, and the Manchester station, called '2ZY' using the Metrovicks studio, started the following day. A General Election was in fact taking place on the day and, after the usual musical items and a 'Kiddies' Corner', election results were broadcast up to 11 p.m.

The new station established its own reputation over the next two years, presenting talks on many subjects, both serious and less so. Music formed a large element of the content, with news, plays and children's programmes. The station at Trafford Park was not destined to last for long, however. Its studio measured only 30 feet by 16 feet, so space was cramped, and the new Company set about finding an alternative site for a permanent station in the area. This finally became operational in July 1923, when the Dickinson Street studios were opened. The Trafford Park studio was maintained on a standby basis for a further month.

During the mid-1990s, Trafford Park again became home to radio, when the commercial station, Fortune Radio, began broadcasting from studios in the Quay West office building.

Associated Companies of Trafford Park Estates

The continued development of the Park in the years of the First World War and thereafter did little to dampen Marshall Stevens's energies. Indeed, some have stated that the decade 1915 to 1924 saw him at his most active in the pursuit of business.

Faced with the setback on the Barton Dock area in 1921, and the difficulties of attracting business for the cold storage associate, the Estates Company created three new companies in the early 1920s to encourage further business and profitability.

The first of these companies, Port of Manchester Road Services Ltd., was formed in 1921. It took over the road transport work of the warehousing and cold storage

47 *Port of Manchester Ltd.'s 'C' warehouse, containing nitrate of soda, being extended in the early 1920s.*

companies, and acquired a fleet of 17 Sentinel steam lorries, some fitted out as insulated vans. These travelled at a speed of eight m.p.h. and were fitted with oil lamps. The company's intention was to provide an efficient road transport service within a 30-mile radius of the Park, an area where local rail transport could not compete. In fact, the new company itself could not compete against the growing band of local road hauliers, equipped with either cheap war surplus or modern road vehicles. The Company failed to survive the Great Depression of 1929, and was wound up the following year.

A second new company, Manchester Consignments Ltd., was formed in 1922, with a third, the Manchester Bacon Factory, in 1923. The Consignments Company was essentially a guarantee organisation, backed by the Estates Company to the amount of £115,000, and by the District Bank Ltd., who lent £225,000. The Company claimed that its object was 'to finance the producer, saving him the long wait for money and by prompt settlement and fair dealing ... [it] takes over the consignments, warehouses them if necessary, watches the manufacturer, acts on instructions given, and delivers the goods to the consumer, who pays a percentage of the value of the produce, and remits the balance after the sale'. In 1922, the Estates Company sent a Mr. C.A. Harrison to New Zealand to canvass traffic, and the following year chartered the SS *Admiral Codrington* to carry produce from New Zealand to Manchester. No lasting success, however, was achieved and trading ceased in mid-1927; the company was wound up in 1929.

The Bacon Factory was set up in premises alongside the Cold Store, equipped to deal with 1,500 animals per week. The initial fortunes of the company were very poor, due to the inability to compete successfully with Danish bacon. An alliance with a Canadian firm, Gunns of Toronto, was in place by 1925, but did not survive long, an additional problem being the lack of support from local farmers. The company reported a loss in 1926, along with the Consignments Company, and it too ceased trading in 1927 and was wound up in 1929.

Changes in the Village 1919-39

No additional houses were to be built in the Village, but several facilities were provided or extended in the period, particularly by the local authorities. The Council School 'tin shed' had been replaced by a permanent building in 1914. A Roman Catholic school, called St Antony's after the adjoining church, was built in 1912-3.

Stretford UDC purchased two acres of land in 1921 for the layout of a children's playground and a local park and in 1927 some further land for a municipal swimming baths, which opened on 18 December 1928, the architect being Percy Howard. A wash house was added in 1931. In June 1936, a library and health clinic opened at a cost of £2,500.

The Methodist and Church of England 'tin sheds' were replaced by permanent buildings, St Cuthbert's being completed in 1926. In 1928, St Cuthbert's became a parish in its own right, enabling weddings to be held in the building.

The front gardens of the houses on Second, Tenth and Eleventh Streets were removed in the early 1930s when the front footpaths were replaced by streets.

The cinema in the old Trafford Hall conservatory, located on Third Avenue, was demolished in the mid-1920s when the site and adjoining land was sold to Richard Johnson Clapham and Morris Ltd. The adjacent bowling greens and tennis courts also disappeared at the same time. These had been operated as adjuncts to the hostel building on Third Avenue, which ceased to be used for this purpose around this time. A British Legion Club was built on Third Avenue in 1938.

The Dwellings Company, regarded by now as an associated company of the Estates Company, finally redeemed the arrears on its Preference Shares interest in 1929, and paid out an ordinary dividend for the first time.

General Development of the Estate 1919-39

The inter-war years saw the continued development of the Park, which, due to the diversity of its industries, largely escaped the economic troubles of the times. The areas sold or let, and therefore, with the exception of the Guinness disposal, largely developed, steadily rose from 731 acres in 1919 to almost 966 acres in 1940. These figures include the areas in the estate used for roads and railways which totalled 115 acres. By 1940, 334 acres had been sold outright, with 478 acres being either sold subject to Chief Rents or leased on a long-term basis subject to Ground Rents. Thirty-eight-and-a-half acres were leased on short-term arrangements. This left some 217 acres for development out of the original purchase, plus about seven acres out of the 37 acres subsequently bought at Barton for the Trafford Park Extension.

Over the period, the rents receivable by the Company stayed roughly constant, as did the dividends, being seven per cent in both 1919 and 1939. The overall capitalisation of the Company fell from £1,219,600 in 1919 to £1,043,400 in 1939, the reduction being due to a gradual redemption of the Debentures that took place over the years.

Ever since Lloyd George's 'Peoples' Budget' of 1909, the Estates Company had faced taxation difficulties, in the form of threatened taxes on the capital values of undeveloped lands, and Excess Profits Duties on sales already undertaken, particularly the Guinness disposal. The Company mounted a vigorous campaign in both cases, drawing comparison in a printed circular to the disadvantageous position it was in compared to its liabilities if the Estate had been developed for housing along the lines of the 1896 Edis plan. The 1909 Land Tax was eventually abandoned in 1920, but the Excess Profit Duties for the Guinness disposal continued to plague the Company until 1933. For a time, it was argued that the threat of such taxation would act as a deterrent to estates similar to Trafford Park being established elsewhere, and hindering the industrial strength of the country in the process. The Estate as a whole, however, did benefit from the partial exemption of industrial premises from the payment of rates that was brought in by statute in 1929, under which factory occupiers escaped three quarters of their rates liability. Warehouses, however, received no such exemption.

The development of the Estate in 1919-39 followed a similar pattern to the early years, with roads and railways following factories. Inevitably, most disposals were in the central and western parts of the Park. In the years immediately prior to the First World War, disposals had started to get larger and sites more spacious. This continued in the inter-war years. Even today, the nature of the western Park is discernibly more spacious than the surviving older areas of the eastern Park, with their close concentrations of brick-built factories and warehouses.

When the First World War ended, Guinness did not develop their site. The contents of the Hall were auctioned in August 1919 by Capes Dunn & Co. The sale realised some £1,544, and included such items as 150 combination bedsteads, 120 Hospital lockers, and blankets. The Hall itself remained vacant until the start of the Second World War, although caretakers lived in part of the older section, the last being the Perrin family, who lived there from 1932-9. Trafford Park Estates agreed to act as Guinness's agents for the site, but it was to remain undeveloped until the 1950s and later.

Important disposals took place in 1919 to Massey Harris on Ashburton Road, Victor Blagden & Co., British Electron Ltd., London Electric Wire and Smiths Ltd. on Mellors Road, and the British Alizarine Co. (later to become part of ICI Ltd.) on Westinghouse Road. Ingersoll Rand and Courtauld's Ltd. followed in 1920. A large site to the west of the Bridgewater Canal at Barton was sold in 1920 to Manchester Corporation, for construction of the large Barton Power Station, finally concluding negotiations dating back to 1913. Work on the new the new station, with its nine steel chimneys, started in April 1920, and the completed building was opened on 11 October 1923 by the Earl of Derby. The station was one of the most technically advanced of its day, and was served by modern coal-receiving facilities for coal brought by barge along the Bridgewater Canal. Its impressive structure earned it the title 'Queen of the North' within the electricity industry, although skippers on the Ship Canal referred to it as the 'Barton Light'. During the building of the power station, a new entrance to the estate was built from Redcliffe Road, using a new road and rail bridge over the Bridgewater Canal. The original bridge, still with the tramroad rails, remained as a footpath, and was only demolished in 1992.

48 *Inside Brooke Bond's tea warehouse, c.1924.*

Brooke Bond Ltd. took a site on the northern side of Trafford Park Road in 1922. In the same year, Nicholls Nagle became Corn Products Ltd. Freedlands Ltd., furniture manufacturers, took a site in 1929. A new stretch of road, built to reach the new factory from Trafford Park Road, was called Tenax Road, after one of the firm's products.

In June 1931, 10 acres of land between Brooke Bond and Nicholls Nagle were leased to Thomas Hedley & Co., a recently acquired subsidiary of the American soap manufacturers Procter and Gamble. Work on the new £100,000 factory started in July 1932, and production started a year later, by which time the site had been purchased outright. A further five acres were bought in 1936 and the factory was substantially extended in 1936-7, when a pipe bridge was also built over the Ship Canal so that oil could be discharged from ships moored on the northern bank. The bend in the canal at this point made it impossible to berth ships adjacent to the factory itself.

In September 1931, the Ford factory closed. The Ford Company had been looking for a new site for some time. Since 1920, it had been subject to a discriminatory system of taxation on the horse power of its engines and this, coupled with competition from U.K. producers, Morris and Austin, caused the firm to seek a larger site closer to the European market for export purposes. Trafford Park could provide neither of these, and the existing works could not be extended to any great degree, although various extensions had taken place in 1920-1, and the former government tractor factories had been rented in 1926 and 1928. As early as 1922, rumours started that the factory would leave the Park, after Ford had bought a site in Southampton. The search started in earnest in 1923, and Dagenham was being considered by 1924. The site, some 300 acres in extent, with its own Thames-side dock and a London County Council housing estate

49 *Aerial view of Turners Asbestos Cement, mid-1920s, with the undeveloped Guinness site on the opposite side of Ashburton Road. In the foreground are the Clarence Avenue houses, erected by Taylors for key staff.*

50 *Exterior of Ford factory on Westinghouse Road, c.1925.*

51 *View of the rear of the Hovis factory, c.1930, showing the staff bowling green. The building was completely destroyed in the Blitz.*

(Becontree) on its doorstep, was bought and work started in May 1929. In the meantime, production had changed over to the 'Model A' in 1927. When the Trafford Park factory closed, 3,100 were employed at the main works with a further 310 at the former Scotts factory. Some 2,000 employees were moved to Dagenham by chartered train over the weekend of 19-20 September. The old factory had produced over 300,000 cars. It was offered for sale or rent, but no buyer could be found. Shortly afterwards it was let to Friedlands, Universal Furniture Products Ltd., and its associated company, Great Universal Stores Ltd., all controlled by Isaac Wolfson. Wolfson later gave his interest in the buildings to his son, Leonard, and for the next two decades the premises were referred to as the 'Leonard Works'.

Over the years, a number of smaller disposals took place, many being for extensions to existing factories. Between 1919 and 1939, disposals averaged about 12 per annum. Some firms left the Park in this period, through removals elsewhere like Fords, bankruptcies and takeovers. In 1935, it was estimated that 35,000 manual workers were employed in the Park, in addition to clerical and managerial staff. In 1937, the Estate's total rateable value was estimated at £303,153. Twenty years earlier, it had been £119,868, a clear indication of the scale of development that had taken place.

In 1936, a spectacular fire took place when three timber yards between Westinghouse and Trafford Park Roads caught fire in hot dry weather. The blaze extended to an area of six acres and lasted three days. The nearby Estate Office was only saved by virtue of the fire brigade playing water onto the roof and walls of the building.

The Estates Company continued to invest in buildings and infrastructure. In 1919, a number of surplus aircraft hangars were bought from the Government for use as temporary factories. Most were built of wood, but two were of steel construction, and after 1923 became the workshops of the Company's Works Department on Mosley Road. In 1922, the entrance lodges opposite the White City entrance on Chester Road were removed at the expense of the Estates Company to form the front entrance to Stretford's Gorse Hill Park, where they remain, albeit rather neglected, to this day.

Roads continued to be built or extended to serve new sites: Richmond Road (1919), Praed Road (1920-1), Mosley Road—between Ashburton Road and Westinghouse Road (1922), Royce Road (1923), Bailey Road (1924), Kilvert Road (1927), and Twining Road and Tenax Road to Friedlands (1929). As in earlier years, most roads were named after past or present directors of the Estates Company or tenants. Clarence Road (later Clarence Avenue) was made up in 1925 by Taylor Brothers. In 1937, it is reported that Ashburton Road had been provided with cycle tracks on each side, although not segregated from other traffic except by a white line. A census of traffic using Trafford Park Road, carried out in 1935, revealed a total of 5,500 vehicles per day using the road, a clear indication of a growing traffic problem for the Park in the future.

During the 1920s, two new entrances to the Park were built by Stretford UDC. The first, the Warwick Road connection to Trafford Park Road, was built in 1920-2 following representations for the Trafford Park Industries Association. This road also served the new Manchester United Football Ground. The second entrance, completed in 1926, was a southwards extension of Mosley Road across the Bridgewater Canal, to meet up with Park Road in the Barton Dock area.

In 1931, the local authorities in the area were reorganised. Davyhulme was taken into Urmston UDC and the boundaries between Urmston and Stretford UDCs were adjusted within the Park to follow logical road boundaries. Two years later, Stretford became a Municipal Borough.

The death of Marshall Stevens, 1936

Marshall Stevens's involvement with the Estates Company began to lessen gradually during the late 1920s. In 1924, his son Colonel T.H.G. (Harry) Stevens, was appointed Joint Managing Director, having worked for the Company since 1920. In February 1925, Marshall Stevens did not offer himself for re-election to the Manchester Chamber of Commerce after the death of Edred Stevens, his sixth and youngest son. In 1927, he revised his will, and the following year ordered his own memorial vault for St Catherine's churchyard at Barton. In 1929, it is reported that he had been ill for much of the year, and he resigned the Chairmanship in favour of T.G. Mellors. In 1932, he resigned as Joint Managing Director, and retired to live on a pension of £500 per annum from the Company. He lived for a number of years at a villa at Cap Martin on the French Riviera, although he continued to maintain his own home at Dingle Bank in Bowden.

He died, aged 84, on a 'farewell' visit to his home town of Plymouth on 12 August 1936. His funeral cortège passed through the Estate, and the roads were lined with the employees of the Estates Company and other firms with which Stevens had been associated. On the form of service for his funeral, were printed some of his words: 'I shall have performed the mould allotted to me, and consequently there should be no mourning at my passing away'.

The vicar, the Rev. Pierce, added, 'He was to live dangerously and splendidly. He was a visionary and a dreamer who by energy and will and the practical bent within him had made his dream come true.'

Stevens was buried in the vault he had ordered at St Catherine's churchyard, where it overlooks both the Ship Canal and Trafford Park, major enterprises in which he played leading rôles.

There is little doubt of the significance of the rôle that Stevens played in both ventures, helping both to succeed where lesser men without tenacity and vision would have failed. His stature in the world of business was recognised internationally. He was a permanent member of the International Congress on Navigation, a member of the Transport Committee of the Federation of British Industries, and a Director of the Manchester Chamber of Commerce. In 1921, T.P. O'Connor, the Liverpool M.P., described Stevens thus: '... that quiet modest man, a little like a French Field Marshal with his white moustache and his white goatee, with all the iron tenacities in the strong jaw which has taken him through gigantic successes, and with good humour and kindly eyes making at once a soft invincibility, and the goodwill and tact which have made him at once popular as he has proved tenacious and successful.'

The final chapter in Stevens's involvement with the Park was the erection of a memorial, at the junction of Ashburton Road and Trafford Park Road, which was unveiled on 1 October 1937. Paid for by subscribing Company shareholders, it was made from a 20-ton block of granite, 16 feet high, taken from a hill top from the

52 *Hedley's factory in June 1933, shortly before production started. The Finished Products Building, since extended, is on the left, while the Glycerine and Kettle Building on the right is still under construction.*

Nefyn area of North Wales. It carried a bronze medallion, provided by Metrovicks, with an inscription carved by Sherwood Edwards, an Ashton on Mersey artist. It contains the words, 'To whose foresight, energy and ability, the successful development of Trafford Park as an industrial area is due'.

Marketing and Publicity for the Estate

From the outset, it was apparent that if development of the Park was to proceed at a rate which would earn early profits for the Company, the latter would have to play a substantially more active rôle than that of a mere passive landowner.

The rôle played by Marshall Stevens has already been outlined. Stevens assiduously sought business contacts anywhere and everywhere, and no doubt used his family's connections in the shipping business in the early years. He also maintained close contact with local politicians of all shades of opinion. He made many trips abroad, including visits in 1904 and 1906 to the United States. A network of foreign representatives was maintained; in the early 1900s, these included Berlin, New York and Toronto, as well as London. From 1923, a London office was maintained at Leadenhall Street. In 1928, it moved to Bush House where it remained until the start of the Second World War. Stevens once estimated that of all his negotiations carried out to bring industries to the Park, only about four per cent were successful. Among firms he did not manage to entice were the Yarrow Shipbuilders from Glasgow who were approached in 1905.

In line with Stevens's manner, the Estates Company set about publicising Trafford Park as a site for industry. The Company's telegraphic address was, not surprisingly, 'Developing'. Port of Manchester Warehouses Ltd. used 'Deposit, Manchester', whilst the cold storage company used 'Freeserve, Manchester'. Great stress was laid on the proximity of the Park to the Manchester docks, and the cost advantages that industrialists could gain through the favourable railway rates negotiated with the Canal Company. Publicity material issued in the late 1900s coined the term 'Traffic Park' to underline this relationship, the leaflets outlining the railway and canal connections, and listing a bewildering number of towns whose nearest ocean terminal was the Manchester docks. Many leaflets issued contained simple diagrammatic illustrations of ships and factories, showing the 6d. per ton charge of the rail connection between the two, and the fact that materials hauled from the factory to eventual domestic destinations could be carried at dock railway rates. A circular letter, publicising both Safes and Hives, issued in January 1910, is a good illustration of this, showing cross sections of both types of building and the loading arrangements and machinery.

From the early years, the Estates Company issued layout maps of the Park. Not only were these useful to industries already established, they also advertised site availability to prospective industrialists. The example would be followed by developers of other industrial estates in the 1920s and 1930s. The earliest plan seems to have been issued with the 1897 Debenture prospectus, and similar layouts would be issued every year or two up to 1939, subject only to a change in the layout style *c*.1914. A plan was incorporated into a poster erected on Company land at the main approach to the Park on Chester Road. The plans, also as a means of encouraging prospective industrialists, contained lists of all the firms present in the Park.

On a number of occasions, the Estates Company invested in lengthier publications. The earliest of these, sold for 2d., was the book *Trafford Park and Ship Canal Guide, Past and Present*, published in 1902. It contained some historical text, plus photographs of established factories, before finishing off with an artist's impression of the newly erected premises of the British Electric Car Company and a full-page advert for the Car Company itself. Further books were brought out after the formation of Port of Manchester Warehouses Ltd. in 1914, including *Then and Now* in 1921, and books appeared throughout the 1920s and 1930s, with titles like *Trafford Park, the Home of Modern Industry* and *Trafford Park in a Nutshell*. Two books appeared in 1931, which were reprinted and updated later in the decade. They were nicknamed the 'Gold' and 'Silver' books on account of their covers. The former, in a softback cover, was entitled *Manchester, the Centre*, and contained paragraphs on Manchester's history, the position of Trafford Park, the Ship Canal, Railways and aviation. Later sections dealt with a wide variety of detail, giving the railway rates, for comparison, to inland destinations from Liverpool, London and Trafford Park, distance tables from the same places, the populations of town in the north west, exports by value from Manchester to various places in the world, and details of statutory services available to industrialists. Also listed were trade associations and local amenities. One section even listed the chemical composition of water obtained from the mains supply, local wells and the Bridgewater and Ship Canals. Its companion volume, in a hard silver back, was entitled *Where should my factory be*. This publication covered the same topics, but with less detail. Photographs, an aerial view of the Park and a list of firms in the Park were included. Attractive sepia photographs of Heaton Park, Little Moreton Hall, the Cheshire Hounds, and other rural scenes completed the volume.

In 1929, the Company arranged for a series of enamel plate posters to be erected at important railway stations advertising Trafford Park as an industrial location.

By the 1920s, publicity for the Company was in the hands of its own Information Bureau, which performed a similar marketing function for the Park to the Industrial Development Officers established by local authorities from the 1960s onwards. Its work was suspended during the Second World War, but it resumed limited activities thereafter before being wound up in the mid-1950s.

The appointment of T.H.G. Stevens as sole managing director saw the introduction by the Company of a Trafford Park handbook, largely written by him. It contained the usual list of firms in the Park together with other publicity material, and advertisements from traders themselves. Publication of these booklets continued every few years, with the exception of the war years, up to 1970.

The growing influence of government and statutory town planning

The inter-war years saw the first tentative steps nationally towards the establishment of a statutory town planning system, designed to exercise control over developments and changes of land use. This process culminated in the 1947 Town and Country Planning Act, which gave local authorities control of development in their areas. Associated with this trend was the increasing concern of local authorities to promote positive planning schemes for their areas.

At first, the town planning system was associated with municipal housing but, after the Act of 1909, subsequent legislation up to 1932 widened the scope of 'town planning' to include infrastructure, preservation of historic buildings, regional planning and the direct control and regulation of individual sites.

The legislation of this period gave only limited development control powers to the local authorities, which had no effect on the Park at this time. The Park was affected, however, by various positive planning schemes and infrastructure provision. In this, the local authorities were carrying out functions which had already been undertaken for the Park by the Company itself.

53 *Estate layout plan, February 1934, issued by Trafford Park Estates Ltd., showing developed and undeveloped sites.*

TRAFFORD PARK, MANCHESTER.

TRAFFORD PARK ESTATES LIMITED,

TRAFFORD PARK, MANCHESTER, ENG. OFFICE

Telephone : 1946 TRAFFORD PARK.

Telegrams : "DEVELOPING, MANCHESTER."

SITES & BUILDINGS AVAILABLE

Scale: Six Inches to One Statute Mile or 880 Feet to One Inch

FEBRUARY 1934

A Manchester and District Regional Town Planning Committee was formed in 1929 under the provisions of the Local Government Act 1929. One of its first suggested schemes was a suggested new arterial road to by-pass Manchester to the west carrying north-south traffic. Its route passed straight through the Park, running up Mosley Road, and then continued at a high level in front of Trafford Hall to pass over the Ship Canal at a height of 80 feet on a 200-foot span bridge. The Estates Company decided to oppose the scheme as it affected many undeveloped sites, and would have caused general disruption to the Estate both during construction and after. The road plan remained a proposal for years, the local authorities possessing neither the finance nor the commitment to carry it out. The idea was dropped in 1937, but was resurrected in a different form after the Second World War and was built over 20 years later.

In February 1937, members of the Regional Town Planning Committee visited Trafford Hall, by then in a semi-derelict condition, though still in Guinness ownership. The Committee decided not to recommend the scheduling of the building as an Ancient Monument, unless the Stretford local authority were willing to bear the costs of restoration.

54 *A 7-ton hammer in use in the Axle Forge, Taylor Bros, 1930s.*

A new Town and Country Planning Act was passed in 1932, which extended the limited powers previously available to local authorities to introduce planning control schemes for their areas. It also provided for councils to recover from land owners increases in land values caused by the introduction of such schemes. The Estates Company was opposed to these provisions and made representations to central government, but no scheme was introduced in the area at the time.

The growth of the town planning system was accompanied by increased interest from both central and local government in the location of industry. In 1931, both the Manchester Development Committee and the Lancashire Industrial Development Council were formed. In 1935, the Manchester Chamber of Commerce formed the Port of Manchester Committee. Its purpose was to attract both shipping to the port and trade from the locality. Colonel Stevens served as the Estates Company's representative on the Committee.

The inter-war years saw the establishment of industrial estates elsewhere in the U.K. The first such estate, the Slough Trading Estate, started in 1920 utilising the buildings of an ex-Government military vehicle repair depot established in the closing days of the First World War. The success of Slough encouraged similar private sector schemes in London and the Midlands using either converted buildings or greenfield sites, mainly on a smaller scale, and Slough became a model which many would copy. Although built on a relatively large scale (the initial site was *c.*668 acres), and possessing both nursery factories,[2] an estate railway and certain services provided by the estate company, Slough differed from Trafford Park in three important respects. Firstly, industrialists could only

55 *Taylor Bros steelworks and the Bridgewater Canal, viewed from the air in 1934. To the right stands Trafford Moss House, the home of Francis Ellis, Sir Humphrey's resident land agent prior to 1896.*

56 *The Anglo American Oil Co.'s tank farm, in 1934, stood on both Estates Company and Ship Canal Company land. A canoe can just be seen on the Lake on the right.*

57   View of W.T. Glover's factory at the junction of Trafford Park Road and Westinghouse Road, late 1930s.

rent buildings from the estate landlord on a rack rental basis; sites for development were not to be made available through either sales or ground leases. The whole estate therefore remained under the control of the landlord. At Trafford Park, relatively few buildings were provided by the Estates Company, apart from the Hives and the warehouse and cold storage buildings for occupation by its associates. Secondly, the difference in types of occupiers was marked; Slough attracted mainly light 'footloose' industries. Even in the 1930s, Trafford Park was still mainly a centre for heavy industry, although lighter industries from then on started to become more numerous. The Crittall Manufacturing Company, manufacturers of window frames, took several units in the Hives during the 1930s. Finally, although Slough was initially formed from buildings originally provided for another purpose, its development followed a more purposeful plan than Trafford Park, and most future industrial or trading estates would be laid out on a planned basis, with features such as landscaping along the main roadways.

Encouraged by the success of Slough, central government itself established industrial estates on greenfield sites in depressed areas to deal with high unemployment. This was done through publicly owned estate companies established under the Special Areas (Development and Improvement) Act 1936. The first such estate was started at Team Valley, near Gateshead, in 1936, followed by Treforest near Cardiff, and Hillington, near Glasgow, both in 1937. They followed Slough as the model, and buildings were only provided by the landlord for letting at rack rents direct to the industrialist. Again, the estates followed a planned layout and the size of the projects was also substantial (Team Valley 700 acres, Treforest 250 acres, Hillington 320 acres). They were provided

58 *Bowdon House, part of the Turners Asbestos Cement site, was built in 1934-7 to a design by Manchester architect P.G. Fairhurst. It has been extended since, but still contains a striking Art Deco entrance foyer, which has featured in television productions, most notably as the reception area to the* Waldorf Astoria Hotel *in Granada T.V.'s 'Brideshead Revisited'.*

with both nursery units,[3] estate railways and landlord-provided services such as steam, hot water and heating, but the type of industries attracted did not mirror the existing Trafford Park occupiers.[4] During the inter-war years, the average size of site sold at Trafford Park tended to increase over that of the earlier disposals, and exceeded the size of site at Slough and the government estates. Although Slough and the first government estates were substantial in area, they did not approach Trafford Park in size, and other government and private sector schemes would be smaller.

Closer to Trafford Park, the local authorities were also involved in the promotion of industrial estates. On its newly developing Wythenshawe Estate, Manchester Corporation established the Sharston Industrial Estate in 1930, designed to provide some local employment for the inhabitants of its new satellite town. Although a much smaller site than Trafford Park, the development followed the Park in some respects: only infrastructure was provided by the landlord, who leased sites on long leases to industrialists. However, the terms

59 *The Marshall Stevens Memorial at the junction of Trafford Park Road and Ashburton Road, shortly after its erection in 1937.*

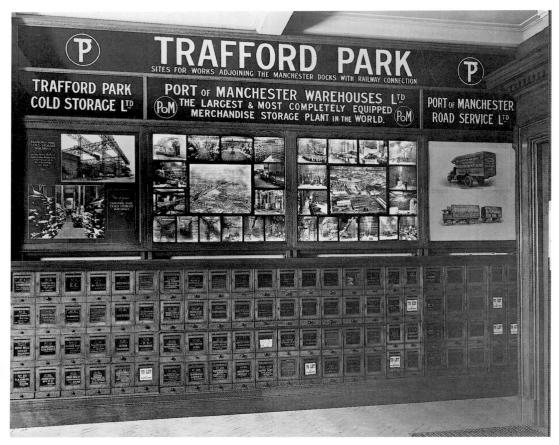

60   *Advertising display for Trafford Park Estates and its associates in Manchester's Royal Exchange, 1920s.*

of such lettings were concessionary in certain cases, and the Corporation also provided favourable finance to assist firms in the building of their factories. Again, the industries attracted were light in their nature. A similar estate was provided by Liverpool Corporation at Speke.

The notion of the north of England as a depressed area occupied many minds in the 1920s and 1930s, and the question of whether trade was 'going south' was aired in the press many times. The public concern was closely monitored by the Estates Company, and eventually caused the Board of Trade to carry out surveys into the pattern of establishment of industry. In one such survey, carried out in 1936, it was found that, out of 551 factories built in the U.K., some 235 had been located in the North and Midlands. The survey also established that there was little evidence of any discernible drift of industry to the south. In 1937, however, the government appointed a Royal Commission to enquire into the causes influencing the geographical distribution of the industrial population. The Estates Company made written submissions to the Commission headed by Sir Montague Barlow. The Barlow Report, as it came to be known, was eventually published in January 1940. It recommended the establishment of a National Industrial Board to oversee the distribution and dispersal of industry in the U.K., to

61 *Extract from* Then and Now, *issued by Port of Manchester Warehouses Ltd. in 1921, which contained illustrations by W. Heath Robinson.*

help to alleviate both unemployment in depressed areas and congestion in other areas. Its recommendation for a National Industrial Board was not adopted by the post-war government, but the influence of the report's contents manifested itself in legislation that would affect Trafford Park.

Notes

1. It appears, however, that ownership of the locomotives remained with the Trafford Park Company. 'Lord Ashburton' and 'Sir Joseph Lyons' were taken out of use *c.*1930, and sold for scrap in 1935. 'Sir William Bailey' was still in use in 1943.
2. Called 'Bijou' factories.
3. Called 'Nest' factories at both Treforest and Hillington, the average size being 1,250-1,500 square feet, rather smaller than the Trafford Park 'Hives' at 2,400 square feet.
4. Ironically, Team Valley did share some matters with Trafford Park. The estate company was based in Metrovick House, Newcastle, and one of its first directors was Colonel George Walton, a director of Thomas Hedley & Co. Ltd.

Chapter IV

The Second World War

By 1939 the Park, although not completely developed, had reached a stage where its strategic importance to the economy of the region was not in dispute. With its concentration of industry, particularly engineering, electrical, oil storage, construction and consumer goods, many of which could be rapidly turned over to the production of war materials, and its immense warehousing and cold storage facilities, its importance to the nation as a whole would soon become apparent.

The threat of war in the late 1930s led to steps being taken prior to the outbreak of hostilities. In October 1937, Colonel Stevens publicly suggested that a series of air-raid wardens be set up to cover the Park. In July 1938, the government asked Metropolitan-Vickers to start production of a heavy bomber, designed by A.V. Roe Ltd., to be known as the 'Manchester'. In August, agreement was reached between the firm and the government for the extension of the West Works within the main site for the manufacture of radar equipment, an area in which the firm with its strong research department was acquiring some expertise. The extensions were completed in only 13 weeks. A further extension to the West Works was started in August 1939 and completed by December.

After the Munich crisis in October 1938, preparations on the Estate began in earnest. In November Metrovicks announced that they would be building an aircraft factory, to be operational in nine months' time. In the same month, Kilvert's started work on a large air-raid shelter for their staff, capable of holding 250 people. It was equipped with radio and telephone links, forced ventilation and emergency lighting. Built with walls three-feet thick, the shelter had three floors. Kilvert's also formed their own First Aid and decontamination squads, and provided tin hats, respirators and protective clothing. Other firms on the Estate made similar preparations. Carborundum's had nine shelters.

Metropolitan-Vickers Electrical Co. Ltd.
TRAFFORD PARK, MANCHESTER, 17.

Air Raid Precautions

A Spaniard who has been through more than 400 raids gives the following advice on how best to conduct oneself in an Air Raid :

1. At the sound of the alarm, keep a cool head, follow instructions, but above all do not rush.

2. Always know the shortest way to the nearest air-raid shelter. Have warm clothing with you in winter.

3. If there is no shelter available, get down into a basement. Keep close to corners. Avoid being near doors and windows.

4. If no warning has been given against gas, keep your windows and doors open. Do not stand in the middle of the room but get close to the main inside walls.

5. If actual bombing finds you in the street, rush into the nearest doorway and lie down flat close to the wall with the head pointing inwards.

6. If caught in the open, far from any shelter or house, lie flat in the lowest ground and if there is grass or soft ground lie there. Bombs falling on soft ground, sink in and the explosion is upwards.

7. Carry with you a lead pencil, a piece of soft rubber or cork to put between your teeth in order to keep the mouth open. This avoids internal injury or the bursting of the ear drums by concussion.

8. If lying in the open, cover your head with a folded coat or an open book to avoid injury from splinters from anti-aircraft gun shells.

9. *For information :* A bomb falling in the immediate vicinity, makes a loud whistling sound. Bombs falling from 100 to 500 yards distance, make a loud hissing sound.

10. Strips of paper pasted over the window panes do not prevent them breaking ; they do keep splinters in place.

62 *Air Raid Precaution leaflet issued by Metropolitan Vickers, September 1939.*

In Spring 1939, Tenax Road was extended to meet Ashburton Road, to open up further land for development if required for wartime production. The Ministry of Transport provided financial help to the Estates Company to meet the cost.

In February, work started on the new Metrovick aircraft factory, on the site owned by the firm to the west of Mosley Road, used for some years as allotments. The firm experienced some difficulties with the government over the size of the factory, which was initially cut back to reduce costs. The factory was a modern structure equipped with a comprehensive system of overhead cranes and all its services underground to minimise disruption from bomb damage. It comprised 18 production bays and was provided with reinforced concrete floors, especially necessary as the site conditions comprised peat and running sand. Air-raid shelters were provided on the new site.

Production of aircraft started early in October 1939, and the building was completed on 22 October. Work on a second phase, necessary to increase production to new levels set by the government, started in January 1940. It added a further 26 bays and increased the size of the completed building to some 800,000 square feet. The second phase was completed in December 1940, one month after the first Manchester bomber had been completed.

In June 1939, the Trafford Park Traders Association arranged for a training school to be opened for the training of volunteers for Air Raid Precautions (ARP) duties.

In August 1939, the Manchester Port Emergency Committee was formed under the 'Control of Traffic at Ports Order'. Colonel Stevens acted as its warehousing member. The committee made many arrangements with owners of buildings in the region for the emergency use of storage space to keep the docksides cleared of stored goods and materials, to allow the efficient discharge of ships' cargoes.

On the outbreak of war in September 1939 small areas under the control of the Estates Company were taken over for the siting of army huts, ack-ack guns and two barrage balloon stations, one of which was close to the Corn Products factory. Two machine guns were positioned on top of the Liverpool Warehousing buildings. Both the Stretford and Urmston local authorities, together with Lancashire County Council and individual firms, dug air-raid shelters at numerous sites all over the Park. Some of the Metrovick air-raid shelters were provided in the huge concrete cavities formed under the floors of the main works where it was positioned over the Manchester Corporation Outfall Sewer. The County Council also provided three decontamination stations. A number of ponds were dug out to aid fire fighting, and a temporary road was laid to the lake for the same purpose.

On 3 September, Trafford Hall, which was vacant apart from a small area occupied by the Perrin family as caretakers, was taken over entirely by the military, who proceeded to erect high fencing around it, and carried out other improvements to render it habitable, including the first electricity supply. It was rumoured at the time that the Hall was to be used for housing either internees or prisoners of war, although it does not appear to have been used for such. The reason for the works soon became apparent because between October 1939 and January 1940 the Hall was used for billeting groups of the Royal Engineers who were using the lake as training for the use of assault bridges.

Two British Restaurants were provided by the local authorities: one was on the bowling green to the rear of the *Trafford Park Hotel* and the other at the junction of Ashburton and Richmond Roads. Both were popular. In the Village area, both St Cuthbert's and St Antony's were open at lunchtimes as rest centres.

The remaining open spaces in the Park, including undeveloped sites, were studded with piles of old road sets to deter the landing of enemy aircraft. A separate ARP scheme was sanctioned by the County Council for the Park area and put into operation on 8 July 1940. Many firms formed their own forces from employees, both for fire-fighting and fire-watching duties.

The Park's own unit of Local Defence Volunteers was formed in May 1940, under the command of Lt. Col. K.G. Maxwell of Metrovicks. The force was initially called the 'R' Company of the Manchester Regiment. It was quickly raised to battalion status and had a total of 4,160 men. Later it became the 'C' Company of the 45th County of Lancaster Home Guard. Over half its strength was comprised of men from Metrovicks Main Works and aircraft factory, although some other factories had their own units and many employees served in units elsewhere nearer their homes. In time, the Park's Home Guard unit became an efficient fighting force.

Many buildings, belonging to both the Estates Company and others, were requisitioned by the government. Some were made available to firms such as Metrovicks to expand armament production. Less essential operations and some office staff were moved away from Trafford Park to make space available for work of higher value to the war effort, and to protect staff from air raids. Metrovicks took factories at Timperley, Sharston, Patricroft and elsewhere, whilst office staff found themselves at leafy locations such as Sale Lido, the Kenwood Club in Stretford and Bowdon Assembly Rooms, as well as large residential properties in the south-western suburbs of the Manchester conurbation.

63 *Hedley's Home Guard unit. It is rumoured that when the unit was first established, although all the men had rifles, the whole unit had only five rounds of ammunition.*

As in the rest of the country at the time, all directional and location signs were removed from the area, along with boards that showed the names of firms on particular roads. Difficulties would be faced over working the estate railways, especially at level crossings. The services of crossing keepers were arranged at 12 crossings during the hours of darkness, and shields were fitted to the 'robot lights'. Normal street lighting was forbidden under the blackout regulations, but special 'Home Office' lights, with an intensity of 0.02 foot candles were provided at road crossings, although even they had to be turned off when a 'Purple Lights' air-raid warning was given. There are reports of columns of employees walking home in the blackout, headed by staff from Hedley's holding lighted candles, which the factory still made at the start of the war. In 1943, controversy arose over the issue of a poster by the Civil Defence authorities, which threatened to reveal the names, offences and fines imposed on people who had contravened the blackout. The proposal was resented, and many refused to display the posters, which were withdrawn after representations were made by a Member of Parliament to the Ministry of Aircraft Production.

Smoke stations were also set up in the streets of Stretford near to the Park: the aim was to provide a smoke barrage to deter recognition of the Park and obscure the view from enemy bombers and reconnaissance aircraft. A similar purpose was behind the reported sprinkling of sawdust onto the Bridgewater Canal. Barton Power Station was painted in camouflage. In October 1940 the distinctive water tower at Metrovicks, over 200 feet high, and so useful in the early radio broadcasts but by now disused, was

64   *Those who worked in Trafford Park during the Second World War have strong reminiscences of the warmth and comradeship of the times, feelings reflected in this atmospheric view of the canteen at Hedley's, complete with Home Guard notices.*

65   *King George VI and Queen Elizabeth paid a visit to Metrovicks on 2 May 1940. They were given an extensive tour of the factory and inspected A.R.P., Fire Service and other staff involved in war work.*

reduced to a height of 50 feet. The aim again was to remove a local landmark which could have been of use to the enemy. The Sheffield scrap metal firm of George Cohens did the work. The remaining part of the tower became a platform for a 4.5 inch anti-aircraft gun.

The defences of Trafford Park were put fully to the test in the Manchester Blitz, which affected the Estate most seriously over two nights, prior to Christmas 1940. The first raid started at 6.45 p.m. on Sunday 22 December, and continued until 6.00 a.m. the following day.

A similar raid started at 6.45 p.m. on the same day, finishing at 1.00 p.m. on 24 December. In the morning, the main entrance to the Park was barricaded due to the large number of unexploded bombs and land mines still uncleared. Large numbers of high-explosive bombs and land mines were dropped on the first night and mainly incendiaries in the following raid. The highest concentration of damage was inflicted around the docks and the eastern parts of the Estate. The resources of the local fire-fighting services were severely stretched, particularly as the Manchester Fire Brigade had sent a large number of men and equipment to Liverpool which had been blitzed the previous night. Assistance in dealing with Trafford Park was rendered from places as far away as Birmingham, Wolverhampton and London.

Damage to factories and warehouses was extensive. The Estates Company lost 10 buildings completely, with a further 23 suffering damage. Three out of the four ware-houses let to the Canal Company were completely destroyed, the fourth only being saved with some difficulty. Port of Manchester Warehouses Ltd. lost 11 out of its 24 buildings, including four cotton safes, representing some 54,999 tons or 60 per cent of its total storage capacity. The arrangements made earlier by the Port Emergency Committee proved of great value in storing the contents of partly damaged warehouses; there are reports of small agricultural buildings on Manchester Corporation's Carrington Estate being pressed into use to store tobacco leaf, saved from damaged bonded stores in the Park.

The Cold Storage Company lost the main storage building of the Cold Store and its contents. The compressor plant, however, was saved. The Cool Store suffered some damage. The Dwellings Company suffered extensive damage to some houses on Eleventh Street, losing seven in total, although nearly all the Village suffered minor damage through broken windows' etc. The front part of Trafford Hall was damaged by a land mine during the first night's raid. Guinness decided to demolish it shortly after the end of the war. The work was done by the local firm Thomas Maidens, and the stone lions which had graced the front steps could be seen for many years outside the garage owned by the same firm in Sale.

Metropolitan-Vickers suffered extensive damage. Two high-explosive bombs were dropped within the main works causing severe damage to the switchgear testing space and staff canteen, and completely demolishing the heat treatment shop. Incendiary damage on the following night led to two major fires in the box factory and the main machine shop. Small-scale damage elsewhere was extensive. A high-explosive bomb

66 *The King and Queen watch activity in 'G' aisle at Metrovicks, 2 May 1940. They paid a return visit after the Blitz, on 13 February 1941.*

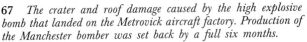

67   The crater and roof damage caused by the high explosive bomb that landed on the Metrovick aircraft factory. Production of the Manchester bomber was set back by a full six months.

68   Bomb damage to the Switchgear Department in the Metrovicks West Works.

also landed in the aircraft factory, completely destroying the first finished Manchester bomber and its 12 successors. Production at the factory was set back by a full six months.

Elsewhere in the Park, damage was extensive. The Hovis Mill and the Grain Elevator were completely destroyed. The estate railway system suffered little direct damage, but rail traffic in the docks was suspended for several days to allow clearance of debris. An underground telephone cable was cut and a messenger service, using boys working for the police, had to be operated for two weeks before the necessary repairs could be completed.

Despite the damage, production in the Park was little affected and in most cases the disruption was only temporary. Three cases from Colonel Stevens's files give a good illustration of the efforts made to maintain production. At the Knowsley Cast Metal Co. Ltd.: 'All roof seriously affected, much glass and roof sheeting gone. In full production if weather fine, otherwise almost stopped'.

At Northern Motor Utilities: 'Building only 50% sound, 50% of roof gone, remainder lifted and twisted. All glass damaged. In full operation.'

The Brooke Bond & Co. Ltd.'s entry reads: 'Considerable damage to roof covering and extensive glass damage. Building apparently badly shaken, details not available yet. All western doors displaced. Production normal'.

Most of the destroyed buildings were not immediately replaced, but those that were only damaged were repaired in record time over the next few months through the fortunate provision of resources, coupled with determination, commitment and ingenuity from the firms involved and their employees. The work undertaken at Metrovicks serves as an example of what was done elsewhere in the Park on a smaller scale.

After the raids, production at both the main works and aircraft factory was virtually stopped. Large numbers of employees, particularly from those departments unable to carry on their normal functions, together with outside contractors, carried out clearance work and emergency repairs. Wintry conditions in the two weeks following the raids made matters difficult. Within a week, some production had resumed, and three weeks later production was 80 per cent of normal. Within six months all the emergency repairs, and some permanent repairs had been completed. During this time replacements were found for tools and machines lost in the raids, although many were salvaged and reconditioned.

At the aircraft factory, in addition to the blast damage, most of the roof had been destroyed, making production difficult by day and impossible during the blackout. Temporary tarpaulins were borrowed from the Air Ministry, but building materials for a more permanent repair were difficult to obtain because of bomb damage in other towns. When the materials were to hand, suitable roof sheeters could not be found until one hundred were supplied by the Ministry of Labour, subject to the firm finding them suitable sleeping quarters. After a time, it was suggested that a train be borrowed for this purpose. The London Midland & Scottish Railway Company duly obliged, and the train was shunted into sidings on the western side of the works, where it was coupled up to the works' boilers to provide heating.

Trafford Park experienced further air raids, but none were as bad as the Blitz of December 1940. In May 1941, 1,850 windows were broken at Barton Power Station, and another raid followed in June. At the Metrovicks spotters' post, a total of 287 'alerts' were noted between September 1940 and September 1944. Of these, only 41 gave rise to 'alarm' warnings, whereby production ceased. That the Park was not seriously attacked again and escaped comparatively lightly must constitute one of the Allies' strokes of good fortune during the Second World War, because it was by now the most formidable arsenal of military production in the country. That it was known to the Germans is not in doubt, as Luftwaffe records recovered after the war included suitably annotated Ordnance Survey maps of the Park, showing some strategically important targets.

Within a year of the outbreak of war, total employment in the Park is estimated to have risen from 50,000 to 75,000. Output at the Carborundum factory rose by 250 per cent over a similar period. Although many employees enlisted in the forces, many occupations were 'protected' and war production was insatiable in its appetite for labour. Employment at Metrovicks increased by 50 per cent, reaching a peak of 30,000 in 1943-4. The Metrovick aircraft factory alone employed 8,411, including 3,500 women, reflecting trends elsewhere in the Park and nationally. In 1943, requests were made to the Stretford Education Committee to provide a nursery school for working mothers in the Park, to occupy the area used by the first-aid post on the first floor of the Council School. No action was taken.

Taylor Bros steelworks produced over 40,000 gun bearings, and a quarter of a million forged steel tracks for Churchill tanks as well as other tank parts. Turners Asbestos produced materials for army camps, huts, munitions factories and for the repair of bomb damage and provision of temporary housing as well as pressure pipes for repairs to damaged water mains. Glover's produced electrical cables, Bailey Bridges, prefabricated aircraft hangars, radar towers, and over 20 miles of the 'Pluto' pipeline that was laid under the English Channel to supply fuel to the Allied armies after the Normandy landings. The new Geigy factory, completed only as war broke out, produced DDT, which was useful in dealing with the 1944 Naples typhoid epidemic as well as for general army use. ICI erected and operated the first plant in the U.K. for the quantity production of penicillin, and manufactured 'monastral blue' for map production, as well as synthetic dyestuffs for use in uniforms and camouflage, and adipic acid for nylon in parachutes. The Trussed Concrete Steel Company produced pre-cast concrete beams for the building of ordnance factories, and units for part of the Mulberry Harbour installations. The command caravan used by Field Marshal Montgomery was built by the British Trailer Company.

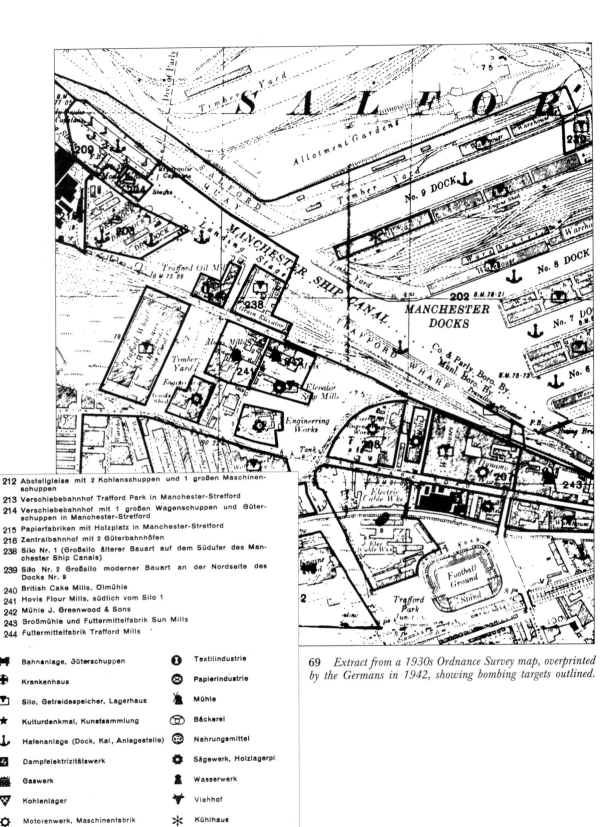

69 *Extract from a 1930s Ordnance Survey map, overprinted by the Germans in 1942, showing bombing targets outlined.*

70   *The significant rôle played by women in providing much needed labour for the war effort was reflected at Trafford Park. Here, women riveters work on part of a Lancaster bomber fuselage in the Metrovick aircraft factory.*

Products from the Superheater Company were used extensively by the Admiralty. The Lancashire Dynamo Company manufactured thousands of shell rings for use in rocket shells. The ordinary products of this company met a heavy demand during the war, and the same applied to many other firms in the Park, including Carborundum's, British Oxygen and Courtaulds Ltd. Parts for Bailey bridges were also built by Banister Walton & Co. (who also produced prefabricated sections for ships), Trafford Park Steel Ltd. and Edward Wood & Co. Parts for the Mulberry Harbour installations also came from Banister Walton & Co., Redpath Brown and Edward Wood & Co. Trafford Park Steel made radar and observation towers. Standard bridging equipment, storage buildings and aircraft hangars were made by Redpath Brown. Frank Rosser Ltd. made furniture and fittings for nearly one hundred aerodromes, produced a million packing cases and supplied timber for other war purposes. The Knowsley Cast Metal Company produced fire-fighting appliances, pumps for tanks and equipment for mine clearance on beaches.

The Second World War led to a return to the Park for the Ford Motor Company, who were to produce, under licence, the Rolls Royce Merlin engine, used in both the Spitfire and the Lancaster. For a short time, the Company reoccupied part of its old works on Westinghouse Road, then still in its ownership. At the same time, the Ministry of Aircraft Production first requisitioned, then bought, some 20.5 acres of Estates Company land on the Trafford Park extension. Together with a larger area of land similarly acquired from the Canal Company, a large factory was started in May 1940 on a 118-

acre site. It was operated by Ford's for the production of Merlin aircraft engines and was built with two distinct sections to minimise bomb damage. It was completed in May 1941, and bombed in the same month. At first, the factory had difficulties in attracting suitable labour, and large numbers of women, youths and untrained men had to be taken on. Despite this, the first Merlin came off the production line one month later. The staff included two resident doctors and nurses. Sixteen acres of adjoining land were cultivated by the staff to produce vegetables for use in the works canteen or for sale to employees. A total of 34,000 such engines, with a combined horsepower of 40,000,000 h.p., were produced while the factory operated. Some 17,316 people worked there, including 7,200 women.

As the war progressed, demands from the government and the armed forces gave rise to further extensions at the Metrovick factories. At the main works, the West Works were again extended in late 1942, and other extensions were completed in 1942-3. In 1941, part of the old Ford factory, the Leonard Works, derelict since the Blitz, were taken over for the manufacture of gun mountings.

During the war, the firm produced a bewildering array of materials, including projectors, sound locators, searchlights, automatic pilots for aircraft, compasses, generators, circuit breakers, degaussing (anti-magnetic mine) equipment, naval switchgear, radar installations, guns and gun mountings, mobile generators for use in Russia, equipment for dealing with unexploded bombs, a mobile land mine (called 'the Beetle'), jet engines, gears for tanks, electrical instruments, polythene mouldings, voltage regulators, relays for submarine mines and mine sweeping, battery chargers for torpedoes, gyroscope protective relays, centralised control systems, hand grenade castings, azimuth brackets as well as many different forms of lighting. In addition the Research Department undertook a number of projects for government on matters such as atomic energy, penicillin drying and acoustics.

At the aircraft factory 43 'Manchester' bombers were produced. The aircraft suffered problems with its Rolls Royce 'Vulture' engines, but the airframe was successful, and was further extended to form the four-engined 'Lancaster' bomber, equipped with 'Merlin' engines. Production started to change to the Lancaster in May 1941, with the first completed aircraft scheduled for January 1942. The target was bettered by a month, and production targets of 30, 35, 40 and then 45 aircraft a month were eventually exceeded. In all, by the close of hostilities, a total of 1,080 Lancasters had been produced, together with spares for a further 64 aircraft. In July 1943 orders were received by the firm for a further and quite different bomber, the 'Lincoln'. A total of 80 Lincolns were built before the end of the war brought an end to production. The aircraft factory also produced 'Messier' and 'Dowty' undercarriages for the Halifax and Lancaster bombers respectively under assembly elsewhere.

Development of the Estate during the war did not cease entirely although, due to severe building controls, any building work carried out had to be justified for war production purposes, and mainly comprised extensions to existing factories. Between November 1940 and summer 1942, substantial extensions were undertaken at Thomas Hedley & Co., including the erection of large external tanks for holding edible oils. The amount of land held by the Estates Company for development fell from 224 acres in 1940 to 167 acres in 1947. The use of the estate railway system reached a peak of over 2.5 million tons in 1940, and over the entire war it was estimated that some 13 million tons of freight was carried over the system.

Trafford Park demonstrated its capabilities during the Second World War. The challenge of the post-war decades would be to maintain that status.

Chapter V

Completion and Decline
1945-1980

Post-War Changes

The end of the war was accompanied by a rapid reversion to peacetime production, although some firms, particularly Metropolitan-Vickers, were able to continue some production in fields they had entered during the war. Overall employment fell back from wartime levels of over 70,000 to about 54,000, estimated to be about 9,000 above 1939 levels, indicating the scale of the Park's development during the war.

Production started to run down at the Metrovick aircraft factory before the war's end, and ceased altogether soon after. Departments from the main works transferred to the building, as others, transferred elsewhere for the duration, moved back to the main site. At first only part of the huge building was occupied, and it would be 1948 before further sections moved in. Metrovicks remained in occupation of Leonard Works. At the Ford factory on Barton Dock Road, production started to run down in August 1945, and finally ceased on 23 March 1946. The building was then taken over by Platts Brothers of Oldham for the manufacture of textile machinery and they used it until the mid-1950s. Thereafter, it did not find a single occupier, being partly used by Massey Ferguson, and partly for a time by the Sivewright Group for warehousing.

71 *1945 view of the Geigy factory from Tenax Road. Building work for the Anglo-Swiss firm had started in early 1939, but was virtually halted when war broke out. It was resumed when it was demonstrated that phosphate plasticisers were useful in aircraft production.*

72 *Hedley's factory 1945, showing the various extensions completed since 1933, and the pipe bridge across the Ship Canal. In the right foreground is the site of Trafford Hall.*

The two British Restaurants remained in operation for a time, reflecting their popularity at a time of continuing food rationing. One was still open in the early 1950s.

Another chapter in the Park's history closed when the last trams of Manchester and Salford Corporations ran on the loop line through the Village on 24 August 1946. The Estates Company expressed some concern about future traffic congestion on the Estate.

The rôle of Metropolitan-Vickers during the war was celebrated in a book the firm published in 1947. Called *Contribution to Victory*, by Frank Rowlinson, it was distributed free to all the firm's staff. The Estates Company itself published a booklet in the same year, to mark the 50th anniversary of the arrival of industries in the Park. Entitled *Some notes on the development of Trafford Park 1897-1947*, it was written by Colonel Stevens.[1] One passage from the end of the booklet is worth quoting as it shrewdly forecasts some of the problems that would beset the Park in the future:

> Whilst the markets of the world remain 'sellers markets' with buyers willing to give any price for goods, the situation of the factory is of little importance, but the time approaches when our factories will have to compete with factories more efficiently sited and employing cheap and efficient labour in China, India, Africa and elsewhere.

Another book was produced by Metropolitan-Vickers in 1949. Written by John Dummelow of the company's publicity department, it was called *1899-1949*, and was a celebration of the 50th anniversary of the firm's taking a site in the Park. Like the earlier book, many copies were printed and were distributed free to members of the

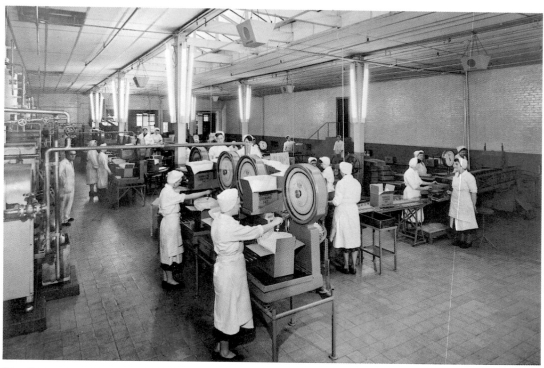

73 *Late 1940s scene in the Southern Oil factory (the word 'cotton' had been dropped from the title in 1922) showing bulk packing of 28lb-cartons of 'Veltex' golden shortening.*

Company's Long Service Association, and to all employees having 25 years' service with the firm.

The connection between the Estates and Dwellings companies was severed in 1948, when the Estates Company's shareholding was sold to the Bradford Property Trust Ltd. The Estates Company's decision no doubt reflected the continuing system of tightly controlled rents on residential property, introduced by government as a temporary measure during the First World War, but retained for reasons of political expediency; it left owning companies little or no financial return for repairs or modernisation. The Bradford Property Trust were associated with a building society, and it is believed that their interest in buying the Dwellings Company was to sell the houses with the aid of mortgages. In the following decades, many of the houses in the Village were sold in this way while others were modernised.

More serious, however, were other measures brought in by the post-war Attlee government. The first was the Distribution of Industry Act 1945, which was the government's response to the Barlow Report's recommendations of 1940. It stimulated a renewal of the government's own programme of building industrial or trading estates in areas of high unemployment, in competition with private sector estates like Trafford Park, in areas without such designation. In particular, a number of large new estates were to be created out of wartime Royal Ordnance Factory sites, the nearest of which was at Kirkby, near Liverpool. Most importantly, the Act vested in the Board of Trade considerable powers and duties to direct the location of industrial production.

These powers were given greater effect when the Town and Country Planning Act was passed in 1947. This established a development control system throughout the U.K., by which all but the most trivial developments could not proceed until planning permission had been granted by the local authority. Outside the 'Development Areas' defined by the government, planning permission for industrial developments exceeding 5,000 square feet in size could not be granted unless the applicants already possessed an Industrial Development Certificate issued by the Board of Trade. In the case of areas outside the Development Areas, such certificates would only be granted for factory alterations and small-scale extensions. For larger schemes, even existing factories wanting to expand substantially would have to consider moving to a Development Area, or splitting operations. In addition, the 1947 Act established a tax of 100 per cent on increases in site values due to the granting of planning permissions, and at the same time set up a fund to partially compensate land owners whose land had decreased in value due to the introduction of planning control schemes in their areas.

The Estates Company were alarmed at these changes, which would effectively stifle any further large-scale industrial development in the Park. The system of building licensing controls, introduced in the war to allocate scarce building materials, also remained in force and would not be relaxed totally until 1954. The Company lodged a claim for £500,000 with the Central Land Board in respect of the depreciation of its interests, and sought legal advice from Arthur Capewell K.C. on the issue of the 100 per cent development charge, particularly over the question of whether the cost of providing roads and railways to service individual sites would be an allowable deduction. The Company also joined with Slough Trading Estates Ltd. in forming the Industrial Estates Association. Its function was to consider, make representation and raise objections to legislation that might adversely affect industrial estates. Colonel Stevens acted as the Company's representative on the Executive Committee of the new association.

The more stringent measures of the 1947 Act, relating to the development charge and compensation, did not survive long on the statute book, and were repealed by the Conservative government in 1953. Planning permissions and the need for Industrial Development Certificates remained. Transport and warehousing developments, however, needed no such certificates, and the legislative system is perhaps part of the explanation why these uses began to become more predominant in the Park at this time.

Overall development on the estate continued nevertheless; the amount of undeveloped land held by the Estates Company decreased from 167 acres in 1947 to 141 acres in 1953, although most disposals were small and for extensions to existing factories. In June 1950, the *Daily Dispatch* reported that 'present conditions are tending to keep back any further development in Trafford Park'.[2]

The Guinness land remained undeveloped, apart from the area to the west of Ashburton Road which was taken over by Turners Asbestos in the late 1940s, although discussions did take place from 1950 between Guinness and the Estates Company, who now acted as Guinness's agents for the disposal and development of the site. In January 1952, the site of the former Trafford Hall was sold to Thomas Hedley & Co. who used it over the next few years as a car and lorry park. Two sites comprising 18 acres to the east of Ashburton Road were sold in 1954 to National Benzole and Victor Blagden & Co. respectively and, the following year, Brown and Polson Ltd. bought 12 acres, including the wharf laid out by Guinness before the First World War. The company built new grain silos and made extensive alterations to their factory. The wharf was first used on 18 September 1956 when SS *Welsh Trader* delivered 9,000 tons of maize. Also, in 1956, work started on 9 September on the construction of Guinness Road, linking

Tenax Road and Ashburton Road, to open up the Guinness land for development. The Estates Company had been seeking to do this since 1950, following the tracks of the estate railway laid along the same route in the late 1920s.

In 1950, the Stretford Labour Exchange reported a shortage of female workers in the Park. Only 50 had applied for 200 vacancies. Employers were encouraged to take on more part-time staff, but apparently were reluctant to do so because full National Insurance contributions still had to be paid for them. Similar general staff shortages were reported in the local press in 1955.

In 1951, a new Shell Mex and B.P. lubricating oil plant was completed at a cost of £500,000 on a bomb-damaged site to the west of Ashburton Road. It was capable of processing 25,000 gallons of oils in 300 different grades. The plant was formally opened by Sir Frederick West, former chairman of the Ship Canal Company.

The following year, rebuilding was completed of the main building, destroyed in the war, of the Trafford Park Cold Storage Company. Work on this had been undertaken in stages, the first third of the building being ready for use in 1949.

The death of E.T. Hooley

In February 1947, Trafford Park's original purchaser, Ernest Terah Hooley, died aged 88 at his birthplace, Long Eaton. Since his bankruptcy in 1898, Hooley's fortunes had continued to rise and fall, though his activities were said to have become even more devious. In autumn 1910, he had been convicted of fraud and sent to prison for 12 months. When released, he re-started as a property speculator. Bankruptcy came again in 1923, and a further fraud conviction, in respect of the flotation and sale of Jubilee Cotton Mills Ltd., followed in 1924, after a trial lasting 26 days, for which he was sentenced to three years' penal servitude. In 1925, he published his autobiographical *Hooley's Confessions*. He became bankrupt again in 1939. At the age of 85, he was still running a modest business as a property dealer.

Dock Railway Rates

1950 was to see the last of the large-scale disputes between the Estates and Ship Canal companies, so characteristic of the early years of the century. The dispute itself was in fact merely a resolution of an issue which had its origins in that era.

The Canal Company from time to time submitted private Bills to Parliament to extend or modify their statutory powers. The Bill for 1950 included clauses that would have enabled them to increase the 6d. a ton charge for rail haulage between docks and factory that had been introduced in the 1898 agreement between the two companies. Any increases had been successfully resisted by the Estates Company.

The Canal Company's first bid to increase the charge had partly succeeded in 1916, when in a court case heard in the King's Bench division it was decided that the 6d. charge did not include storage or sheeting services, for which the trader would have to pay extra. Further negotiations took place in 1920-1, but the traders and the Estates Company stood firm, and the Canal Company reluctantly had to accept the fact that the 6d. charge was a binding obligation. When in 1930 the agreement was entered into between the two companies relating to the extension of the estate railway into the Barton Dock area, the 6d. per ton charge was continued in the new agreement.

The Canal Company sought to increase the charges to 1s. 9d. a ton, or 1s. 4d. if the traders' own rolling stock was being used. The suggested charges were strenuously opposed by the Estates Company and its statutory subsidiary, the Trafford Park Company, who were supported by the Trafford Park Traders Association.[3] The arguments were heard by a House of Commons Select Committee, and all the parties employed eminent counsel to put their cases.

The Canal Company argued that there was some evidence that 6d. a ton was even an uneconomic charge in 1898, when the cost was more like 8d. a ton. They estimated that the current charge should be more in the order of 3s. 6d. a ton, or 2s. 6d. if traders' own wagons were being used. The rates they were seeking in the Bill were still a concession on their part.

Expert witnesses for both sides appeared before the committee. The petitioners' experts cast doubts on the accuracy of the Ship Canal's costings, and others made the point that the Canal Company was enjoying a period of very high profits at the time. The latter point must have had an effect, as the committee ruled that the charges should rise, but only to 1s. 3d. and 1s. 0d. per ton respectively. Subsequent legislation obtained by the Canal Company finally increased the charges to 1s. 8d. a ton by the early 1960s.

Westinghouse Road

Another long-standing dispute was settled in 1954. This was with Stretford Borough Council over Westinghouse Road, a dispute which had started back in 1907 and had involved litigation at the time. Over the years, parts of the road had been adopted by

74 *The Estates Company's Works Department undertook a wide range of contracting activities. Here, c.1947, estate railway track at the junction of Trafford Park Road and Westinghouse Road is relaid. In the right background, the Hovis flour mill, destroyed in the Blitz, is being rebuilt.*

the local authority, between Trafford Park Road and First Avenue in 1930, and as far as Mosley Road in 1942. The agreement related to the remaining length, then a cul de sac, and also provided for the total reconstruction of the section west of Fraser Road by the Estates Company.

As a result, the estate railway track, which previously ran unguarded down the centre of the road, was set in a central reservation. The work cost £16,000 and was completed in three months. It was formally opened by the mayor, Councillor Richard Lee, and was hailed as the first length of dual carriageway to be built in Stretford.

Road connections to the Estate

The 1950s were to see the start of the decline in the use of the estate railway system, and the consequent increased usage by traders of road transport. At the same time, workers in the Park increasingly used their own transport, contributing to a growing congestion problem at peak hours.

The idea of a north-south arterial road, passing either through or close to the Park, canvassed as part of the regional planning initiatives of the 1930s, now began to be taken seriously. Representations were made as early as 1950 for a high-level bridge over the Ship Canal, itself part of the problem, as increasing use of the canal in the 1950s caused greater delays at the bottleneck of the Barton Swing Bridge. In 1954, following a meeting between W.T. Proctor, M.P. for Eccles, and the Eccles Trades and Labour Council, the trades unions within the Park arranged for hundreds of postcards to be sent to M.P.s from workers seeking support for such a bridge, and citing lost time and wages due to delays at the swing bridge. Shortly after, a group of Conservative and Labour M.P.s went to see R.A. Butler, the Minister of Transport.

The following year, the government announced a four-year national road plan, with the new bridge high on the agenda. Work started in 1957 under the auspices of Lancashire County Council, who through County Surveyor Sir James Drake had long campaigned for a national motorway network. The Ministry of Transport contributed 75 per cent of the cost. Construction took a long time, partly due to the largely urban nature of the route, but also due to variable soil conditions, including peat deposits and mining subsidence. Industrial waste had to be used to form the high embankments leading to the new bridge over the Ship Canal.

The motorway and bridge became part of what at the time was an isolated stretch of the M62 motorway, running from the A56 at Stretford to the A57 at Eccles.[4] At the same time, the road linking the Redcliffe and Dumplington roundabouts was turned into a dual carriageway. The new two-lane motorway opened for use on 29 October 1961, the opening ceremony being performed by Alderman Sir Anthony Smith, leader of the County Council. The previous day had seen the bridge opened to pedestrians, and engineers in kiosks answered queries about the new road. It would be the only instance of pedestrians being able to use the motorway-standard road.

By the early 1960s, congestion within the Park itself had been recognised as a problem. Increasing car ownership and use, coupled with the fact that employment levels were still high within the estate, were the causes. AEI itself still employed 23,000 in 1962. The firm organised its own traffic survey over a 14-month period ending in November 1962. A Trafford Park Traffic Congestion Committee was formed. This resulted in the introduction of waiting and loading restrictions on Ashburton, Trafford Park and Westinghouse Roads in January 1963. During 1963-4 part of Trafford Park Road was widened, between the Lancashire Dynamo and Knowsley Cast Metal factories, through the agreed removal of a stretch of estate railway on the northern side of the road at this point. In late 1966, work started on a £522,000 scheme to improve the main Chester Road entrance to the estate. The road layout was re-formed into a gyratory system. At the same time, the road linking Trafford Park Road with Chester Road was rebuilt with new bridges over the Bridgewater Canal and railway respectively. The loading capacity of the bridges was increased ten-fold, for the transport of heavy machinery and goods from the estate. The scheme took 18 months to complete.

Further progress was made in 1965 when the County Council started work on 'Route 232', a scheme which had been discussed by the Estates Company and County Council many times in the 1950s, and which in 1961 had been the subject of representations by the Trafford Park Industries Association, who again cited time lost to firms and employees through congestion. This had recently been exacerbated by reductions in the average working week from 47 to 41 hours, which made staggering of worktimes less feasible. The new road was a dual carriageway linking the M62 at Urmston with a landscaped roundabout within the Park at the junction of Ashburton and Tenax Roads. Originally it had been intended to link the new road and Ashburton Road by a flyover, but shortage of funds caused this to be dropped. At the same time, the westerly stub of Westinghouse Road was connected to the new roundabout, located on the site of 'Boggy Hills'.

The new road, called 'The Parkway' after its extensive landscaping, entered the estate through some of the last remaining undeveloped land under Estates Company control. The land not required for the scheme was developed as the Longwood Road Estate. The Parkway, which also included slip roads to the Barton Dock area, finally opened in 1967 at a cost of over £1 million.

The SELNEC Transportation Plan, issued in the early 1970s, proposed a £2.5 million busway linking the estate and stations on the Manchester-Altrincham commuter railway. It was never built.

Road congestion in the Park gradually diminished after the 1960s, largely as a consequence of the continuing decline in employment levels, particularly among the larger firms.

Changes in the Estates Company

In 1954, Colonel Stevens resigned as Managing Director of the Estates Company, and became the Chairman. Unlike his father, he never combined the two posts. After Marshall Stevens's own resignation, the Chairman's position had been taken by T.G. Mellors (1930-43), G.R.T. Taylor (1943-9),[5] and Sir Joseph Nall (1949-54).

The Company's influence on the estate declined in the late 1940s and 1950s. In

75   T.H.G. or 'Colonel' Stevens, from a photograph taken in the late 1940s, when he was Managing Directory of Trafford Park Estates Ltd.

76 *Kilvert's factory and the Warwick Road (since 1994 Sir Matt Busby Way) bridge in 1949, with a queue of Manchester United fans waiting to enter the ground, recently reopened after war damage.*

77 *The Mosley Road premises of the Trafford Park Cold Storage Ltd., complete with delivery vans, in 1951, shortly after completion of the post-war rebuilding work.*

1953, its ownership, including all properties let on short-term leases, undeveloped sites and land used for roads and railways, amounted to just over 23 per cent of the entire estate, and this declined further over the next decade. The Company's income would be derived from lettings of buildings or sites let on short-term leases, from its interests in the warehousing and cold storage companies, from fixed chief rents, and from a declining estate railway system. Little income could be expected from large-scale disposals of development sites.

The company had cleared all its Debenture borrowings during the Second World War, and made no new borrowings during the 1950s. Its rental income held up during this period and, despite the punitive taxation of the late 1940s, managed to pay out dividends of between 8 per cent and 15 per cent during the years 1949-56. As building controls and licensing became easier, it became possible to undertake large-scale re-pairs. 'A', 'B' and 'D' Warehouses were substantially re-roofed in 1957 by Port of Manchester Warehouses Ltd., who in 1956-7 built two new adjacent warehouses between Trafford Park and Westinghouse Roads, on the site of 'P', 'U' and 'W' Warehouses destroyed during the war. Named the Stevens and Telford Warehouses respectively, after former managing directors of both Estates and Warehousing companies, they were used by Carreras Ltd., part of the Imperial Tobacco Company, as bonded tobacco warehouses. The Telford Warehouse was extended in 1959. From the mid-1950s onwards the warehousing associate concentrated all its activities on the storage of tobacco, completing a gradual change of emphasis, which had been apparent since the 1930s, away from storage of other types of merchandise.

During the late 1950s a number of changes were initiated which led the Company in the following decade to invest outside the Park. Firstly a review of all remaining undeveloped sites in Company ownership assessed their development potential. In 1958, this amounted to only 8 per cent of the Park area. Three years later, it was down to 6 per cent or 73 acres. Secondly, the Company began to pursue a course that would give it greater financial control over its subsidiaries. Thus minority interests were bought out of the Warehousing, Cold Storage and Grain Elevator Estate companies from 1958, although all would remain separate companies.[6]

In 1961, Stevens resigned as Chairman of Trafford Park Estates, although he remained as Chairman of Port of Manchester Warehouses Ltd. until August 1964. At the Estates Company, his place was taken by C.E.W. Lavender. In May 1962, Neil Westbrook, a Manchester chartered surveyor, was engaged as a consultant for the Company. Rather surprisingly for a property company, none of its staff or Board members in recent years had held any qualifications in property management or development, and Mr. Westbrook was brought in to fill that gap. By the end of the year, at the suggestion of Baring's, he was invited to join the Board.

Neil Westbrook's influence within the Company was to be quickly felt. At an early date, the old policy of selling sites was ended. The granting of fixed chief or ground rents usually associated with this practice was an anachronism, particularly in a period when general inflation was increasing, so that such fixed rents soon lost their value. Another Westbrook proposal to be adopted was the decision to invest outside the Park. He initiated the acquisition of three small trading estates at Hereford in 1964 through a newly formed subsidiary, Trafford Industrial Buildings Ltd. Further buildings would be added to all three estates. Further developments followed elsewhere at Wythenshawe (1965) by Trafford Extensions Ltd., at Sunderland (1967), and at Hooton and Wigan (1973) by Trafford Industrial Buildings Ltd. A joint venture, called Calder Vale Estates Ltd., with Trafford Park Estates holding 51 per cent of the shareholding, was set up in

78   *Ladies and children of St Antony's queue up in 'Sunday best' outside the church on Our Lady's Sunday, May 1949.*

79   *1953 Coronation street party on Tenth Street, looking eastwards.*

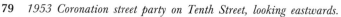

1968 with Charles Roberts & Co. Ltd. to develop part of that company's former engineering works on a 32-acre site at Wakefield. In 1972, a similar joint venture company,
Ringway International Development Ltd., was set up to acquire and develop a large
area of land on the northern side of Manchester Airport. In that year, as a reflection
of his growing influence within the Company over the previous decade and the increase
in its fortunes that had resulted, Neil Westbrook was appointed Chairman of the Company on the retirement of C.E.W. Lavender. By 1977, he had become Chief Executive
as well, being the first person to combine both positions since Marshall Stevens.

To enable the Company to undertake all these developments, it was necessary to
expand its capital base. During 1962-5, various amounts in the company's reserves were
converted into additional shareholdings and issued as bonus shares. This effectively
divided the 'cake' up into smaller slices, but enabled the Company to have a nominal
shareholding greater than £1 million, which qualified the shares for investment by the
financial institutions as trustee investments and thus made them more saleable. In 1965,
Baring Bros floated £1.25 million-worth of First Mortgage Debenture Stock at an interest rate of 7.25 per cent. Four years later, the same merchant bank placed £2 million-
worth of First Mortgage Debenture Stock at 9 per cent.

The 1960s also saw the company investing again in the Park. The first instance of
this was a small development on Fraser Road, built in 1964. A much larger development was the Longwood Road Estate, named after one of the old woods in the pre-1896
Park, where a total of 19 units were built by the Company's own Works Department

80 *In 1960, the Ashburton Chemical Co., a subsidiary of Geigy, completed a new administrative building, with
a drawing office on the top floor. Office furniture and work attire of the era is clearly evident in this view taken
that year.*

in 1965-8. It was necessary for the company to purchase two small areas of land to complete the development.

In 1967, Trafford Industrial Buildings Ltd. bought the recently closed Kilverts factory at the junction of Trafford Park and Warwick Roads. This was developed in 1970 as the Warwick Place Trading Estate with 10 units. Other developments of small industrial buildings were carried out on former railway land, reflecting the gradual abandonment of parts of the system. Such developments included Taylor Road (1966), Nash Road (1968), Richmond Road (1969), and Guinness Road (1969) where the estate railway had been taken up at an early date due to lack of demand.

Work started in 1968 on a new temperature-controlled warehouse on Westinghouse Road for the Cold Storage Company. This had a total capacity of 3.5 million cubic feet, and was completed in 1970. Two years later, the entire Cold Storage Company was sold by the Estates Company to the Transport Development Group, who retain ownership to this day, the Mosley Road site trading under the 'Novacold' name. The entire transaction was said to be worth £1 million. The Westinghouse Road building was initially leased to the new owners, but it was subsequently bought outright.

81 *Unloading grain from the SS* Sils *at the Brown and Polson (originally Guinness) wharf, early 1960s. The Barton High Level Bridge is just visible in the left background.*

The first large-scale factory closures

The fortunes of the Park had managed to hold up reasonably well until the mid-1960s, although employment levels in 1965, estimated at 52,000, were virtually the same as post-war levels. Employment densities, however, had clearly started to decline, as the Park had continued to develop, albeit on a more limited scale since 1945. The development was now complete, apart from odd pockets of Guinness land, which would not be developed until the 1980s. Although the need to obtain Industrial Development Certificates still applied, they had become easier to obtain in the 1960s, particularly when the threat of growing unemployment started to loom large in the latter half of the decade. In July 1962, Thomas Hedley & Co. adopted the name of its American owners, Procter and Gamble. The factory continued to expand, taking over a 23-acre site for expansion adjacent to Brooke Bond in 1962, and in 1965-8 building in two stages a large warehouse on the site of Trafford Hall, which was linked to the main factory by a bridge.

82 *In July 1961, Soviet cosmonaut Yuri Gagarin made a one-day visit to Manchester at the invitation of the metal workers union, visiting Manchester Airport, the Town Hall and AEI. Despite his limited English and heavy KGB 'protection', evident in this picture, his genuine friendliness and enthusiasm was felt by all he met, and he was mobbed by adoring crowds everywhere.*

The 1960s were a period of large-scale industrial reorganisation, partly encouraged by the Labour Government's Industrial Reorganisation Corporation, set up to encourage greater efficiency through amalgamations of firms. Some old established names in the Park became parts of larger organisations, who would then proceed to rationalise capacity, and close down the older and less efficient plant. Other firms might in the short term benefit from such a process. Glover's, as an example, who had works on both sides of the Bridgewater Canal, became part of the B.I.C.C. Group. In 1966, it was announced that the capacity of the plant was to be increased by 50 per cent to meet increased demand. Yet, only three years later, the firm shed 400 staff, and in 1970 closed completely, lead-

83   *Two minutes past five and the late afternoon exodus from AEI, 1962. A row of Salford Corporation buses waits on Third Avenue. On the corner is Crayfield House, originally a hostel for visiting workers, which was demolished in 1994.*

84 *The Southern Oil Company's factory was in the hands of Kraft by the time this 1962 view of the laboratory within the egg processing plant was taken.*

ing to a further 750 redundancies, the remaining work transferring to a BICC plant in North Wales.

Many long established names would disappear in this period. Kilvert's has already been mentioned. Lancashire Dynamo and Crypto were taken over by GEC and closed at the end of 1967, with the loss of 400 jobs. The old Ford factory, the Leonard Works, were closed down in the same year by AEI, the name under which Metropolitan-Vickers had been operating since 1958. The steel producers, Edward Wood and Co., ceased operations at the end of 1969. The Lancashire Wire Co. and Truscon Concrete were two other names that disappeared in the late 1960s. The Superheater Co. laid off 100 staff in 1970; like Glover's, this firm had expanded in 1966. In 1969, rumours circulated about a possible rundown in Taylor Bros steelworks, by now part of the nationalised British Steel Corporation. By 1973, this rundown had produced 15 acres of surplus land next to the Parkway which was being considered for a joint development scheme between British Steel and Trafford Park Estates. The main spine road serving the estate was to have been called Melchett Way after the then Chairman of British Steel, but the scheme did not proceed because of the collapse of the property market in 1974.

In late 1967, Associated Electrical Industries Ltd. was subjected to a take-over bid from its smaller rival, GEC Ltd., headed by Arnold Weinstock. At the time, in financial and industrial circles, the bid was considered somewhat audacious, and the AEI chairman, Sir Charles Wilson, urged shareholders not to accept the bid, said to be worth £124 million. AEI however, was a relatively poor performer, and the bid was success-

85 *Layout plan, January 1963, issued by the Ship Canal Company, showing both Trafford Park and surrounding Canal Company-owned land, including Barton Dock.*

DOCK OFFICE

For particulars of sites on the Comp___
estate application should be made t___
Company's Land Agents.

86 *Growing traffic congestion problems in the Park are illustrated well by this evocative* Manchester Evening News *picture of the Mosley Road/Westinghouse Road junction, taken on a dark night in February 1966.*

ful. Rationalisation of the Trafford Park factory followed with inevitable job losses. An area adjacent to Fraser Road was leased out in 1969 as the Allens International Freight Forwarders Estate, a facility associated with the new Freightliner Depot. In April 1970, the former Apprentice Training School on Moss Road was sold to the local authority.[7] Its functions were slimmed down and transferred within the main site. At the end of the year, the former aircraft factory on Mosley Road closed with some 900 redundancies.

The immediate result of these closures was a glut on the local property market of the redundant buildings and sites. Large-scale occupiers were no longer available to take over such old buildings, and many would remain on the market for some time. Others would be bought for investment or development purposes, for subdivision or demolition. The former Leonard Works was bought by the Springfield Warehousing and Transport Group in 1969, an estate occupier since the 1950s, to be turned into the Springfield Trading Estate of small units converted from existing buildings. In 1970, the same group bought the Edward Wood site, which was subsequently adapted as the 'Ocean Estate' devoted to transport and warehousing functions.

The Estates Company itself acquired the former Glover's factory in 1972. The part on the eastern side of the Bridgewater Canal was renamed the 'United Trading Estate' on account of its proximity to the Manchester United football ground, and was subdivided for letting and partial redevelopment. Substantial parts were still vacant in 1976. The Mosley Road aircraft factory was bought in 1972 by the Property Security Investment Trust. The building was subsequently subdivided and partly demolished to create 44 separate units, called 'Central Park'. The estate still had substantial vacancies in 1980, despite lettings to Schrieber's, Kellogg's and others.

Formation of the Trafford Park Industrial Council

Recognition of the Park's decline stimulated action to combat the problem. Following a meeting in November 1970 between Geoffrey Thomas, chairman of the Springfield Group, and the area's M.P., Winston Churchill, early in 1971 Stretford Council considered setting up a representative body to halt the Park's decline. A meeting was held on 9 July at Stretford Town Hall, and on 30 July the formation of the Trafford Park Industrial Council, or TRAFIC, was announced by Councillor Warbrick, leader of the council, at a luncheon held for industrialists after Winston Churchill had unveiled a plaque at the Springfield site, commemorating Ford's years at the premises.

87   *General view of Trafford Park Estates's Longwood Road development in November 1966, shortly after the completion of its first phase. In the background is the I.C.I. (ex British Alizarine) factory.*

Thomas himself was inaugural chairman of the new body, which was to be non-political in nature, and open to all firms in the Park and Barton Dock, including the local authorities. It met every three months and soon attracted a membership of over 60. At the luncheon, Churchill said:

> Unless we can get grants to demolish old factory buildings, Trafford Park will be less attractive to new industrialists than a green field site. If the green acres of Trafford Park could attract industry 76 years ago, then it can do so again.

One of TRAFIC's first moves was to encourage an element of self improvement to the Park's environment by firms still active on the estate. Each year, TRAFIC would present a green pennant to the firm that had done the most to improve its surroundings by way of landscaping etc. The first award, presented by Sir William Mather, Chairman of the North West Economic Planning Council, went to Carborundum's. The following year's award went to the Barton Oil Terminal.

Less tangible work was done on the political front. Representations were made at the absence of Development or Intermediate Area status for any of the Park, whereby government grants for the demolition of old buildings were not available. Similar complaints were made about the Industrial Development Certificate system, which resulted in some planning permissions for developments in the Park being refused. In a reply, Churchill stated that no such certificates had been refused since the Conservatives had come to power in 1970.

The Civic Trust Report 1972-74

Another manifestation of the growing awareness of the Park's problems came with the commissioning, at a cost of £5,000, of a report on the area from the Civic Trust for the North West. In the early 1970s there was growth in public interest in the environment, reflected in the B.B.C.'s screening of the series 'Doomwatch' and by the government which created the Department of the Environment under Peter Walker. Local govern-

88 *The main gate of the Park's largest employer was often the scene for demonstrations and picketing. In 1972, a token presence stands at the G.E.C. gates during a dispute which affected all engineering employers in the area.*

ment at the time was busy with 'Operation Eyesore', cleaning up and landscaping der-elict sites through government grants.

The Civic Trust were a natural choice for the work—the problems at the time were felt to be environmental in nature, stemming from the decline of an estate whose build-ings were now past their prime. The costs of the study were met by Stretford and Urmston Councils, with a substantial contribution from the Estates Company, and a nominal £100 from TRAFIC.

The report was completed and published in March 1974, a few weeks before the local authorities in the area were amalgamated, as part of central government's reorganisa-tion of local government, into a new author-ity, Trafford Metropolitan Borough.

The report had some harsh words about the condition of the Park. 'The Workshop of the World' had become 'a mere collection of factories and warehouses' ... 'One can only remark at the lack of attention paid to it over many years' ... 'The rebuilding of some order and organisation is the key to any lasting improvement.'

The root causes of the problems were environmental, including the diversity of land ownership, the obsolescence of the estate railway system, the inadequacies of the road system, the lack of immediately available expansion space for many of the remaining industries, the general air of decay and the varying levels of ability of firms to finance any improvements themselves.

On the face of it, the report could have been interpreted as an indictment of the Park's key players, namely the Estates Company and the local authorities. However, the former now only owned a limited proportion of the estate, and the powers and finance available to the latter were limited. Neither was to blame for national economic condi-tions and the industrial restructuring that had taken place and affected the Park. Most of all, the key players were aware of the problem, and had taken the first tentative steps towards a solution.

The outline recommendations of the report, reflecting the modest nature of the commission, centred on a four-point plan:

1. The formation of a Committee supported and financed by businesses in the Park to help solve some of the environmental problems.
2. Individual firms could continue to be encouraged to carry out their own improve-ment works.

3. Railway land should be bought for landscaping and improvement.

4. The new Trafford Council should start more fundamental studies to cover matters such as the economic future, pollution, social problems and the internal transport system.

Later in 1974, the new local authority and TRAFIC decided to form the Trafford Park Environmental Committee. It held its first meeting in September 1975, and its membership comprised local and central government representatives, the statutory undertakers, the CBI, the Civic Trust, TRAFIC, along with the Ship Canal and Estates Companies. Its remit was very wide.

Environmental improvements in the meantime had started in the Park, partly in response to the 'Operation Eyesore' initiative, and the 'Plant a Tree in '73' campaign. Shell Mex and B.P. spent £2,000 renovating the boundaries of the Barton Oil Terminal. The surroundings to the Marshall Stevens monument at Ashburton Road were tidied up by Stretford Council, whilst the monument itself was sandblasted by Metallisation Services Ltd. Elsewhere, some of the newly lifted railway tracks were landscaped. The central reservation on Westinghouse Road was grassed over and 50 trees were planted, paid for by Winston Churchill reputedly out of the proceeds of a libel action he had won against the satirical magazine *Private Eye*. In 1974, TRAFIC made a suggestion that the festering eyesore, previously the Lake, should be restored.

The demolition of St Catherine's Church

St Catherine's Church was demolished in 1972. Although slightly outside the Park, its connection with the estate stemmed from both the part played in its founding by the de Traffords, and the fact that the churchyard contains the Stevens memorial vault.

The building had been remodelled at a cost of £2,500 in 1962, when bomb damage from the war was rectified. At the time, the steeple and part of the tower were removed, along with the clock provided in 1903 by a Mr. Fogg, and the church's eight bells, seven of which had been provided in 1921 as a World War I memorial.

St Catherine's ceased to be used for regular worship in September 1970 when the St Mark's Chapel opened in the Godfrey Ermen Memorial School in Eccles, following the amalgamation of the parish with St Michael and All Angels, Peel Green. At the time, the stained glass windows from St Catherine's were installed in the new chapel. Afterwards, only weddings and funerals and eight major services a year were held at St Catherine's.

Demolition came in late 1972, after extensive dry rot had been found in the roof. At the time, hopes were expressed that the building's foundations would remain. At the time of writing, the churchyard remains with some gravestones tended. From time to time, the local press expresses concern at its condition, especially the Stevens memorial, which now has an unkempt look and has recently suffered vandalism.

The death of T.H.G. Stevens

T.H.G. (Harry or 'Colonel') Stevens died on 12 December 1970, in a nursing home at the age of 87. The obituaries of the time dubbed him 'Mr Trafford Park'. Although he had not been actively involved in the Estates Company for a number of years, his passing effectively marked the end of an era for the Company.

T.H.G. Stevens had spent his early years in the Park, in the days before industry began to encroach upon Trafford Hall. As a boy, he would exercise his elder brother's

89 *Aerial view of the Quicks Truck depot on Mosley Road, which opened in 1972 on the Truscon site. The firm moved its truck department to part of the former aircraft factory in 1994, when this site was redeveloped.*

(Blamey's) polo ponies along the leafy lanes of the Park. From 1897 to 1900, he attended King William's College in the Isle of Man. In 1900, he was sent to the Royal Indian Engineering College at Coopers Hill. From 1903 to 1920 he worked as a civil engineer for the Public Works Department in Burma, where he built many roads and railways. This service was broken for active service in Mesopotamia during the First World War for which he received the O.B.E. He was mentioned three times in dispatches. After the war, he remained a Lieutenant Colonel (a title by which he was often addressed) in the Indian Army Reserve of Officers.

He became a member of the Worshipful Company of Glaziers in 1939, and married rather late in life, in 1946, Margaret McKechnie Dickson. They lived at the home he had inherited from his father at Dingle Bank, Bowdon.

Stevens was a contrast to his father. Although just as keen to promote the Park, he was a less aggressive character; disputes of the type that characterised the early years of the Company did not occur, and old disputes were eventually resolved through his co-operative approach. Described as a kind and generous man, he demonstrated his organisational capabilities during the Second World War, and he set the company off on its wider path in the late 1950s.

Stevens was a keen gardener, writing *Trees and Shrubs in my Garden* which was published in 1939. Although modestly declaring 'I am not a historian', he published *Manchester of Yesterday* in 1959, and his 1947 work on Trafford Park itself has already been mentioned. His contribution to students of Trafford Park's history is immense.

The decline of the Estate railway system

Usage of the estate's internal railway system, linking factories to both the Docks and the main lines, reached a peak in 1940 when a total of 2,553,511 tons was carried. An analysis of the following year's total, 2,242,254 tons, is available. Of this, the majority (1.46 million tons) was traffic destined for the main lines. Slightly over 0.5 million tons was traffic between the Docks and the main line, and only about 0.25 million tons was traffic between the Docks and the Park. The remainder comprised transfers within the Estate, the Trafford Park Extension and Barton Dock estate.

After the war, traffic tailed off to 1,877,489 tons in 1946, but recovered somewhat by 1951, when 2,045,815 tons were carried. Thereafter, a relentless decline set in throughout the next two decades as firms started to utilise road transport on a large scale. By 1962, total traffic had declined to 770,703 tons, although surprisingly, despite the increased haulage charges by the Ship Canal Company, traffic to and from the Docks was slightly higher than wartime levels; at 300,000 tons a similar figure to that for 1950 when the charges were first raised from 6d. per ton. Local traffic within the estates was now negligible and would soon cease altogether. Three years later, the total traffic had declined to 515,882 tons, and in 1971 it was 234,459 tons.

Traffic on the Canal Company's own railway system had undergone a similar decline, and between 1966 and 1970 both the Canal Company and British Rail through a joint working party studied how best to tackle the problem. In June 1970, the working party recommended closure of the dock railway facilities, although this would not necessarily mean closure of other railway functions carried out by the Canal Company, including their rôle in the Park. At the same time, the Canal Company gave formal notice to firms using its system that, unless such firms could guarantee continued usage of the railway at viable levels, the Canal Company would be unable to continue the services beyond the end of 1970. Many of the remaining users of the railway went over to road transport at this time.

Manchester Docks lost their rail facilities in autumn 1972, and the Trafford Park 'B' Sidings went out of use at the same time.

A separate working party, comprising representatives from the Canal Company, British Rail, and The Trafford Park Company, since 1969 had been looking into the operation of the estate railway system, and in particular into the expected traffics over the next 10 years. Their report appeared in October 1972. It recommended changing

90   *The Park saw political rallies of all types. One of the last was this address by Harold Wilson, on the Metrovick bus park next to Redpath Browns, during the February 1974 General Election.*

the basis of payment by British Railways and discontinuing the fixed sums payable under the early agreements. Its main recommendation, however, was to reduce the size of the railway system, then standing at 26.75 miles (reflecting abandonments of over six miles since 1950) to six and a third miles, leaving in use only the line along Trafford Park Road and part of the Ashburton Road line, as far as British Steel.

The system was gradually reduced during the 1970s, being about eight miles by 1979. In that year, only 84,374 tons were being carried, being mainly coal to Corn Products Ltd. and railway wheelsets from British Steel. The remaining system, now looking distinctly down at heel, had been minimally maintained, and was still laid out to Victorian standards, being unable because of the tightness of the curves to take long wheelbase high-capacity freight wagons then in increasing use on main line railways.

The local authority expressed a wish in 1979 to abandon the remaining system, to use the roadside strips for highway widening or landscaping. No steps, however, were taken to achieve this, and the Estates Company were opposed to the idea.

Trafford Park as a railfreight distribution centre

The rapid establishment of containerised systems for the transport of freight by sea, rail and road took place in the late 1960s. This led to vast changes in ports, and shifts in the location of transhipment activity.

In Trafford Park, these developments established the area as a centre for freight distribution, coincidentally whilst the internal railway system continued to decline.

The first new facility was established in 1968 by the Canal Company in conjunction with shipping and transport interests, on the Barton Dock Estate. Called 'Containerbase', it was served by the Canal Company's own railway. After experiencing some industrial relations difficulties in its early years, the facility was expanded in 1973 at a cost of £2.2 million.

Next to appear was the Freightliner Depot, which opened at the end of 1969 on the site of the old Trafford Park main line locomotive depot, to the east of the Bridgewater Canal. The main vehicular access through the Park was by a bridge across the Canal to join Westinghouse Road.

The third facility was located next to the Freightliner Depot and shared its road access. Called the Manchester International Freight Terminal or MIFT, it was developed jointly by a consortium of freight forwarding companies. Opening in 1974, it comprised a group of five cargo and receiving sheds, each with their own rail sidings, marshalling areas and vehicle maintenance facilities.

Changes on the Estate 1970-1980

The estate's employment at the start of the 1970s had fallen to $c.$40,000. Despite all the tentative initiatives outlined, it fell further, to 38,000 in 1975, and to 24,500 by 1985. Concern about the Park had been registered by central government, and in September 1971, a visit took place by Sir John Eden, the Minister for Industry. Little immediate action followed apart from a promise further to relax the already nominal controls exercised through the Industrial Development Certificate system. The Park was, however, granted Intermediate Area status with effect from March 1972. In 1970, Geigy became Ciba-Geigy, and the plant was extended in 1975.

Press reports following the setting up of TRAFIC talked optimistically about the revival of the Park. Expansion at CPC was highlighted and a British Road Services Depot, which had recently closed, reopened in 1972 although closures continued period-

91   *General view of Ciba-Geigy in the 1970s. The large multi-purpose building on the left was built to deal with organic chemicals. It was designed by architects Scherrer and Hicks to a vaguely Corbusier style, and along with All Saints and Barton Power Station merited a mention by Pevsner. It was demolished in the early 1990s.*

ically during the decade. In 1971, the British Trailer Company, located in Phoenix Works on Richmond Road, closed. The site was subsequently developed for car auctions. In September 1972, a new Quicks truck depot opened on Mosley Road at a cost of £250,000, occupying the old Truscon Concrete site. The opening ceremony, performed by the Head of Ford's U.K. operation, featured the appearance of an Indian elephant, which subsequently travelled through the streets to central Manchester. Also in 1972, the engineering firm of Morrell Mills, a subsidiary of Manchester Liners and a long standing occupier on Trafford Wharf Road, successfully acquired the Manchester Dry Docks on the northern side of the road. An expansion programme was planned and two years later the firm purchased parts of the Lancashire Dynamo and Crypto site, reopening the old Armstrong Works in the process. This piece of good news was yet another that turned out to be short-lived. Manchester Dry Docks closed later in the 1970s and the Morrell Mills site was sold in 1978, after the firm went into liquidation.

In 1972, Port of Manchester Warehouses Ltd. moved out of their head office on Ashburton Road and relocated within the Estates Office. The Ashburton Road building was subsequently taken over by Laing National Ltd.

The oil industry saw a massive investment in the Park between 1972 and 1975. In 1972, work started on a pipeline linking Manchester with the oil port of Milford Haven. The Manchester end was a vastly increased tank farm at Trafford Park, on the area to the north of the old lake. The new facility increased the storage capacity from one million to 15 million gallons. The old Esso site, on the banks of the Ship Canal, was extended both towards the lake, the site of which was bought, and also onto the site of the old Manchester Corporation Foreign Animals Wharf, on Ship Canal Co. land, which had closed in 1966. Trafford Wharf Road was shortened in the process and joined Trafford Park Road by a new link built in the late 1970s called Churchill Way, after the local M.P., on the site east of the lake. The new facility, operated by Esso, was officially opened by the mayor of Trafford, Councillor Colin Warbrick. In 1972, however, the Burmah Oil Refinery, located on two sites, on Twining and Nash Roads, closed with the loss of 400 jobs. The Twining Road site was later taken over by Texaco.

Another portion of the Guinness site was developed in 1973, when a factory was developed for Leathers Chemicals Ltd.

In 1973, Stretford Council took the first moves to clear the Village area, by now considered to be slum property, an unsuitable location for housing. A report recommended the demolition of a first phase of 298 houses between Westinghouse Road and Fifth Street. Subsequently, a Compulsory Purchase Order was prepared and a Public Inquiry was called to hear objections. The Order was confirmed by government in February 1976, and demolition soon followed.

The area between Westinghouse Road and Fourth Street from 1977 was developed by the local authority, now Trafford Metropolitan Borough, as the Westinghouse Industrial Estate of small units for local businesses. Alongside, in 1980 the Council built a depot for its Environmental Health Department. Other small plots, on a site called Westinghouse Phase 2, between First and Second Avenues, were leased for direct development by industrialists, following an outline planning brief by the Council in

92 *Trafford Park Road in the mid-1970s, with Trafford Park Power Station in the background. The double track estate railway line was singled shortly after.*

1977. Four such units had been built by 1983.

The Cooperative Wholesale Society's Sun Flour Mills were substantially damaged by fire in 1974. The building was eventually acquired by the Spillers Group, who demolished it in mid-1980. Also in 1974, the Coop announced that its tea factory would be closing, and transferred the work to Crewe. In March, Lancashire County Council turned down a planning application for a new-style hypermarket in the Park. In the same month, Barton Power Station finally closed. Towards the end of the year appeared reports of a proposed helicopter base being established on the old Courtaulds Chemicals site on Westinghouse and Textilose Roads, which had recently closed. Although a demonstration was ar-

93 *View of Ingersoll Rand showing environmental improvements of the type undertaken by firms during the 1970s. First established on Ashburton Road in the 1930s, the firm left the estate in the early 1980s, its premises now being occupied by Trafford Park Bakers.*

ranged by Suttons Helicopters Ltd., nothing came of the plan, and the site from 1975-81 was developed in phases by the Norwich Union Insurance Group as the Severnside Trading Estate of industrial units.

The Manpower Services Commission, a government agency, took over part of the old Guinness site, at the junction of Guinness and Ashburton Roads, in 1975 for the development of a skill centre for training the unemployed.

By mid-1976, clearance of the Village area had begun, and proposals were brought forward for the next phase of clearance. The residents responded by holding a local Pageant in June, the first in the area for 10 years. Twelve floats paraded through the streets, including one representing the 'Good Old Days', containing elderly residents in period dress, including one 75-year-old lady said to have been the first baby to be born in the Village. The following year, the Queen's Silver Jubilee saw street parties in the area. Late in 1977, Trafford Metropolitan Borough received a formal request from the remaining shopkeepers on Third Avenue, who feared loss of business when the remaining population left. They asked the Council to subsidise them after demolition, arguing that lack of shops would hinder firms trying to recruit staff. Nothing seems to have come from the approach.

The certainty of further clearances led the Manchester Studies unit of Manchester Polytechnic to carry out a large-scale study into the Village and its remaining inhabitants, which involved the collection of family photographs, and the recording of over 30 hours of taped reminiscences of life in the Park and Village. The results were exhibited, initially at four venues but later extended to 13 because of the level of interest aroused. A selection of the material was included in the book *Trafford Park 1896-1939* published by the Polytechnic in 1979. Both study and book were timely in capturing documents and information that would soon have been spread far and wide.

In July 1979, it was announced that the Gulf Oil plant on Ashburton Road would close with the loss of 50 jobs. This site had originally been occupied by the Patent Fuel Works and the Caucasian Oil Company, and later the Homelight Oil Company. The site was subsequently taken over by Edgar Vaughan & Co. Other closures in 1979 included the Rank (originally Greenwoods) Flour Mill on Trafford Wharf Road, and a large part of the Turner and Newall site, which was drastically reduced from 48 to eight acres, after the closure of the firm's building material manufacturing facility in the Park, partly as a result of health scares and the associated litigation that affected the entire asbestos industry from the late 1970s onwards.

In 1979, the local authority published its long awaited second slum clearance Compulsory Purchase Order, and the inevitable Public Inquiry was held in November. Some 325 houses and business premises on Fifth and Sixth Streets and between Eighth and Twelfth Streets were involved. The Orders were confirmed in June 1980 and demolition started shortly afterwards. Clearance would then leave only 84 houses, originally the largest in the Village, in the area bounded by Third Avenue, Ninth Street, Fourth Avenue and Eleventh Street. Being unable to justify the demolition of them on Slum Clearance grounds, the Council in 1980 promoted a separate Compulsory Purchase Order under the Community Land Act, a piece of legislation brought in by the previous Labour Government designed to help developers to prepare sites for development. A Public Inquiry was held in November 1980, before the Order was confirmed in May 1981.

The Council School, experiencing a declining attendance as a result of the slum clearances, finally closed in December 1981. Also closed at the same time were the baths, health centre, recreation ground and the Trafford Park Language Centre, which had originally been set up in part of the School buildings in 1972. The Roman Catholic School closed in 1982.

The clearance of the remaining part of the Village stirred considerable ill-feeling among the residents, over half of whom were opposed to the proposals. An Advice Centre was set up and a Residents Association actively campaigned on the issue, and published a newspaper, the *Park Times*, for a number of years. Towards the end, the remaining residents became resigned to the clearance, and articles in the paper concentrated on interviews with Council officials responsible for rehousing and compensation. An annual reunion of residents was arranged, which takes place every autumn in St Antony's Centre on Third Avenue. One of the principal organisers of the event was disappointed when 'only 400' turned up in 1994.

The Trafford Park District Plan 1979-80

In 1979, both Trafford and Salford Councils jointly issued a draft District Plan, covering the Park and the Salford Docks area. The latter area was seen to have similar problems to the Park and the days of the Docks operation were clearly numbered, as ships using the upper reaches of the Canal continued to decline.

Preparatory work on the Plan had started in 1976. It contains some interesting statistics on the state of the Park's economic decline and employment levels. Employment levels had declined from 50,700 in 1965, just before the first large scale closures, to 37,600 in 1976, of whom 7,000 worked at the GEC factory. Approximately 14 per cent of the workforce was female. Some 70 per cent of the total were engaged in engineering, food and drink, tobacco, chemicals, building materials and transport. This compared with 21 per cent engaged in similar industries nationally.

After a period of consultation, the Plan was formally adopted by the Council in 1980. It was essentially a 'development control' document, i.e. one that merely set out a framework of those developments which it would favour when deciding planning applications. Its 'positive planning' contents, i.e. those to be carried out directly by the local authorities, are contained in outline only, with few details of when schemes would be implemented, which would depend on a range of factors, including the availability of finance.

The Plan envisaged the closure of the remaining estate railways and their use for road widening or landscaping, the creation of a system of cycleways, the use of the Bridgewater Canal for recreation, and the creation of specific zones where 'unsightly industries' such as scrap metal yards could be located. A new road would be built linking Westinghouse and Ashburton Roads replacing Third Avenue, Trafford Park Road between Ashburton Road and the gyratory system would be widened, whilst Westinghouse Road would be realigned near to First Avenue, and widened at the access to the Freightliner Depot and MIFT. A new cycleway and footpath would link Westinghouse Road and the United Trading Estate across the Bridgewater Canal. The Plan indicated that the Council had spent some £75,000 on landscaping since 1974, as well as many more proposals for environmental improvement.

In formal planning terms, the District Plan had a very short 'life', being largely supplanted by the Enterprise Zone proposals of 1980-1. However, many of the positive planning proposals in the Plan have remained, in modified form, in the various initiatives taken since then to regenerate the area.

Notes

1. The Estates Company later updated this booklet in a typewritten version issued *c*.1962.
2. 28 June 1950.
3. Sometimes also referred to as the Trafford Park Industrialists Association. This body had an office on Third Avenue. It ceased to be active a few years before the formation of TRAFIC.
4. It was re-numbered M63 after the completion of the M62 between Manchester and Liverpool.
5. Taylor, from the steelworks of the same name, had served on the Board since 1921 and had been the first instance of a Park occupier being invited onto the Board of Trafford Park Estates.
6. Grain Elevator Estate Ltd. ended its separate existence in 1979.
7. It is now part of North Trafford College.

Chapter VI

Rebirth of the Park
1980-Present

The Enterprise Zone 'Experiment'

The large-scale closures of the 1960s and 1970s resulted in some sites being converted into mini-industrial estates. First pioneered by Trafford Park Estates on those estates described in the previous chapter, they were followed in the 1970s by Trafford Council's Westinghouse Industrial Estate, and by the private sector which had undertaken subdivision schemes on existing buildings at Central Park, Springfield Trading Estate and the Allens Freight Forwarders Estate. Only Severnside was a totally new private sector estate started in this era. More would have been achieved had not the property industry suffered a severe crash in 1974 after the inflationary boom years of the Heath government.

By 1980, following more closures, further estates had been started. The Estates Company in that year started work on a central spine road, costing £350,000, through the 12 acres that comprised the former 'B' Sidings. This was developed from 1982 as the Westbrook Road Estate providing about 200,000 square feet of space.

In 1980, the Estates Property Investment Company (EPIC) completed a small development, called the Monarch Trading Estate, on a 2.5-acre site previously occupied by Hall and Pickles Ltd. on Trafford Park Road. Ten small units provided 53,000 square feet. On Guinness Road, the Prudential Assurance Company had bought a 10-acre site off Ciba-Geigy to develop the Guinness Road Trading Estate, with a total area of over 100,000 square feet. The surplus 40 acres released from the severe rationalisation of Turner and Newall in 1979 had produced two sites for development. The site to the west of the remaining factory, initially called 'Broadoak 1' but later called the Royce Trading Estate, was taken over by Trust Securities who undertook a combination of new building with conversion and subdivision of former buildings. The other site, on the eastern side of the Turner and Newall site, was developed in phases with new units by Pentith Developments as the Broadoak Trading Estate. Finally, the surplus land from the British Steel site, considered for a joint scheme with the Estates Company before 1974, was developed by Tarmac Developments as the Parkway Industrial Estate, the first phase being completed in late 1980.

The take up of all this new and planned space was relatively slow, and one Manchester property agent expressed the view that there would be an over-supply of space for some time. He cited difficulties of attracting suitable labour, especially female workers, peak hour congestion, lack of shops, public houses and other facilities, and that smaller developments away from main roads would have difficulty in establishing their own marketing identities. Much of the demand was from transport-orientated organisations who either had trades-union difficulties over requirements to employ only Dock labour, or who faced developers who insisted on filling sites with buildings leaving insufficient space for parking and manoeuvring.

Into this scenario came the Conservative government's Enterprise Zone 'experiment'. Elected in 1979 on a mandate of rolling back the frontiers of state control, the Margaret Thatcher government was convinced that one of the solutions to the country's economic plight was to encourage industry by reducing or removing official hurdles to private enterprise.

The concept of bureaucracy-free zones came from the Fabian Peter Hall, Head of Geography at Reading University. First expounded in the early 1970s, his ideas had crystallised following a visit to the Far East in 1977. Thereafter, they were taken up with enthusiasm by the Conservatives. In January 1980, it was announced that four such zones would be set up. On 26 March, Geoffrey Howe, the Chancellor, invited interest from selected local authorities for the establishment of three to four zones in England, and one each in Scotland, Wales and Northern Ireland.

The zones would last for 10 years, would extend to about 500 acres each, and would not be part of existing regional, inner city or derelict land policies. They were to be an experiment: 'On a few sites to see how far industrial and commercial activity can be encouraged by the removal of certain fiscal burdens, and by the removal or streamlined administration of certain statutory or administrative controls.'

Premises and developments within such Enterprise Zones could expect exemptions from Development Land Tax, levies from Industrial Training Boards, Industrial Development Certificates and, most importantly, local authority rates (the government would reimburse Councils their lost income). Planning permissions would not be required for most types of development, and 100 per cent capital allowances would be given on all industrial and commercial buildings. Certain Customs benefits would be available and the government itself would keep to a minimum its own demands for statistical information.

On the same day as Geoffrey Howe's announcement, both Trafford and Salford councils received invitations from the government to set up a zone to cover both Salford Docks and Trafford Park. The process effectively asked the local authorities to put in draft submissions to be considered in competition with bids from elsewhere. Government advice stressed that the deciding factor would be the attitudes to development that Councils could demonstrate within their submissions.

Despite reservations about certain aspects, Trafford decided to make a submission jointly with Salford. Local support for the zone idea was strong, including TRAFIC and the Manchester Chamber of Commerce and Industry. With a 500-acre site limitation, including Salford Docks, it was clear that only a limited part of the Park could benefit. The prospect of a separate zone in Salford was one which the Council could not afford to ignore.

The joint submission, made after extensive consultations with local civil servants, was made on 30 May. It did not include a defined boundary for the Park, but set out

94 *Demolition of the Cooperative Wholesale Society's Sun Mills on Trafford Wharf Road, 1980.*

four options, all including Salford Docks. Option 'A' was basically a scatter of undeveloped sites, 'B' concentrated on the western side of the Park and 'C' on the eastern end. Option 'D' was similar to 'C' but included other land in the Cornbrook area. The government's response arrived on 29 July, indicating acceptance to both councils, along with zones at Speke, Tyne Valley (which included part of Team Valley Industrial Estate) and the Isle of Dogs. Both Councils now had to prepare formal schemes for submission to government, including defined boundaries, which would be advertised and modified after receipt of objections. The Secretary of State for the Environment would then grant formal approval through a Designation Order.

Success in the initial stage led to further discussions with local civil servants and with affected industrialists and developers. Major concerns were now raised over the possibility of large retail schemes within the zones, which it was felt would be detrimental to existing retail centres. Concern over this was heightened in August when Hypermarket Holdings Ltd. submitted a planning application for a store on Trafford Road in Salford. Representations were made to government ministers, including Lord Bellwin, and to Tom King who visited the Park on 24 October. The Greater Manchester Association of Metropolitan Authorities expressed similar concerns to the government. Trafford Council originally wanted a 5,000-square ft. size limit on retail schemes, later modified to 10,000 square ft. Similar concerns had been registered by other local authorities affected by Enterprise Zone proposals. These combined to have effect as the government accepted a limit of 16,000 square ft. for retail development in the Park, coupled with a larger allowance in Salford. This seemed to satisfy the Council and the concerns of local shopkeepers expressed through local Chambers of Trade.

The other major issue was the zone's boundary, and the effect on both industrialists and developers of new and existing space that the freedom from rates would have on the attractiveness of properties on either side of the zone boundaries. In drawing up the boundaries, the government wished to keep its own liabilities (i.e. the cost of rate reimbursement) to a minimum, and the intention therefore was to include few existing premises. Some, however, had to be included: for example, Turner and Newall and parts of sites owned by Shell, as the zone had to be a contiguous area and not a scatter of undeveloped sites. The zone also had to be limited to about 500 acres in total, including Salford, although many of the zones created, including Trafford Park, finished up larger. Existing industrialists saw potential rate savings from inclusion in the zone, whilst developers of new space feared loss of interest from potential tenants if their schemes did not end up within the zone. Until the final boundaries were known, the whole estate could be blighted to a degree from the uncertainty created.

In discussions between the Council's officers and the Department of the Environment, an initial scheme had been drawn up comprising parts of options 'B', 'C' and 'D'. Effectively, three separate areas were zoned within the Park, the eastern end including the Pomona Docks and Cornbrook areas. The Council made its own submission on 24 November, and the government's response, which reduced the size of the Council's bid, was received on 18 December. The suggested boundaries were first formally published on this date, and comments were invited from affected parties. Many representations were received by the Council from developers, including many on the adjacent Barton Dock Estate (which had been totally excluded from the zone). The developers of the small Monarch Estate stated that their (as yet mainly unlet) estate would suffer by being immediately adjacent to zone land. The Estates Company, who had yet to start building work at Westbrook Road, could not understand why their site had been excluded whilst other nearby undeveloped sites or recently completed schemes like Guin-

ness Road had been included. Industrialists were also dismayed by exclusions. The
old established but clearly struggling firm
of Banister Walton expressed the hope that
demand for its products would be increased
from developments undertaken within the
nearby zone. Doug Edwards of GEC regretted that the zone had not included parts
of the GEC site, then in the course of being
further vacated, as otherwise he could have
secured the relocation of another part of
GEC from elsewhere in the U.K., bringing
400 jobs in the process. He made the very
pertinent point that the quickest way to
create additional employment was to encourage existing industry. The zone idea
did nothing to assist such firms as all the

95 *The old and the new in the Park in 1981. A new warehouse
building off Trafford Wharf Road for freight forwarders L.E.P.,
whilst behind the old Greenwoods/Rank flour mills are being
demolished.*

benefits were geared towards provision of buildings and not additional plant and equipment, which was a considerable outlay in capital-intensive heavy industry. Others made
the more general point that few occupiers would see the benefits of the rate free
allowances as rents for new space would be driven up, leaving only developers and
selling landowners as the main beneficiaries. Only where those landowners were existing Park firms selling spare land would any benefit be felt by Park employers.

The Council duly passed on all such comments to the government, adding its own
special plea in respect of the Village area, left out of the zone by the local civil servants.
It feared that the zone would stifle any occupier or developer interest in the areas of
former housing land in the Village cleared after the compulsory purchase orders.

The Enterprise Zone finally came into effect on 12 August 1981. On 1 August, the
Government announced that it was to withdraw Intermediate Area status to the Park
along with other parts of Greater Manchester with effect from 1 August 1982.[1] The final
area within Trafford Metropolitan Borough was 438 acres. Both Monarch and Westbrook
Road estates were included, but Severnside, the Village and estates within Barton Dock
were excluded.

The Enterprise Zone in operation

The declaration led to the increased take-up of space in estates within the zone, and to
the building of further estates. Adjacent to the Guinness Road Estate, the Harp Estate
was built in phases and, further along the same road, the Enterprise Trading Estate.
Both Broadoak 2 and Westbrook Road were built, and a second phase of the Parkway
Estate was completed. A development of small industrial units was completed on Canal
Company land to the north of Trafford Wharf Road, called the Waterway Enterprise
Park. Some owner-occupied development took place, most notably the ex-Shell site to
the north of Ashburton Road where the National Freight Consortium built a transport
and distribution depot for its Exel Logistics subsidiary, for use in connection with work
for Kellogg's.

In January 1982, a two-day Enterprise Zone exhibition was held at Longford Hall
in Stretford. It was opened by Lord Bellwin, Parliamentary Under Secretary for the
Environment.

Enterprise Zones continued to feature as part of government economic policy for a few years, and more zones would be declared. It was fairly soon apparent that they would not be the panacea for the U.K.'s industrial decline. They did not *per se* secure the provision of the necessary infrastructure to service new industries, and the planning-free régimes could have served to harm the poor physical environments of the zones. Most importantly, there would always be the debate about how much totally new economic activity had been created within them, and how much was due to the attraction of footloose industries drawn by the prospect of rate-free allowances.

The limitations of the policy were recognised by Trafford Metropolitan Borough, and in mid-1983 the Council's Policy Committee considered the need to adapt a new strategy to facilitate the Park's revival. Reference was made to the original rôle of the Trafford Park Environmental Committee, first established in 1975. Over the years, '... the steam has leaked out of this initiative. The broad approach has shrunk to a long term derelict land reclamation and landscaping programme. Valuable though this is, it is by itself an inadequate response.' [2]

In March, the Environmental Committee voted to return to its original aim and renamed itself the Trafford Park Joint Committee. Subordinate working parties were proposed dealing with matters such as infrastructure, landscaping and promotion. A series of conferences was suggested, both at local and national level, with the aim of attracting long-term property investment funds of the major financial institutions. Little came directly out of these suggestions, but the need for further specific action was not in doubt.

About the same time, the Council issued a draft Planning Brief for the Village, designed to promote private sector involvement in the areas it owned. The draft Brief caused concern locally when it proposed major changes to one of the few areas of the Village left relatively unchanged by the clearances, namely the St Antony's Church, Presbytery and former school. The Brief envisaged demolition of the school, turned since closure into a christian centre by industrialist Kevin Flanagan, and converting the Presbytery into offices and its garden into a lorry park. The final version, approved by the Council in November, fortunately omitted these proposals. The Brief envisaged the Village road network being amended, with Second Avenue being widened and turned into a through route, and Third Avenue being blocked to through traffic. Other streets would either be upgraded or closed in parts to enable viable development sites to be assembled. Car and lorry parks would be provided, along with public open space, landscaping, public toilets and a system of pedestrian routes. Existing businesses would be encouraged to remain or expand. The former Council School would remain and was, along with the former Library and Health Centre buildings, already in the process of being relet by the Council in parts as small industrial workshops. A similar proposal to convert the houses between Ninth and Eleventh Streets, then being acquired by the Council under the Community Land Act, into industrial workshops was ruled out when it was decided that such a use could have caused legal challenges over the basis of the Council's acquisition of the houses.

The Village Planning Brief was adopted by the Council, but led to no direct work being undertaken, private sector involvement being limited to a couple of small extensions to existing businesses. Although initial steps were taken by the Council to achieve some of its positive planning initiatives, implementation would largely depend on whether the Council could secure Derelict Land Grant funding from government. In subsequent discussions with the Department of the Environment, the Brief was further modified as the commercial content was scaled down, and Third Avenue was retained

96 *'Trafford Park, the ideal site for your factory' from* The Organiser, *December 1919, Trafford Park Estates Ltd.'s first advertisement for the Park after the First World War. Some 75 years later, the slogan has lost none of its relevance.*

as a through route when the government decided not to fund the extension of Second Avenue.

The limitations of the Enterprise Zone policy towards the Park were highlighted by Stretford Labour M.P., Tony Lloyd, in a short adjournment debate in the House of Commons in June 1984. He called for fresh government assistance and described the area's decline as 'spectacular and disastrous'. In August, Lloyd and his Conservative colleague for Urmston, Winston Churchill, accompanied by senior Trafford officers and representatives of the 'Major Manufacturers' consortium (a group of seven Park firms led by GEC) went to see David Trippier. Shortly after, requests were made to both the Environment Secretary, Patrick Jenkin, and to Norman Tebbitt, then the Trade Secretary, to make a 'flying visit' to the area, in the manner that the previous Environment Secretary, Michael Hesletine, had undertaken frequently in Liverpool. The government's response, on 10 August, was to award Trafford Council £1.5 million in grants for derelict land reclamation. Although welcomed, Doug Edwards of GEC remarked that it would need £20 million just to tidy up the Park. A request in December to designate the area an Inner City Partnership Area, which would have brought forth further government funding, was turned down. In November, however, the Park was restored as an Intermediate Area.

Progress continued to be slow. Against a target of 7,000 new jobs over 10 years, only 2,557 had been achieved by February 1986. This total had been negated by the job losses within GEC alone, which had shrunk from 6,000 to 3,500 over the same period. Other firms had continued to close or to shed labour. Uniroyal, the successors to the Rubber Regenerating Company who had taken over part of the former Ford factory at the end of the war, closed at the end of 1981 with 125 redundancies. In Autumn 1983, Frederick Smith's of Anaconda Works on Mellors Road, another long-standing Park firm, closed with 310 redundancies due to intense competition and lack of demand for its products. In 1980, the same firm had employed 650. Other firms that went in this period included Schrieber's, NEI, Coventry Climax, Burmah Oil and Ingersoll Rand.

The period 1983-6 saw intense effort on the part of the Council to secure the revival of the Park. New firms were attracted, although many merely replaced firms that had closed. One notable success was the establishment in 1984-6 of Trafford Park Printers on Ashburton Road, on a site held for a time for expansion by Ciba-Geigy, which had been released when the British Steel site was first rationalised in the early 1970s. The success was achieved after personal appeals by senior officers of the Council, including Michael Shields, the Chief Executive, and Roger Dodsworth, the Industrial Development Officer. The new plant, with 270 employees, first operated on 2 January 1986, printing the *Daily Telegraph* and other papers. The Guardian and Manchester Evening News Ltd. later bought a 50 per cent stake in Trafford Park Printers.

The Trafford Park Investment Strategy 1985-6

The need to achieve something more fundamental for the Park was mulled over by the various authorities for some time, particularly as the limitations of the Enterprise Zone policy had to be clearly demonstrated. In September 1985, it was decided by the parties that a detailed study into the problem was needed. The Borough Council, the local offices of the Departments of Trade and Environment, and the 'Major Manufacturers' consortium commissioned at a cost of £100,000 the Trafford Park Investment Strategy. The local trades unions also lent their support to the study.

Work on the Strategy started in November, and was undertaken by a combination of consultants, Roger Tym and Partners (planners and economists), the Franklin Stafford Partnership (architects) and Sykes Waterhouse (chartered surveyors).

Preliminary work done for the report echoed many of the points made over a decade earlier by the Civic Trust:

> Environmental problems mean that in its present condition the Park cannot hope to compete for investment with alternative greenfield sites. Moreover, the multiplicity of land ownerships, and the lack of a single estate manager, means that there has never been a mechanism for putting things right.

The Enterprise Zone had brought few benefits, but the Park had a powerful strategic location, being close to Manchester's buoyant city centre and airport, accessible to a diverse and highly skilled workforce, and with access to one of the largest concentrations of technological higher education in Europe.

An interim report was ready by March 1986 and the final report appeared the following August. A copy was sent to Nicholas Ridley, the Secretary of State for the Environment.

The main recommendation of the report was the establishment of an Urban Development Corporation (UDC), similar to those established in Merseyside and London Docklands slightly before the Enterprise Zone policy, and which had been regarded as successful in bringing about regeneration of their areas. The UDC, which would be a 'special kind of UDC', working in close cooperation with the local authority on such matters as land assembly and industrial promotion, would invest about £90 million of public money on infrastructure and promotion, intended to generate over its five- to ten-year 'life' over £550 million of private sector investment. Targets of nine million square feet of new space, and 16,000 new jobs, would be set requiring the acquisition of 430 acres of land. A new road network would be built with a link across the Ship Canal. Existing buildings to be retained would be given substantial facelifts, and major land reclamation and structural landscaping would be undertaken. An association of Park firms should be set up to become an Enterprise Trust, initially to promote business development, but eventually to take over the UDC's assets when it was disbanded.

The Government accepted most of the proposals and in fact increased the amount of money promised to the new body to £160 million. The decision to set up the UDC, which was in fact a Development Corporation on standard lines, was announced, along with three others, at the 1986 Conservative Party Conference. The UDCs would take over the planning functions and some land assets of the local authorities within the designated areas. In the case of the Trafford Park UDC its remit would extend not only to the Park proper, but also to Barton Dock, to parts of Stretford adjoining Cornbrook (known as the Hadfield Street area), to parts of Salford Quays (as the former Salford Docks area was now known) and to the Irlam Steelworks site (to be called Northbank).

Trafford Metropolitan Borough welcomed the plan but was disappointed over the loss of planning powers and the fact that it had not secured a larger rôle for itself. One prominent member of an adjoining local authority described the plan as 'yet another mouse sized idea for coping with the mammoth sized problems in the area'.[3]

Revival of the Estate Railway system

In the early 1980s, usage of the remaining parts of the rail system declined further, and in 1984 both remaining regular users, British Steel and Corn Products, ceased their

97   *Aerial view of Trafford Ecology Park, created out of the remains of the old Trafford Park Lake.*

98   *Architect's perspective of the ambitious but abortive Rosehaugh-Trafford scheme for the development of Wharfside, submitted in 1989.*

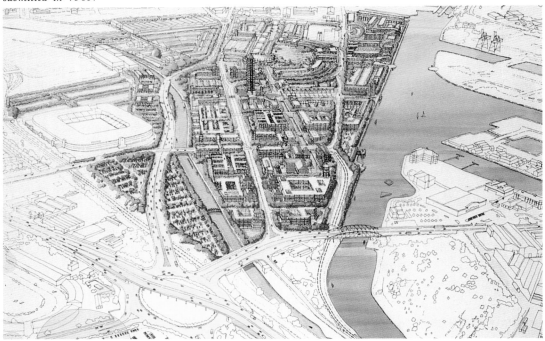

traffics, leaving only occasional traffics—imported containerised tobacco for Port of Manchester Warehouses, which was unloaded on Mosley Road, and isolated single van loads of chemicals sent to Ciba-Geigy from Switzerland.

At this point, The Trafford Park Company decided to terminate the long-standing agreement with the Canal Company for haulage within the Park. The share received by The Trafford Park Company for the surviving traffic was too small to meet track maintenance costs. The Company were also unhappy because of damage to the track by the poor condition of the Canal Company's locomotives, and its lack of control over the movement of traffic within the system. The Trafford Park Company purchased two second-hand shunting engines to handle the traffic.

In 1985, Corn Products undertook some trials using high capacity bulk powder wagons to distribute its products via the British Rail network. The trials were successful and the firm hired 22 bulk wagons for long-term use. At the time, the strength and condition of the track within Trafford Park was insufficient to permit their use, and the products had to be taken by road to Ardwick to be loaded. The following year, the old Ananconda Works on Mellors Road was taken over by S. Norton & Co., scrap metal merchants. This firm wished to send scrap steel to Cardiff by rail, but again were obliged to tranship at Ardwick.

With definite prospects of regular traffic for the Trafford Park Road line, the Estates Company decided to invest about £100,000 in upgrading the track, and purchased two heavier-duty diesel locomotives from British Rail. Freight from both Norton's and Corn Products, since 1987 known as Cerestar, started in 1989, the latter being given a champagne send off by Sir Neil Westbrook and Cerestar Managing Director, Tony Ratcliffe. Cerestar invested £675,000 in 1992 in a further nine vehicles, capable of travelling by rail to continental destinations.

The rail revival to date has been modest compared with the hey-day of the system. About 100,000 tons are carried per annum, and this is reported to be increasing, although the traffic from Norton's has recently ceased. Further upgradings of track have taken place since 1989, to the Ashburton road line as far as ABB Wheelset, formerly British Steel, and FMC, formerly Ciba-Geigy, although at present neither firm uses the system. Occasional traffics have been handled to Novacold on Mosley Road, and a new siding, partly to serve this firm, was laid on former trackbed in August 1992. From time to time, the prospects of restoring the link into Procter & Gamble are aired.

The impact of the UDC's highway proposals, particularly the Europa Way link, on the rail network resulted after many delays in the signing of a formal agreement between the UDC and the Estates Company in February 1992, under which a new length of track was built between Trafford Park and Westinghouse Roads. This takes a more direct route with gentler curves than the previous direct connection, and allows the Cerestar traffic, which could not take the old direct route, to avoid reversing along Trafford Park Road. The final link, crossing the new Europa Way roundabout at its junction with Trafford Park Road, was laid in December 1995. As a result, part of the Trafford Park Road line leading towards Trafford Road has been abandoned, although part of the Westinghouse Road line will be retained to serve Estates Company-owned land recently let to a company which will import cars to the site by rail.

Development of the Ecology Park

Trafford Park's Lake was a prominent feature of the early years, when the westerly parts of the estate remained semi-rural, and when the recreational facilities offered by Will

Crookes were appreciated. Gradually, industries increased in the vicinity of the Lake. By 1906, the Liverpool Storage Co. had premises alongside and the L.N.W.R. had a depot nearby. In 1913, the Carborundum factory opened on the opposite side of Trafford Park Road and by the early 1920s the site was virtually surrounded by industry.

Crookes appears to have given up his lease in about 1922, following which the boating operation was taken over by Rathbones, who ran the long established boatyard near Longford Bridge on the Bridgewater Canal. A café operated on the site since the days of the First World War in a building built at the edge of the lake on wooden stilts. In 1916, the adjoining Top Lake was filled in.

The condition of the Lake deteriorated during the 1920s and 1930s. In August 1923, tipping from the Carborundum works was reported on the south-east corner of the site. The water in the lake itself was polluted by both asbestos and by oil seepage from the adjacent depot of the Anglo American Oil Co. Ducks and fish had long since disappeared from its water. By 1930, infilling continued, although boating continued on a smaller scale before ceasing totally later in the decade. The café remained in operation, and the site was still visited by workers for recreation, sometimes bringing portable gramophones for entertainment.

Taylor Bros started to use the site during the Second World War for tipping. This took place on a revolving basis, the clinker-slag material being removed from time to time when quantities were sold for construction purposes. The situation was regularised between Taylor's and the Estates Company in 1946, and the licence was extended in 1956 before the site was bought outright by Taylor's in 1958. Tipping temporarily ceased c.1957, but the material was excavated later for building the embankments to the Barton High Level Bridge. Tipping resumed in the early 1960s, although the lake was never completely filled, and a small part always remained in water.

The site was bought by Esso in 1974 in connection with the extension of the adjoining tank farm. The company used the land to improve the frontage to their own site, and levelled and seeded the western part of the site. A large sign was erected at the junction of Mosley Road North and Trafford Park Road.

Increasing awareness of the poor condition of the Park's environment heightened concern over the Lake, and in 1974 TRAFIC made a suggestion that it should be restored. Little direct action followed but Trafford Metropolitan Borough thought the idea worthwhile. By 1980, plans began to take shape, following consultations with and representations from the Ecological Parks Trust, the Cheshire Wildlife Trust and others, and a biological study of the site by individuals from Manchester and Salford Universities. The water in the lake in 1983 was said to be 'remarkably unpolluted' and wildlife in the form of herons, foxes, rabbits and ducks had already returned to the site.

Negotiations to buy the 11-acre site from Esso were completed by late 1982, the purchase price being £50,000. In April 1983, the deeds were handed over to the Mayor of Trafford, Councillor Dan Sullivan. The proposals centred around re-establishing the lake to be run by a charitable trust as an Ecology Park. The work would take some two years to complete. The Park was intended to demonstrate ecological principles alaid out in three distinct parts. Firstly, the eastern part of the site, including the lake itself, would comprise a 'wildlife area'. The public would not have access to this area so that its existing wildlife could be enhanced. Secondly, a 'study area' would be formed on the western part of the site, to include hedge and woodland planting, meadows, experimental and demonstration ponds, a mound and an experimental area for use by children. Finally, along the Trafford Park Road frontage, a public nature park would be created for informal recreation.

In the years 1983-7, the local authority implemented their scheme. Both the start on the scheme and its completion were delayed when government spending restrictions led to delays in supplying the grant moneys. At first, the government did not regard the site as derelict, but in the end were persuaded to contribute towards the costs. Some preliminary work was done in 1983, but the first main phase—ground shaping, path construction, landscaping to the wildlife area—did not get under way until the end of 1984. Some tree planting was undertaken by the British Trust for Conservation Volunteers. The second phase started in Summer 1985, finishing in 1986. It was to comprise the initial visitor and ranger buildings, bird hides, further earthworks and signs. The Salford and Trafford Groundwork Trust acted in an advisory rôle to the Council, and much of the work was undertaken by labour secured through the government-sponsored Community Programme. Due to shortage of funds, some works were postponed: five demonstration ponds and a public bird hide were not provided until 1987 and 1988 respectively.

During 1985-8, the Council considered how the completed site could best be managed. The initial plan was for an independent charitable trust to run the completed site with no further financial input from the Council. This was over optimistic; both the Countryside Commission and Esso, who were financially supporting the Park's running costs on a short-term basis, did not wish to support an independent trust when a larger but similar body already existed in the Salford and Trafford Groundwork Trust. In December 1985, the Council agreed in principle to this course of action. Negotiations between Council and Trust, about whether the Trust should take a lease of the site or act as the Council's agent, continued until August 1987 when a formal 'Task-Partner Agreement' was completed, it being intended to grant a formal lease after a trial period. The first staff to look after the site arrived in November 1987, and it was opened to the public, albeit only for specially-booked parties and educational visits.

The question of management of the site was overtaken by the vesting of the site in the UDC, which took effect in Spring 1988. In July, it was agreed that the Trust would act as the Corporation's managers, with direct funding of running costs.

In the years since, further works have been undertaken to the Park both by the UDC directly and also by the Trust, although some of the original plans have been modified. The public nature park was landscaped in 1987-8 along more formal lines with areas of hard landscaping, and a pergola since removed. A boardwalk along part of the lakeside, allowing disabled access, was completed in 1992, using grant aid from the Mersey Basin Campaign and ICI. Some of the demonstration ponds have been removed to improve access to the outdoor teaching area. Further buildings have been added and an observation beehive has been provided, the latter funded by Esso. The public bird hide now displays on its wall a mural, painted by volunteers from adult day centres in Salford and incorporating ideas from the children of Lostock Hall High School in Stretford. The Study area contains a small memorial, incorporating a weather and pollution monitoring station, to Major Bill Lloyd, the energetic and dedicated Secretary and later Chairman of TRAFIC, who died in 1989.

The site was opened to the public on a regular basis in April 1990, and is now managed by a small team from Salford and Trafford Groundwork, who also use it as a base for contract work carried out elsewhere. In its first two years of operation, 4,100 and 7,400 visitors came to the Park and it remains popular with school parties. A number of public events are organised in the Park.

A wide variety of flora and fauna are already evident, including foxes, weasels, rabbits, hedgehogs, lapwings, kestrels, herons, coot and Canada Geese. Wild orchids

99 *Aerial view of the striking Quay West office building with the former Salford Docks, now Salford Quays, in the background.*

100 *View of Quay West and the Hovis Flour Mill from Salford Quays, showing the promenade on both sides of the Ship Canal provided by the UDC. On the extreme right is HMS* Bronington.

and herbs also grow. Common frogs and several types of newt breed in the lake, including Great Crested Newts rescued from Parbold Quarry.

Formation of the Trafford Park Urban Development Corporation

Government was quick to get the new UDC in operation, and promoted through Parliament the Trafford Park Development Corporation (Area Constitution) Order, which formally established the UDC on 10 February 1987. Its designated Urban Development Area (UDA) was 3,130 acres, over twice the area of the Park proper. Control of the new body was through a Board, comprising eight members from local business and property circles, but including a single councillor from Salford and two from Trafford. The Chairman, Yorkshireman Peter Hadfield, had recently retired as managing director and chairman of Bass North-West Ltd., and was chairman of the local Residuary Body, charged with winding up the affairs of the former Greater Manchester County Council, which had been abolished in Spring 1986. In its first year of operation, the UDC was based at the former County Hall in Piccadilly Gardens, Manchester, before moving to its own offices built at the Wharfside Business Centre on Trafford Wharf Road.

The new organisation started with no staff of its own, and relied heavily in its first year on seconded staff from local authorities and the local offices of the civil service, together with a wide range of consultants. By March 1990, the UDC had gradually built up a staff of over forty.

An early decision, which helped to defuse suspicions by the local authorities, was to use planning departments from both councils to undertake development control as agents for the UDC. The UDC also took over the local authorities' rôle for the Enterprise Zone areas, which continued to run until 1991.

In May 1987, it was announced that the UDC's Chief Executive would be Durham-born, 44-year-old Michael Shields, who reportedly beat off 400 other candidates. Shields, who took up his duties on 1 October, was well placed for the post, having been the Chief Executive of Trafford Council for four years, and before that Chief Technical Services Officer of Salford, where he was involved in the joint Enterprise Zone submission.

The UDC's initial year was largely involved in planning, land purchase, marketing and promotion. Large area developments and road schemes would take time to implement, due to the length of the Compulsory Purchase process necessary to buy land from unwilling vendors. The UDC's strategy would be two-fold. Firstly, to undertake measures to benefit the UDA as a whole, including infrastructure, landscaping, marketing and promotion, support to industry, and measures designed to translate the benefits of regeneration to the wider community outside the UDA, for example, through training and community group support. The second aim of the strategy was to undertake four large area redevelopment schemes. Two of these, at Hadfield Street and Northbank, Irlam, were outside the Park proper, whilst Wharfside and the Village were within the Park.

Wharfside

Wharfside extended to over 200 acres at the eastern end of the Park, incorporating Ship Canal Company land to the north of Trafford Wharf Road as far west as the former dry docks. The UDC intended Wharfside to be a flagship site, providing prestigious office, retail, leisure and 'hi-tech' industrial accommodation in a landscaped parkland setting, with generous water features. Vastly different from the residual industry that still existed in parts, it was designed to capitalise on the area's proximity to the city centre, and to mirror the successful developments, in design terms, developments undertaken at Salford Quays.

Planning and feasibility work was undertaken in 1987-8 by architects, Building Design Partnership. In May 1988, the UDC's master plan was unveiled and interest from developers was sought. Responses were received from a wide variety of parties including the Estates Company, who owned the western parts of the area, and from Rosehaugh, a London-based development company, headed by the reclusive Geoffrey Bradman and involved in the imaginative scheme at Broadgate near Liverpool Street station.

In May, Rosehaugh-Trafford Developments was formed as a joint venture. In October, the joint company was declared the UDC's preferred developer for most of the area, along with the Ship Canal Company who would develop land already in its control. Press reports of the time also mentioned Amec and Heron, who envisaged developing smaller schemes of their own.

The joint developers set to work to design a scheme in line with the UDC's requirements. The economy was enjoying a credit-led 'boom' and such schemes were seen as the path to the future. By August 1989, the UDC received formal plans, which were publicised. The scheme was massive in scale, although it would take until the late 1990s to complete. It would cost over £500 million and would house some 10-12,000 jobs. The accommodation was designed to attract firms relocating from the South East and European firms looking for a U.K. location. Designed by architects, Shepherd Epstein and Hunter,[4] the scheme provided high quality space in a parkland setting around an artificial lake, with squares, water features and promenades. All buildings would be served by a centralised heating system under which tenants could save some 40 per cent of their usual energy bills. Trafford Park Road would be diverted along a new alignment following the Bridgewater Canal, called Bridgewater Boulevard. Overall, the scheme was designed to be '... the most spectacular and exciting development ever proposed for the North West ... the flagship of the North West and Trafford Park in particular'.

Two other schemes in the meantime had been started within Wharfside in accordance with the UDC's plans. These were Samuel Platt's public house and restaurant, located on the banks of the Ship Canal, which was completed in 1990, and Quay West, a nine-storey office building built by Ship Canal Investments Ltd., a joint venture between the Canal Company and G.R. Morris Ltd., near where the Grain Elevator had once stood. Work on the £7-million building, designed by the John Ratcliffe Partnership and built with pink reflective glass cladding, started in February 1989 when the first sod was ceremonially cut by Environment Minister, David Trippier, who was served a glass of pink champagne to celebrate the occasion. It was completed in May 1991, and occupied partly by the Canal Company itself, who moved its head office there, by Peel Holdings, the Canal Company's owners, and later by other tenants.

Progress on the Rosehaugh-Trafford scheme was not going well. The 1980s boom ended rapidly in late 1989 and the property industry quickly lost confidence. Schemes like Wharfside began to look hopelessly idealistic. In discussions between the UDC and developers, the scheme was dramatically reduced in scale. The financial status of Rosehaugh, heavily involved elsewhere, began to look shaky; soon the firm went bankrupt. By February 1990, the developers and the UDC jointly agreed to terminate the preferred-developer status of Rosehaugh-Trafford. By coincidence, outline planning permission for the full scheme, originally applied for in September, was granted in the same month by the UDC.

The UDC sought interest from other developers, although now its aspirations for Wharfside were more modest. A revised master plan was issued in August 1990, which envisaged a phase 1 development, 'pump primed' by the UDC. It was hoped that this would create the necessary momentum to secure the development of the rest of Wharfside over a timescale extending beyond the UDC's term. In early 1990, negotiations were held with the Charter Group, who had undertaken a striking development called Exchange Quay in Salford. Their interest was conditional upon the inclusion of a hotel and ended when the hotel operator, brought in as partner, experienced financial problems. The UDC in the meantime decided to start acquiring land, and defined the boundaries of four Compulsory Purchase Orders. In June 1990, the first Compulsory Purchase Order was promoted, covering a modest 21 acres. After the usual public inquiry into objections, it was granted in April 1991. It included the Monarch Industrial Estate, completed only in 1980. Clearance of buildings started quickly, with two long-standing Park firms relocating elsewhere in the Park. Knowsley SK went to the Centrepoint development and Illingworth Ingham moved to Ashburton Road where the Superheater Co had once been. Another Compulsory Purchase Order, No. 2, was promoted in October 1990 for the land required to widen and improve Trafford Wharf Road, which started in 1991. In the meantime, reclamation work had been undertaken on parts of the site and by March 1990 work had started on the promenade along the Ship Canal.

In mid-1991, a development agreement was signed with Amec in respect of 3.5 acres at the eastern end of the area with Amec, although no work was undertaken as the developers were unable to secure lettings for any buildings. The agreement was terminated in 1994. The Estates Company also started work on a development of industrial units, called Canalside North, on the site of 'A' Safes on Westinghouse Road, which had been demolished. An extension to Warwick Road North, called Water's Reach, was started in the year, and a central spine road, called Waterside, led off this, serving the Phase 1 site. These works were completed in September 1992 when Environment Minister, Robin Squire, UDC chairman Bill Morgan, and Board member Councillor Colin Warbrick cut the ceremonial tape.

In January 1992, the UDC's aspirations turned to attracting owner-occupied or bespoke developments. The initiative was launched under the slogans 'Create your own Masterpiece', and 'Our Canvas–Your Creation'. Again, little came directly from this, as the national economy was slow to recover from the 1990 recession. Further canalside promenade was completed in 1992-3. In March 1992, the final Wharfside Compulsory Purchase Order was promoted. Named No. 6 (nos 3 to 5 had not been activated), it was confirmed in November 1993. It completed the land assembly required for Phase 1 of the revised master plan and included the Waterway Enterprise Park, erected only in the early 1980s, which did not fit in with the UDC's aspirations for the area, and which was demolished in December 1994.

In October 1992, HMS *Bronington*, the minesweeper formerly commanded by H.R.H. The Prince of Wales, was officially opened by Prince Charles as a tourist attraction on Trafford Wharf Road. The UDC gave the Bronington Trust, who had bought the boat, £25,000 towards the purchase price, paid for its refurbishment and then leased it for operation as a tourist attraction. It is open to the public during the spring and summer months. The public are able to listen to a taped commentary introduced by Prince Charles.

Work also started in late 1992 on a scheme by Amec on a head office building for Combined Power Systems. This is located on the site of Greenwood's flour mills.

101   *The end of an era in the Village, on 28 February 1993, the last day of trading in Cooper's newsagents, Third Avenue, with Chris and Teresa Cooper, customers and old shop fittings.*

102   *St Antony's, after refurbishment in 1993. The church contains the altar and a stained glass window from the Trafford Hall chapel, the transfer of which to St Antony's was paid for by Lady Annette de Trafford.*

During 1994, developers again started to show interest in the Wharfside phase 1 site and towards the end of 1995 the UDC was reported to be in advanced negotiations with a potential developer and several major owner occupiers.

The Village

The UDC's strategy for the Village was substantially different from Wharfside. The scale was smaller, only 55 acres, and most of the vacant land had been inherited by the UDC from Trafford Council. The UDC wanted to create a thriving focal point to service the whole Park and in particular to cater for the needs of smaller firms in particular.

At an early date, Wimpey Property Holdings were selected as the UDC's preferred developer of phase 1 of the area proposals, with an option to develop the remainder. Phase 1, located either side of Third Avenue, between Fifth and Eleventh Streets, would comprise about 100,000 square ft. of space, catering for firms wanting 100-1,000 square ft. Two thousand jobs would be housed in the completed phase 1 development, containing offices, shops, managed workspace, exhibition and conference facilities. The ultimate scheme was to be some 870,000 square ft. in size. Elsewhere, the UDC intended to generate the provision of new and improved banks, shops, leisure and health facilities, public houses, restaurants and cafés, together with additional managed workspace and small industrial units. The UDC's proposals for the Village were more radical than the previous Borough Council plans of 1983, and involved demolishing most of the remaining buildings, by now in a poor physical condition, and unlikely to be improved by owners or occupiers. The UDC started to acquire properties and some demolition work was undertaken in 1988, along with landscaping and the construction of a temporary car park to the west of Third Avenue. A Compulsory Purchase Order was submitted in December 1989.

Discussions between Wimpey and UDC centred on an agreed masterplan for the entire Village, but the scheme was affected by the same economic problems that beset Wharfside. When it became apparent in January 1990 that Wimpey could not start due to lack of demand, it was agreed that the preferred-developer status should be ended. The UDC carried on with property acquisitions, demolitions and the provision of structural landscaping at various locations. Land purchase proved difficult, with a public inquiry in January 1991, and the Compulsory Purchase Order was not being confirmed until June 1992, the longest delay that the UDC has experienced. Several companies in the area were helped to relocate. Firms on the Westinghouse Phase 2 site were helped to extend or to improve their premises. Printsearch and SWS Metals both benefited from UDC grants. In 1991-2, Eighth Street was extended to provide a new access to the temporary car park. In Summer 1992, Second Avenue and a number of adjoining streets were improved.

The UDC attempted, without success, to interest other developers in the area. By the end of 1992, the UDC had decided to take a more active rôle itself and to open sites for owner-occupiers, particularly smaller schemes. It modified somewhat its proposals to clear most of the older buildings in the area and decided to undertake some developments itself.

Opening on 21 September 1992, Trafford Park Arts arranged an exhibition in the St Antony's Centre. Called 'Third Avenue–Dawn 'til Dusk', it used photographs by Chris Thomond, sketches by Sarah Wray and creative writings by John Cannon to tell the story of one day in the life of the street. This was particularly pertinent in view of the clearance of much of what remained of the Village.

In March 1993, work started on the refurbishment of St Antony's Church, Centre and Presbytery. The work, costing £500,000, was funded by the UDC and the Diocese of Salford. The Centre, which had been temporarily housed opposite in the Barclays Bank building, reopened in January 1994 as the St Antony's Centre for Church and Industry, offering community and training facilities, having gained an extra floor. At the reopening ceremony, the keys were handed over by the UDC Chairman to the Bishop of Salford, and the following day former footballer Denis Law unveiled a portrait of himself taken from the original Trafford Park Mural.

The Centre's work concentrates on links between local industry, churches and the community, and is the base for several Trafford Park organisations, including the Trafford Park Arts Project and the Village Traders Association. It also incorporates the Trafford Park Heritage Centre, comprising displays on the history and life of the Park and Village.

Work also started in 1993 on the refurbishment of one of the former retail blocks on the western side of Third Avenue. At a cost of over £500,000, the UDC itself undertook the work which was finished in 1994. It houses a range of shops, some relocated from elsewhere in the Village. It includes the Trafford Park Business Centre, housing six business support groups, including TRAFIC, the Trafford Business Venture, Trafford Park Business Watch, Trafford Business Education Partnership, Business Link Trafford and the Greater Manchester Business Innovation Centre. The refurbished building is called Lloyd House after the former Secretary and Chairman of TRAFIC, who was born on Ninth Street. It was opened by William Lloyd, his 9-year-old grandson. In 1994, work started on the refurbishment of a second block. Completed in June 1995, it is named Cooper House after Cooper's Newsagents, who were based in the Village from 1906-94. New public car parks were built behind both blocks and a new set of public toilets, the design of which imaginatively uses the 'Boys' and 'Girls' signs from the former Council School.

In late 1994, work started on a major refurbishment of the former School, clinic and library buildings, which the UDC had cleared of its former tenants. Using £1 million of grant moneys, developers Urban Splash began turning the buildings into seven two-storey units of between 1,000-5,000 square ft.

In March 1994, an agreement was signed between the UDC and Heath Investments Ltd. for a first phase of speculative industrial development to the east of First Avenue, on which work soon started, with options for subsequent phases. One of the first tenants is the American company A.T. & T. The same developers were expected to commit themselves to a second phase in late 1995. Other owner-occupied developments were undertaken between First and Second Avenues, including new buildings for Avoca Textiles, Europa Freight, the Midland Bank and others. First Avenue itself was improved and further landscaping provided. Both the *Village* public house, converted from the former British Legion Club in the late 1980s, and the *Trafford Park Hotel,* now a Grade 2 Listed Building, are in the course of receiving facelifts and new car parks. In February 1995, Third Avenue was severed as a through route, although it was later reopened with one-way sections.

Towards the end of 1995, the UDC's hopes for the Village are nearing completion, and developments are well under way on the eastern side of Third Avenue. Development of the western area is not progressing as fast because another road between Westinghouse Road and Ashburton Road, called Fifth Avenue, designed to make the area more attractive to developers, is yet to be built and may require a further Compulsory Purchase Order. The outcome of this, at the time of writing, is unknown.

Roads and Infrastructure

From its inception, the UDC regarded the upgrading if the Park's infrastructure as essential to the regeneration of the area. In 1993-4, at £13.6 million, it amounted to 40 per cent of the UDC's expenditure for that year. The UDC's aims have been to improve the links into the UDA particularly along an axis between the Parkway and a new bridge across the Ship Canal near Eccles, but also between the Park and the City Centre. An additional aim is to upgrade the Park's primary and secondary roads.

The route of the Parkway/M602 Link was determined in April 1989 following a public-consultation exercise on four options. Detailed design started in early 1990 and Compulsory Purchase Orders were submitted in July. After a public inquiry, the Order was confirmed in April 1992, and work started on the £36-million scheme in November. The bridge over the Ship Canal was originally intended to be a double leaf bascule structure, but by 1991 was being described as a swing bridge. The final design was for a lift bridge, said to be the largest of its kind in the U.K., and spanning the canal for a width of 41 metres. Its deck can be lifted up to 16 metres giving a clearance of 23 metres above the canal level. The bridge was formally opened on 1 December 1994 by Her Majesty The Queen. To commemorate the centenary of the Ship Canal, being celebrated that year, it was named the Centenary Bridge. The roadway leading from the Park, called Centenary Way, divided Procter & Gamble from Cerestar and necessitated the demolition of the latter firm's offices. These were replaced by a new building fronting Guinness Road, completed in late 1994. The Parkway/M602 Link scheme also involved the dualling of Tenax Road and a new dual carriageway to the north of the Ship Canal, completed about the same time.

The improved links to the City Centre were to be provided by a combination of schemes, called the Eastern Spine, White City Junction and City Link. Compulsory Purchase Orders for these were granted in January 1995, although work has not yet started. The White City Junction and City Link schemes are to be implemented and funded by Trafford Borough Council. Only the Eastern Spine, including the former Bridgewater Boulevard concept, is within the Park itself; it involves the dualling of parts of Ashburton Road East and Trafford Park Road. Work on it will start following completion of detailed design and land purchase. When it is finished, part of Trafford Park Road will be re-named Wharfside Way.

Improvements of primary and secondary roads have included the upgrading of Trafford Wharf Road, carried out in 1991-2, and a new road between Ashburton Road and Westinghouse Road. Originally called Zero Avenue, this was opened in late 1994 as Europa Way. It was built on land acquired under the Village Compulsory Purchase Order. Both the Springfield Trading Estate and the former Uniroyal factory, comprising the former Ford works, were demolished as part of this process. The eastern section of Westinghouse Road was cut off for a time as a result of these works, but was reconnected in December 1995 when this stretch of road was renamed John Gilbert Way. In late 1995, work was in hand to extend Europa Way northwards to link up to Trafford Wharf Road. The single carriageway extension is to be called Warren Bruce Road, after a former Docks Manager of the Ship Canal. Another road improvement scheme was a new access to Euroterminal, MIFT and the Freightliner Depot, completed in April 1993. Additional northbound slip roads, linking the Parkway and Barton Dock Road, were also built in 1994.

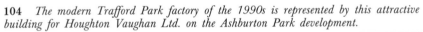

103   *This new canal footbridge over the Bridgewater Canal at Throstle Nest was built by the UDC in 1990 as part of its environmental improvement programme. The bridge in the background carries Trafford Road.*

104   *The modern Trafford Park factory of the 1990s is represented by this attractive building for Houghton Vaughan Ltd. on the Ashburton Park development.*

As well as the road system, the UDC wished to improve access to the Park by public transport. Since the mid-1980s, this had been limited to peak-hour-only bus services, and even these continued to decline in usage and frequency. In 1988-9, the UDC helped to finance a feasibility study, carried by the local Passenger Transport Executive, into providing a proposed branch of the Metrolink light rail system into the Park. Financial support was also given to the cost of seeking the Parliamentary approval for the line, obtained in 1992. The UDC agreed the route alignment, which enters the estate along Trafford Wharf Road, and runs via Water's Reach, Trafford Park Road, Ashburton Road East, Third Avenue, Westinghouse Road, under the Parkway and through Taylor Road to end at the site of the Trafford Centre. A start on the scheme is dependent on financial support from the developers of the centre, and contributions from government and the European Regional Development Fund.

The UDC in 1989 initiated financial support for two local bus routes, running at off-peak times through the Park. Initially, these were provided by blue liveried mini-buses, bearing publicity material for the UDC. The UDC has also grant-aided part of the cost of improvements to the upper reaches of the Ship Canal undertaken by the Canal Company.

Environmental Improvements, Public Art and All Saints Church

Land reclamation and landscaping have been undertaken on a large scale by the UDC. Up to summer 1995, over 355 acres have been reclaimed, and 250 individual environmental improvement schemes have been completed at a total cost to the UDC of £21.7 million, including the planting of some 800,000 trees and shrubs. Such works have usually been relatively easy to undertake and were a continuation of previous work on a more modest scale by the Borough Council. Usually, the schemes did not conflict with the needs of existing industry (unlike the road and area development schemes) and could be used to promote rapidly a new image for the Park, particularly when undertaken in 'clusters' at main entry points to the area and along main highway corridors.

In the UDC's first year, landscaping was undertaken in the Village, and frontage schemes, often involving grant aid for planting or work to improve the façades of buildings, were carried out. The Trafford Road Swing Bridge was painted and work was started at the Ecology Park, where at the perimeter stood the sculpture 'Ten Stones' made from Yorkshire stone by David Haigh. In 1989, a scheme was completed near Barton Swing Bridge, incorporating a new frontage to the Ship Canal, a pergola and a 10-foot-high steel structure made from maritime articles called 'Stevedore' by sculptor Brian Fell. Two new footbridges over the Bridgewater Canal at Waters Meeting and Throstle Nest Lane were built in 1990. The first two phases of a scheme to provide a public promenade along the Ship Canal were completed.

In 1992-3, the UDC's landscaping activity was extended to include marking the entrances to the UDA and key locations within it. A series of arched signs was erected along roads and a new series of names was arranged to help those visiting firms to find their way around. Thus the long standing Central, East and West Parks disappeared from road signs to be replaced by new locations such as Ashburton, Mosley, Newbridge, Wharfside and the Village. In addition, location signs appeared on road overbridges owned by FMC and Carborundum, similar to one which the UDC had instigated on the Kellogg's overbridge in 1990. Existing Park firms were actively encouraged to use Trafford Park in their title, company logo or postal address.

In September 1992, the Marshall Stevens Memorial was removed from the junction of Trafford Park and Ashburton Roads, where it was in the way of the Europa Way proposals. It was cleaned and repositioned in a new site on Trafford Wharf Road in a new landscaped setting, at a cost of £38,000. The work was carried out by Park stone-masons, Mather & Ellis. It was formally unveiled in March 1993 by Sir Dermot de Trafford, the grandson of Sir Humphrey Francis de Trafford.

On 1 November 1993, a new Trafford Park Mural by Walter Kershaw was unveiled by Denis Law on the wall of the old Liverpool Warehouse building at the Trafford Road entrance to the Park, replacing the earlier mural, also by Kershaw, from 1982 which was in need of attention. The £38,000 cost was supported by contributions from firms depicted on the mural. It is reputedly the largest piece of industrial art in Europe. Nearby is a spectacular sculpture, commissioned by the UDC in 1995, a pair of 17-metre-high 'Skyhooks', designed by Brian Fell, which appear to lift the island gyratory system out of the nearby Ship Canal.

In 1986-91, All Saints Church at Barton was restored. Since the days of patronage by the de Traffords, its fortunes had gradually declined. During the 1950s, it was common for parish masses to be delayed because the parishioners, mostly from Eccles, were held up at Barton Swing Bridge. In 1959, the parish was enlarged and a new church was built at Patricroft. Regular services ceased in 1961 although complete closure did not last long; in 1962 the building was taken over by a Franciscan Order, the Friars Minor Conventual. Barton on Irwell was declared a Conservation Area in July 1975, and in 1978 the church was declared a Grade 1 Listed Building. In 1979, the church bell tower was taken down as it was leaning and dangerous. The stones were numbered and stored for future use.

Restoration was proposed in 1985 and the following year both Trafford Council and English Heritage promised grants towards restoration, which started on 1 November. The first phase involved masonry cleaning, dry rot eradication, roof repairs and restoration of the impressive sanctuary mural, thought to be by Joseph Pippet, which contains caricatures of the fourth Sir Humphrey, his wife Lady Annette, and Pugin with a plan of the church. Phase 2 started in March 1990, and included strengthening the west wall, restoration of the colourful rose window and rebuilding the bell tower. The work was completed in 1991. Subsequently, a second-hand pipe organ has been installed and restoration of the friary garden to its Victorian design was undertaken in 1994. As well as the original grants, support has been received from the Historic Churches Preservation Council, the Getty Grant Programme and the Laing Charities. The UDC contributed over £290,000 of the total cost of more than £1 million. Sir Dermot de Trafford made a substantial personal contribution to the restoration of the de Trafford Chapel within the church.

Human Infrastructure and Community Initiatives

The UDC has been keen to promote activities to benefit the wider community, particularly those who might not otherwise gain from the arrival of new industries. This is seen as especially important as the UDA contains virtually no resident population.

Public consultation has been undertaken on the UDC's area development and highway schemes. A Trafford Park Community Liaison Forum has been established, meeting bi-monthly. Its membership comprises local councillors, trades unions, enterprise agencies, the churches, business and community organisations. Financial support is given to TRAFIC and in 1988 a Business Watch crime prevention scheme was launched. A Business Watch Manager was appointed in 1989, and over 600 firms were participating in the scheme by 1991. In 1992, a national 'Secured by Design-Commercial' scheme was initiated in the Park, intended to raise awareness of security in design of industrial and commercial buildings.

The UDC helped to form the Trafford Park Arts in Industry Committee which organised a 'People of the Park' arts festival in October 1988. In the same year, a survey of 930 firms in the UDA was undertaken with the aim of identifying deficiencies in training, particularly for the long-term unemployed. At an early date, the UDC contributed towards the 'Bridge Training' scheme based at the St Antony's Centre, dealing with groups of unemployed from inner-city areas.

By 1989, the UDC's employment and training team offered a variety of support including assistance to firms providing customised training for the local unemployed, specific training courses for known skills shortages, a Job Club for 16-18 year olds, and grants to encourage employers to upgrade the skills of existing employees whilst bringing long-term unemployed onto the payroll. Grants have also been made to the voluntary sector to develop social skills in young people and the disabled. Organisations as diverse as scout groups, amateur football clubs and the Old Trafford Women's Health and Fitness Club have benefited from such support.

The training programme was re-launched in 1990 as the 'Skills Resource Initiative'. The same year saw support for the Business/Education Partnership in Trafford involving local schools, which was staffed by company executives and teaching staff on secondment. The Partnership encourages schoolchildren to gain experience by contact with local industry. Two-hundred-and-fifty items of computer equipment costing the UDC £300,000 were installed in 52 inner-city schools, and equipment was provided at a local college to help blind and partially-sighted people improve their job prospects. A community newspaper 'Link Up', advertising jobs available within the Park, was launched and circulated free to 150,000 households every two months.

1991 saw job preparation courses for Asian women, a 'Clerical Skills Programme' aimed at women 'returners', higher secretarial courses, and opportunities for construction training on the UDC's own contracts, secured through a voluntary code of conduct whereby contractors undertook to employ 50 per cent of labour locally, and 10 per cent as trainees. A Community Arts Officer was appointed, funded jointly with Cerestar, to encourage the creation of a positive community spirit amongst Park firms and employees through arts activities. The Trafford Park Education National Curriculum Project was launched, initially involving 15 schools studying, through the issue of a teaching pack, the historical, environmental and industrial issues of the Park. A similar project had been undertaken by the firm Ciba-Geigy, shortly to become FMC, who issued a 'Bicycle Pack' designed to make real and palatable the scientific themes involved in an everyday object, the bicycle. The Bicycle Pack was a huge success and was eventually distributed nationally to all schools.

In September 1991, the Trafford Park Performance and Quality Forum was established by the UDC in conjunction with Park firms and other organisations in the Manchester area. The initiative is run by Park firms in order to share knowledge and good practice, and thereby improve the overall performance of Park companies and the quality of their products. It provides advice, guest speakers, a forum for debate, a resources facility, links with higher education, training and other functions on the subject of quality in both industrial production and service industry. The Forum first met on 15 June 1992 at the World Trade Centre, Exchange Quay. The meeting was hosted by T.V. personality, Chris Searle. By April 1994, it had some 250 members.

Training activities in 1992 included a 'Drive Start' course enabling 32 women to take driving and fork-lift truck driving tests, a 'prepare to work' course for the disabled, a computer-aided design course for the unemployed and the 'Reaction Scheme', which provided grants to employers offering redundancy counselling. In October 1992, coinciding with the formal opening of HMS *Bronington*, the 'Ship Ahoy' project was launched. This involved some 70 schoolchildren who researched and produced souvenirs for the ship. Some of the UDC's training courses were run at the Chester Road Training Centre, established in 1992 in a Victorian building refurbished by the UDC at Old Trafford. In 1993, a language training laboratory was established to teach English as a second language, and over 700 Trafford schoolchildren were involved in 'Crucial Crew'– a multi-agency safety programme.

By June 1995, over 3,191 training places had been assisted by the UDC, and by Summer 1995 over 400 voluntary and community groups had received money. From 1991-4, preparatory work was undertaken on the Trafford Park Manufacturing Institute, a partnership between 'leading edge' manufacturing companies and local universities designed to ensure the provision of quality education and training for manufacturing and process industry. This will allow standards to be targeted and the prosperity of Park industry safeguarded. The facility finally became operational in the Quay West building in January 1995.

Marketing, job creation and other developments in the Park 1987-95

As well as training and environmental grants, the UDC administered a wide range of direct financial assistance to generate development and job creation. These included City Grants, Rent Grants and Derelict Land Grants. The UDC was also able to promote the availability of Regional Selective Assistance administered by government and available because of the continuing designation of the Park as an Assisted Area, a status which the UDC has successfully campaigned to retain.

In its early years, marketing and promotion concentrated on improving the general awareness and image of the UDA. In 1988, a survey of UDA firms was carried out which gleaned valuable information. In Spring 1989, a press and television campaign was undertaken in the south east, and consultants were appointed to carry on marketing activities in the USA and Canada.

The UDC gave financial support to Manchester's bid to hold the 1996 Olympic Games, and subsequently to the bid for the 2000 Olympics. Feasibility studies were also undertaken into a proposal to locate an industrial heritage museum in the area and a visitor centre at Barton.

Job creation in the early years was small, amounting to hundreds only. In January 1990, UDC chairman Peter Hadfield informed the government that he did not wish a second three-year term, and resigned the following month. No specific reasons were given, but it was thought that he felt frustrated at the slow progress of the area development and highway schemes, and the evaporation of developer interest following the end of the late 1980s boom. His place was taken temporarily by his deputy, F.A. Russell, until September 1990 when J.W. (Bill) Morgan, a former Chairman of Amec and a past director of GEC, was appointed.

The Park continued to develop. In 1987-8, a third rail freight facility was built adjacent to MIFT, with a derelict land grant from the UDC. It is operated by Harris Distribution, part of the Transport Development Group, whose subsidiaries are well represented throughout the Park. Building work also started at the Wharfside Business Centre, partly to be occupied by the UDC itself, and at the site of the old ICI factory on Westinghouse Road, which was bought in 1988 by Monde Developments. Part of

105 *The crowing glory of the UDC has been the Centenary Bridge. Proctor & Gamble and Cerestar are visible on the right.*

106 *The old Liverpool Warehousing building has been the location of two huge murals by Walter Kershaw, depicting industries of the Park. The first, dating from October 1982, was replaced by this version, first unveiled in November 1993.*

the 22-acre site, comprising a section of the wartime penicillin plant, was retained as the Monde Trading Estate, but the rest was developed in phases as the Centrepoint scheme, partly funded by a City Grant from the UDC. One of its roads is named Marshall Stevens Way. Another part of the old British Steel site, now operating as ABB Wheelset, was declared surplus. This adjoined the Broadoak Trading Estate and included the site of the Clarence Avenue houses, the last of which had been demolished in the early 1980s. In 1988-9 this was developed as the Westpoint Enterprise Park by Baltic Developments. The old aircraft factory office block was occupied by H. & J. Quick Ltd. as its head office from April 1988.

1989 saw an amalgamation between GEC, still the Park's largest employer, and the company Alsthom, part of the French-owned Thompson group. The operation is now known as GEC Alsthom. Jobs at the complex continued to decline and large areas of the site became vacant, occupied by other associated companies or let to other firms. The West Works had been occupied since the early 1980s by Hotpoint, part of GEC, as a storage depot. In 1988-9 it was refurbished at a cost of nearly £3 million. The UDC contributed towards the cost of recladding the building's exterior. Other uses of the site in the 1990s included an off-airport car park.

Despite the work of the UDC, older Park firms continued to close or to shed labour. Early in the UDC's existence, the old established firm of Banister Walton, which had supplied the steelwork for the building of Manchester's Central Reference Library, closed. The ICI (ex-British Alizarine) plant, after a long period of run down, finally ceased production in Autumn 1987, and the buildings were cleared shortly after for the Centrepoint development. Another long-standing Park firm was Redpath Dorman Long, previously Redpath Brown, which closed at the end of 1989 with the loss of 250 jobs. The buildings were quickly demolished and the site was redeveloped in 1992-4 to provide a new packaging plant for Blagden Industries, a long-standing Park firm. In the late 1980s, Cerestar virtually halved its workforce.

By 1990, however, despite the economic recession and the setbacks to the area development schemes, the UDC's activities were beginning to bear fruit. By March 1990, some 2,700 jobs had been attracted and one year later this figure stood at 3,500. Since 1987, some 1.3 million square feet of new developments had been built, with 16 major new schemes either under way or complete. Major investment by existing firms, including Procter & Gamble, Brooke Bond and Rank Hovis McDougall, had also taken place.

In 1990, the UDC launched a quarterly magazine aimed at the business sector, called *Trafford Park Profile and Property News*. A three-dimensional model of the UDA was also completed for display in the reception area of the UDC's offices. A separate newspaper, *Trafford Park Today*, was launched by an independent publisher in the same year. This continues as *Business Today*, serving a wider area.

A development called Unison, by London and Metropolitan Developments plc, was completed in September 1990. It is located on part of the old CEGB coal-yard site on Taylor Road, originally acquired by Trafford Council for industrial development in the 1980s. Another development on the same land was the Bridgewater Centre, built by Pilkington Property Developments Ltd., which was completed in September 1991. This scheme provides 21 small units available on short-term lettings.

In October 1991 it was announced that British Rail was to build a new European Freight terminal next to the Harris Distribution facility. Called Euroterminal, it was intended to be open at the same time as the Channel Tunnel. A £1.75-million extension to the Houghton Vaughan plant on Ashburton Road was commenced, along with a £5-

million workshop and office scheme for GKN Chep, also on Ashburton Road, which was finished at the end of 1992. Both were on land sold by the UDC.

From February 1992, the UDC's Board was expanded to 11 members, although this has subsequently been reduced to 10 members.

Around this time, Winston Churchill M.P. suggested to the Imperial War Museum that the Park would make an ideal site for its relocation. One project that did get under way and opened in 1992 was the Heritage Centre at Salford Quays. Funded by Salford City Council, it includes photographic displays of working life in both Salford Docks and Trafford Park. The book *Bridging the Years* was prepared by members of the project staff, and supported by the UDC.

In April 1992 it was announced that the old Ford Merlin engine plant on Barton Dock Road, owned but only partly occupied by Massey Ferguson, was to be demolished. The Massey Ferguson parts operation, employing 300, closed in 1993 and the activities transferred to the Midlands and to Irlam. Thirty acres of the site were bought by Gazeley Properties for development of an Asda store and a distribution park, called North West Direct. Another 40 acres of the site were bought by the UDC to be developed by Amec. The latter site, named Giants Field for marketing purposes, was publicly launched in late summer. Manchester United footballers Neil Webb and Bryan Robson attended, and there were cheerleaders and a field marked out as a U.S.-style softball diamond. Over 600,000 square ft. of space would be built on the site.

In May, GEC Alsthom announced that a further 500 jobs would be axed over the next two years, due to the rapid reduction in demand for steam turbine equipment. This would leave less than 2,000 employed people at the complex, mostly office-based project staff working on power station and traction contracts elsewhere. Only about 95 blue collar staff would be retained for a small low pressure turbine maintenance facility.

July saw the start of work on Euroterminal, when Transport Minister Roger Freeman cut the first sod. The scheme, covering a 20-acre site and costing £11 million, was to be equipped with two huge gantry cranes, an office block, container storage and a workshop for mobile handling equipment. The terminal would have capacity to deal with 35 trains a day or about 40,000 containers a year, rising eventually to 100,000 by the year 2000. Jointly financed by Railfreight Distribution and the UDC, it would initially employ 40 but in the longer term would generate many more jobs.

In November, a 'Business to Business' exhibition, the first to be held in the Park, was organised by the UDC and TRAFIC at the Unison development. A further initiative by the UDC was the opening of a North American office in St Louis, Missouri. The attempt to attract further investment in the Park was appropriate, bearing in mind the historical links with earlier investors such as Westinghouse and Ford, followed by companies like Procter & Gamble, Massey Ferguson, Kellogg's and the FMC Corporation. By March 1994, at least eight more North American companies had made commitments to develop.

In 1992-3, the UDC started to lay out Ashburton Park on the site of the former Shell lubricating oils plant. This scheme was intended to accommodate firms displaced from the Village and elsewhere. By March 1994, it housed a number of companies, all relocated from the Village.

In October 1993, Euroterminal was officially opened by British Rail chairman, Sir Bob Reid, almost a full year earlier than the often delayed Channel Tunnel. Despite handling lower than predicted traffic volume, the terminal has still caused complaints from local residents in the Gorse Hill area over the noise levels created by its huge cranes. A further development at the World Freight Centre, as the complex was now

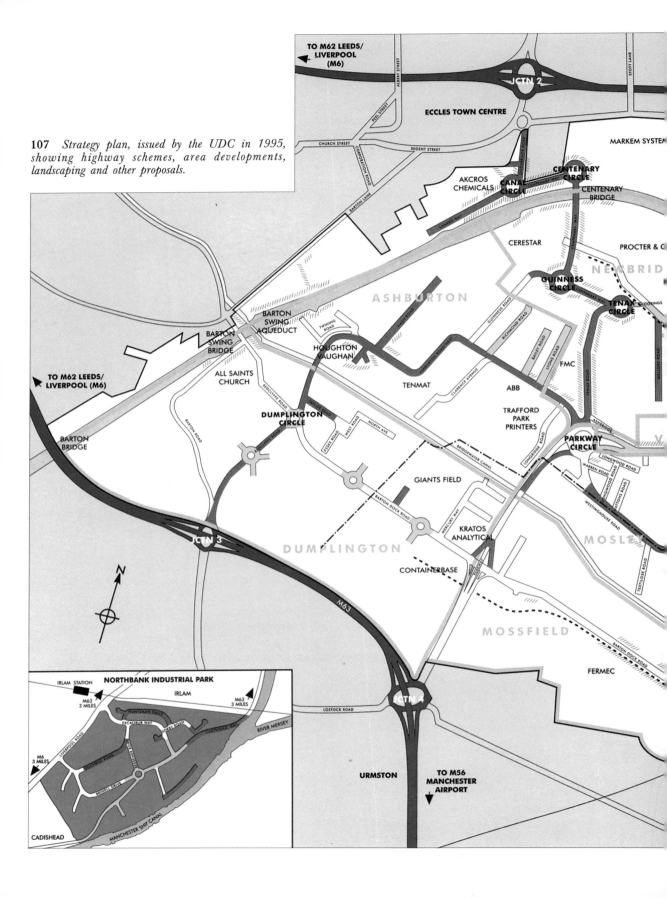

107 *Strategy plan, issued by the UDC in 1995, showing highway schemes, area developments, landscaping and other proposals.*

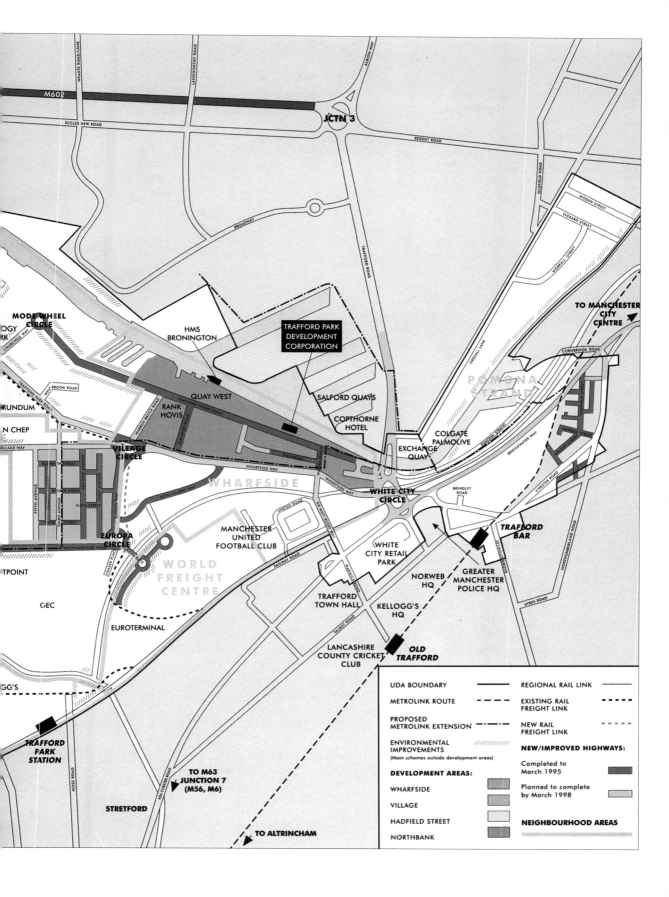

called, was a facility for Davies Turner, which was completed in early 1994. A new distribution facility for Business Post was completed at the end of 1993 on Guinness Road.

Between May and the end of 1994 the Ship Canal Company, together with the UDC, Salford and Trafford Councils, celebrated the centenary of the opening of the Ship Canal. As part of this, the Ecology Park was transformed for a day as the venue for a Victorian 'Picnic in the Past'. The celebrations culminated in the opening of the Centenary Bridge in December.

In early 1994, 47 acres at the eastern end of the GEC Alsthom site were offered for sale. By autumn, it was announced that the site was to be acquired jointly by Gazeley Properties and Trafford Park estates, for high bay warehousing and industrial units. The sale has now taken place but the vacation of this area has yet to be completed.

In summer 1994, work started on a large distribution centre for Robert Wiseman Dairies, a large Scottish milk producer, who had bought 19 acres from Esso on Mosley Road North. The development was expected to create 100 jobs. At the same time, work started on a 350,000-square ft. warehouse for the Manchester Tobacco Company, a subsidiary of Japan Tobacco, at the Giant's Field site. The £47 million investment, negotiated by the UDC, protected 250 jobs in Manchester and was expected to create a further 150 within two years. By the end of September 1995, some 183 staff were already at the site which is expected to be fully operational in 1996. The adjoining Asda store, together with a petrol station, opened on 20 August 1995. A Costco discount store on an adjacent site, opened at Christmas 1995. Both buildings will be dwarfed by the scale of the Trafford Centre, on the south side of Barton Dock Road, on which work started in early 1996.

Trafford Park Estates P.L.C.

The Estates Company continued to prosper in the 1980s and 1990s as an independent company, although rumours of take-over bids circulated briefly in mid-1985. It continued to develop sites away from the Park, including Bristol, Redditch, Heathrow and a notable 'science park' scheme at Cambridge. Although some retail and residential schemes have been carried out, the emphasis of its developments remains industrial and warehousing property. Its chairman and chief executive, Neil Westbrook, was knighted in 1988 in recognition of his services to politics.

Within the Park, the Company's influence has begun to extend again due to the re-purchase of sites, long since sold, for redevelopment. Apart from the joint acquisition of part of the GEC Alsthom site, in recent years the Company has bought the former Texaco site on Twining Road, which had closed in 1992, and most of the Barton Power Station site. In November 1992 the Company moved out of the Estates Office to a new office building, called Neil House, which it had built on Ashburton Road West. In early 1995, contrary to the firm's policy since the early 1960s, the United Trading Estate was sold to the Manchester United Football Club, to enable the long-awaited extension to the football ground to begin.

Relations between the Estates Company and the UDC have at times been strained, arising naturally from the differing aims and objectives of each party. Frequently, Estates Company land and buildings have been included in the UDC's Compulsory Purchase Orders, and the Estates Company has appeared as objectors at numerous public inquiries.

In early 1995, the Company received notice that the remaining contracts operated by Port of Manchester Warehouses Ltd. would be terminated. The operations of the warehousing subsidiary, which since 1986 had been limited to a handling function only, after the remaining warehouses had been leased to the tobacco companies, ceased at the end of 1995.

Winding down of the Development Corporation

The UDC was initially intended to run for 10 years only, ending on 31 March 1997. In line with its original objectives, the UDC has managed to secure a substantial level of private investment in the UDA; at the end of June 1995 this stood at £926 million, which had been 'levered in' by a public expenditure of £202 million, or a ratio of approximately 4.5 to 1. The public moneys have substantially improved the Park's accessibility and appearance, created a positive image for the area and benefited sections of the local community. In gross terms, the original job creation target of 16,000 has already been met; in December 1995 this stood at 18,243. Because jobs have continued to be lost during this period, the net gain has been somewhat less, being a little over 10,466. The UDC has had its critics. Not all have approved of its area-development and highway schemes, including the displacement of some businesses. Along with other UDCs, it has been accused of not being totally under the control of local elected representatives, and therefore 'undemocratic' in its operation.

In early 1995, the UDC started preparations, as required by government, for its 'Exit Strategy'. Many of the UDC's continuing functions will devolve to the local authorities. In an attempt to capitalise on the wider benefits to the region that the UDC has brought, a continuation of its marketing and promotion function was proposed, called the Manchester Investment and Development Agency Service (MIDAS), jointly with local authorities and other bodies such as Manchester Airport.

The timescale for establishing MIDAS has been extended, as in mid-1995 the government granted a one-year extension to the UDC, to March 1998, allowing it more time to secure further jobs, to complete its area developments and to wind down its general activities.

The UDC considers the interest of inward investors in the Park to be now at a peak in terms of both quantity and quality and sees the benefits of its activities continuing for some time after its own demise. The main questions for the future are: whether this dynamic process will continue; whether anyone else will successfully take over the advocacy of the Park; and whether Trafford Park, during its second century, will retain the strengths and identities it possessed during its first 100 years.

Notes
1. Fortunately, a return to Industrial Development Certificates was not involved after the government suspended operation of the system in December 1981.
2. Report of the Chief Executive and Chief Planning Officer to Trafford Borough Council Policy Committee, 18 April and 20 June 1983.
3. *Manchester Evening News*, 21 November 1986.
4. This firm had been substantially involved in the design of the Salford Quays scheme.

Conclusion

In 1996, Trafford Park celebrates its centenary so it is appropriate and timely to look back and determine the historical significance of the story of this estate.

Undoubtedly, it is hailed as Britain's, if not the world's, first industrial estate. Its development was planned within finite boundaries, although there was little fixed development, and growth over the years was opportunistic and piecemeal. The development of the Park, however, was not in the hands of some aristocratic landowner, seeking to maintain his wealth and status amongst the new industrialists through the judicious disposal of his lands. It was the responsibility of an estates company specifically formed to undertake the development, initially in such a way as to contribute to and derive benefit from the Manchester Ship Canal.

The Estates Company over the years battled against all comers. It ploughed a lonely furrow and was a pioneer in more senses than one. Among its 'firsts' were nursery factories, fireproof warehouses and a diversification of activities not common among later property companies. It provided an extensive and still partly functioning roadside railway system. In some respects, Slough and later estates followed Trafford Park.

The rôle played by certain individuals in the company merits mention. E.T. Hooley, the initial buyer, remains a shadowy figure. His involvement lasted less than two years. For him, it was just another 'deal'—one of many that he undertook during his life. He was, however, the essential link between the de Traffords and the successful industrial estate. He was the person who recruited Marshall Stevens to be managing director of the company.

Stevens was the founder of the industrial estate: the man who, according to Dr. Farnie, turned the aristocratic estate into 'a seed bed of modern technology and a quietly humming mass of capital intensive industry'. Having achieved what to many would have been a lifetime's ambition, namely that of seeing the Ship Canal through to completion, he embarked in his mid-40s on a second career. His vision, boldness and energy were what Trafford Park needed to be successful, and he provided them in great quantities. The four per cent of Stevens's negotiations that were fruitful ensured the success of Trafford Park.

Trafford Park was also the birthplace of many industries and products. It was the place where many industries grew larger. The stories of Royce, Fords, Westinghouse and others have been outlined. The Park housed Manchester's first aerodrome, radio station, and a unique residential area. Its place in the history of labour relations deserves mention and its largest employer sent several ex-employees to be Members of Parliament. Another was Arthur Whitten Brown, of Alcock and Brown fame.

The contribution Trafford Park made during the Second World War was truly remarkable. It was Britain's armaments centre, producing *en masse* a wide range of war materials that was vital to the successful outcome of the conflict. Its industry proved itself capable, inventive and innovative enough to adapt readily to war production.

The Trafford Park of today is no longer a quietly humming mass of capital-intensive industry. Its air is not pierced at shift changeover times by the different-sounding hooters and whistles of its various factories, nor do its roads witness vast convoys of red or green municipal buses carrying its workers home to the far corners of Greater Manchester. The names of some of its past products, like Traffolite, Scobrit, Oxydol and the Turnall Trafford Tile, are also subject matter for the history books.

Trafford Park, however, is not dead nor dying any more. It is enjoying a revival and rebirth and is again a seed bed of modern technology. Its companies now run into many hundreds, and they have a habit of changing their identities and locations at a bewildering frequency. Many of them only employ scores of staff; only two employ over one thousand. Its factories today are brighter, cleaner and in pleasant surroundings. The more modern buildings can be quite eye catching. It is a place of enterprise and optimism, and of an active business community. It is also a place that is conscious of its past.

Tracing Trafford Park's history has been a fascinating exercise. There is no comparable area in the U.K. Although vastly different now to the days of the de Traffords, the Park retains its identity, on its island bounded by canals. Its scale and character remain unique and symbolise the mixture of old and new that make up Britain's industrial capacity today.

It is a unique area with a unique history.

Source Material

Archive files, plans & publicity material, Trafford Park Estates plc
De Trafford papers, Lancashire County Record Office
Manchester Ship Canal Company collection, Greater Manchester County Record Office
Trafford Park collections, Manchester Central Reference Library, Salford Local Studies
    Library, Sale, Stretford and Urmston District Libraries
Light Railway Orders, records of defunct companies, Public Record Office
House of Lords Committee papers, House of Commons Committee papers, House of
    Lords Record Office
Special Committee Minutes, City of Manchester
Annual Reports & publicity material, Trafford Park Development Corporation
Enterprise Zone files, Economic Development Unit, Trafford Metropolitan Borough
Unpublished theses by V. MacBride (1978), J. Estowski (1980) & G. Stevens (1981)

Newspapers & Periodicals

Daily Dispatch
Daily Telegraph
Eccles Chronicle
Eccles & Patricroft Journal
Estates Times
Executive Insight
Financial Times
Groundwork Now (Summer 1991)
Illustrated London News (3 March 1897)
Link Up
Manchester Evening News
Manchester Guardian & the Guardian
Manchester Metro News
Manchester Weekly Times
Manchester Courier
Manchester City News
Manchester Weekly Gazette
Manchester Evening Chronicle
Motive Power (March 1990)
Sale Guardian
Salford City Reporter
Stretford and Urmston Journal
Trafford Park Profile & Property News
Trafford Park Today & Business Today
The Harvest

Select Bibliography

Aiken, J., *A description of the country from 30-40 miles around Manchester* (1795)

Aspin, C., *Dizzy Heights* (1988)

Atherton, J.G., *Home to Stay—Stretford in the Second World War* (1991)

Baines, E., *History of Lancashire Vol.1* (1836)

Blundell, Fr. B., *All Saints Church, Barton on Irwell, Restoration 1985-91* (1991)

Blundell, Fr. O., *Old Catholic Lancashire* (1938)

Brooks, R., *Quicks—the First 75 Years* (1987)

Bruce, W., *With the Manchester Ship Canal Company 1894-1945* (1990)

Cassell, M., *Long Lease* (1990)

Collins, P., & Stratton, M., *British Car Factories from 1896* (1993)

Crick, S., *Trafford Edible Oil Refiners, the first 50 years, 1908-58* (1995)

Crofton, H.T., *History of the Ancient Chapel of Stretford* (1903)

Dummelow, J., *1899-1949* (1949)

Farnie, D.A., *The Manchester Ship Canal and the Rise of the Port of Manchester* (1980)

Farnie, D.A., *Seven Manchester Men*

Frost, R., *Electricity in Manchester* (1993)

Gill, K., *Transport Treasuries of Trafford Park* (1973)

Gray, E., *Trafford Park Tramways* (1964)

Green, D., *CPC (United Kingdom): A History* (1979)

Harford, I., *Manchester and its Ship Canal Movement* (1994)

Hartley, I., *2ZY to NBH* (1987)

Hayes, C., *This was Trafford Park* (1994)

Holt, J., *General view of the Agriculture of the County of Lancashire* (1795)

Hooley, E.T., *Hooley's Confessions* (1925)

James, B., *Ciba-Geigy, the Trafford Park Story* (1990)

Jones, E., *Industrial Architecture in Britain, 1750-1939* (1985)

Joyce, J., *Roads and Rails of Manchester, 1900-1950* (1982)

Kirby, A.K., *Dan Boyle's Railway* (1974)

Leech, B., *The history of the Manchester Ship Canal* (1907)

Massey, S., *A History of Stretford* (1976)

Newhill, J., *50 years of change. The story of Procter & Gamble in Trafford Park* (1984)

Nicholls, R., *Manchester's Narrow Gauge Railways* (1985)

O'Gorman, Fr. E., *The History of All Saints Church* (1988)

Owen, D., *The Manchester Ship Canal* (1983)

Percival, G., *The Government's Industrial Estates in Wales* (1975)

Robinson, B.R., *Aviation in Manchester* (1980)

Rowlinson, F., *Contribution to Victory* (1947)

Russell, D. & Walker, G., *Trafford Park 1896-1939* (1979)

Simpson, R., *Novel and Unorthodox, The Story of English Estates, 1934-1994* (1994)

Stevens, T.H.G., *Manchester of Yesterday* (1958)

Stevens, T.H.G., *Some notes on the development of Trafford Park* (1947)

Thorpe, D., *The Railways of the Manchester Ship Canal* (1984)

Manchester Faces & Places—vol. 8

Who Was Who

Bridging the Years (1992)

Report of the Royal Commission on the Distribution of Industrial Population. Cmd.6153, H.M.S.O.

Index